D1711574

Red Ties and Residential Schools

Red Ties and Residential Schools

Indigenous Siberians in a Post-Soviet State

Alexia Bloch

PENN

University of Pennsylvania Press

Philadelphia

Printed in the United States of America on acid-free paper

10 9 8 7 6 5 4 3 2 1

Published by
University of Pennsylvania Press
Philadelphia, Pennsylvania 19104-4011

Library of Congress Cataloging-in-Publication Data

Bloch, Alexia.
Red ties and residential schools : indigenous Siberians in a post-Soviet state / Alexia Bloch.
p. cm.
Includes bibliographical references and index.
ISBN 0-8122-3759-5 (cloth : alk. paper)
1. Evenki (Asian people)—Education—Russia (Federation)—çvenkiæskiæ avtonomnyæ okrug—History. 2. Ethnology—Russia (Federation)—çvenkiæskiæ avtonomnyæ okrug. I. Title.
LA1394.E84B56 2003
371.829941—dc21 2003056123

To those who continue to dream of utopia

. . . and for Mira Rubina

Contents

Illustrations

Note on Transliteration and Translation

The Library of Congress system is used in transliterating Russian and Evenk terms except when there is a commonly used English version. Thus Moscow and not Moskva is used in the text.

When terms in Russian and Evenk are used in the text, they are explained with the first usage. All translations are my own. For the reader's reference, with the exception of ethnonyms, terms indicated as Russian in origin are in italics, while those Evenk in origin are in italics and underlined.

Unless noted otherwise, ethnonyms are transliterations of the Russian terms and appear in roman typeface; for instance, throughout the text the term "Evenki" is used instead of "Evenkil," the Evenk term. The Russian term "Evenki" in the plural form refers to the people, while "Evenk" is used as an adjective (such as "Evenk language," "Evenk children," or "Evenk surnames").

Preface

For many indigenous Siberians, the collapse of the Soviet Union (USSR) has brought about hardships resulting from the breakdown of government infrastructure such as state farms, medical units, and rural schooling. At the same time, the new era has also presented possibilities for self-representation and self-determination that were absent during Soviet times, and now people are immersed in reconfiguring relationships to local and translocal identities. This book focuses on the experiences of a community of Evenki, an indigenous Siberian group concentrated in central Siberia, to consider how the institution of residential schooling has influenced lives in the Soviet and post-Soviet era. Residential schools established in the 1920s brought indigenous Siberians under the purview of the state, and more than any other institution, came to define the identities of the Evenki. In the post-Soviet period, the relations of power in this central Siberian community, and by extension in broader Russia, are vividly refracted through the lens of the schooling system.

This is an ethnography that weaves together portraits of several layers of community in a central Siberian town to provide insight into a time of jarring social change. I take the residential school as the central axis for considering a range of ways Evenki are redefining their relationships with the post-Soviet state. I consider the place of the residential school from a contemporary as well as historical perspective, because the school continues to be an important nexus for debates about Evenk cultural revitalization. In these pages I seek to provide a sense of the considerable diversity in Evenk perspectives regarding the impact of Soviet cultural practices and institutions on their lives. I examine how Evenk identities were taking shape in the 1990s in conjunction with a wide range of factors, including regional, political, and generational affiliation as well as household strategies for economic survival. Given that Evenk women in particular have been caught between Soviet cultural practices of the past and the emerging market trends, a gendered perspective extends through the chapters. For almost all Evenk men and women, however, the experience of residential schooling is one they share with their children, parents, and sometimes grandparents. Residential schooling continues to be a significant defining feature of what it is to be Evenki.

Children have been taken away from parents to attend residential schools across the globe in Canada, New Zealand, Australia, the United States, parts of Africa, China, and Russia, but their plights have been quite different according to the contexts in which the schools have operated. In some cases, students suffered psychological, physical, or sexual abuse, as recent accounts increasingly indicate. At the very least, no matter what type of ideology existed, many students were homesick, anxious about being in an unfamiliar setting, and numbed by institutional homogeneity. For the indigenous Siberians I came to know, there was a wide range of perspectives on residential schooling, some negative but also many positive; residential schooling has continued to be one of the common factors defining indigenous Siberians even after the fall of the Soviet Union in 1991.

It is difficult to overemphasize how the attendance of more than three generations of indigenous Siberians at boarding schools from age six to sixteen affected their sense of identity. This schooling was not just a matter of learning to read and write; in fact, in the early years when policymakers were involved in crafting the Soviet residential schooling system for indigenous Siberians there was widespread debate about the exact purpose of the institution. Some firmly believed that the schools should refrain from disrupting the native subsistence patterns, while others saw this as the primary purpose. In the early to mid-1920s, many of those cautioning against assimilation were ethnographers working as advisors for the newly created Committee of the North (Komitet Severa) that was charged with overseeing the economic and sociopolitical transformation of indigenous Siberian communities.[1] In a 1926 meeting in Moscow where a program of study for indigenous Siberians was being created, an established Soviet ethnographer concluded:

> It would be a grave mistake to think that the aim of our work is to transmit our ways to the natives. . . . We should approach the tranquility of the natives' lives with great care. It's not hard to destroy these ways, but this will only lead to sure death. . . . The school . . . should only educate natives in such a way that they will not be torn from their way of life. They should not become unfamiliar with their regular subsistence activities. (Leonov 1928: 120)

Ultimately, other positions had more weight. By the early 1930s, the proponents of the residential school as a place to inculcate Soviet values were in charge of designing the residential schooling programs. The residential school system that developed in the 1920s throughout Siberia served as the key element in indigenous Siberians' fundamental shift away from subsistence lifeways. By the late 1980s, only a portion of Siberian indigenous communities continued to live lives primarily based on hunting and gathering, reindeer herding, and fishing; most increasingly found themselves living with strong ties to new industrial-based Soviet cultural practices such as wage labor, biomedicine, and formal education.

As the Russian Federation moved toward a market-based system in the 1990s, the government-financed education system came under increasing threat.[2] This crisis coexisted with growing efforts to dispense with the government supports that had existed for decades to promote indigenous Siberian representation in government, education, and medicine. In this context the residential schools sometimes became important loci for indigenous intellectuals' attempts to reinvigorate native languages and knowledge of local heritages.[3] In examining these identity politics, this ethnography privileges the experience of people over dense theorization on so-called "nationalism" among indigenous Siberians. "Education," per se, is also not the focus of this work.[4] What this book does is examine several aspects of the negotiations around Evenk identities in the mid-1990s and the continuing salience of shared Soviet cultural practices and ideas about belonging to a collective. With the residential school as a key axis of these identity politics, the book explores layers of historical consciousness among a variety of people—elders, students, reindeer herders, entrepreneurs, and nurses, among others—in the central Siberian town of Tura.

In 1995, Evenki in Tura officially comprised about 700 people, over 15 percent of the town's population of about 6,000 people. (This figure, however, included only those who were registered with the town passport bureau.)[5] In the mid-1990s, in addition to permanent households, there were also many individuals temporarily residing in Tura. By 1998 the proportion of Evenki to non-Evenki in Tura was growing steadily as some Evenki left their villages, which had been virtually abandoned by the regional government, and more and more Russians left Tura to seek work in southern urban centers. This was not the first time Tura's population had undergone rapid change.

After World War II the population of Tura grew rapidly as local Evenki came for veterinary and medical assistance, as well as schooling, and Katanga Evenki from the neighboring region and Russians found positions as doctors, educators, administrators, and service personnel. Volga Germans and Baltic peoples were also exiled to the region (Habeck 1997).[6] In the late 1960s and 1970s, there was again a population boom as extensive Soviet natural resource exploitation expanded in the North (Miller 1994: 340–42). Several thousand people (mostly Russian and

Ukrainian men) were drawn to the Evenk Autonomous District (Evenkiiskii Avtonomnyi Okrug) as well-paid employment opportunities in the oil and mineral exploration outfits sharply increased in the area. By the 1970s a type of welfare state colonialism had developed in which prized natural resources such as coal, oil, quartz, and timber were extracted from these areas in exchange for state-guaranteed provision of subsistence needs, schooling, health facilities, and some political representation. Evenki were virtually guaranteed a living wage as members of the state bureaucratic infrastructure, either as members of "collective farms" (state cooperatives for hunting, fur processing, and reindeer herding) or as recipients of entitlements (such as pensions and child benefits). The "newcomers" (priezzhii), mostly Russians and Ukrainians, who came to the area for work received two to three times the local wages as hardship pay. This all changed in the early 1990s as political power at federal, regional, and local levels was contested and instability became a defining feature of daily life throughout Russia.

Political-economic autonomy in the Evenk Autonomous District (hereafter Evenk District or Evenkiia) in the 1990s was multilayered and interwoven with issues of regional autonomy and Evenk claims to subsistence land. The administrative configurations within the Russian Federation remained largely as they were in the Soviet period, with the same town government structures, the same regional parliament, and a parliament or Duma at the national level. Beginning with the elections held in December 1993, however, there was a range of parties competing during each of the campaigns to fill elected offices. Significantly for many regions of Siberia like the Krasnoiarsk Territory and the Evenk District, jurisdictional hierarchies did shift.[7] Since the early 1990s, regions, territories, and republics have had equal access in appealing to Moscow, rather than relying on a intricate hierarchy of chains of command, as they did in the Soviet period.[8] Beginning in the early 1990s, many Evenk and newcomer politicians sought to place the Evenk District directly subject to Moscow bureaucracies instead of it remaining under the sovereignty of the Krasnoiarsk Territory. Bureaucrats and common people alike often thought that this new arrangement would allow the district organs of power to have direct control over the exploitation of the region's natural resources and also allow the district to receive government subsidies and supports without Krasnoiarsk bureaucracies siphoning off a portion.

In conjunction with questions of regional governance, indigenous land claims became a key issue in the Evenk District in the 1990s. As the Russian Parliament considered propositions for privatizing lands, district level administrations attempted to temporarily regulate land use (Fondhal 1998). An uneasy balance existed between private interests renting land from district administrations and the demands of indigenous leaders to have priority over the land on which their peoples had historically depended for subsistence. In connection with these issues in the Evenk District, the Association for Peoples of the North, or _Arun_ ("Awakening" in Evenk) came into existence in 1990. One of its mandates has been to mobilize Evenki to demand indigenous priority over the mineral and forest revenue generated in the Evenk District.[9] Although funded primarily through the Russian Federation central government, the fledgling organization of _Arun_ was also outspoken about local inequities such as the hardship pay allocated only for newcomers and the meager resources directed toward indigenous peoples' needs. As discussed further in Chapter 6, in addition to supporting Evenk cultural revitalization efforts, _Arun_ also attempted to ease some of the pressures of the market economy by providing Evenki with social services—emergency loans and food, gratis helicopter flights for transporting children back to villages at the end of the school year, and small grants for college students. The organization also gained some input into the regional Department of Education's selection of the residential school director in 1994.

Arun directed its attention to the residential school as the primary nexus of Evenk identity and sought to expand course offerings on Evenk cultural practices and Evenk language in the residential school curriculum. As discussed in Chapters 5 and 6, many Evenk intellectuals viewed the residential school as the primary institution for fostering a common sense of Evenk community. The contest over defining Evenk identities was becoming increasingly complex, however, as factions competed for limited natural resources and growing Evenk class divisions threatened to split the collective indigenous interests promoted by the fledgling Association for Peoples of the North. As some Evenk intellectuals attempted to safeguard access to political and economic power for Evenki in the district in 1993, emerging social stratification challenged their call for Evenki to rally around the collective good of their community.

Situating the Project

My interest in the Evenki was sparked in 1988 when I was a student at the Herzen Pedagogical Institute in what was then Leningrad. When I arrived to study Russian there for a semester, I already had a keen interest in learning more about the contemporary lives of indigenous Siberians; my studies had recently taken on new meaning when I enrolled in an ethnography class focusing on minority populations in the Soviet Union. I was pleased to learn that I would be studying at this institute that had a long history as the foremost center of higher education for indigenous Siberians.[10] Since I did not initially encounter students from the North, I set out to make their acquaintance.

I found the Northern Faculty had been relocated to a branch of the campus on the other side of Leningrad. Climbing the dim stairway to the combined dormitory/classroom building, I was disappointed to find that classes were not in session and no faculty were around; it was the end of the spring term. I was fortunate, however, to meet up with an Evenk man who was at the institute on business. Over a cup of tea and a piece of dried fish he had brought from his home in central Siberia, Vladimir explained to me that he was an admissions officer from Krasnoiarsk who was in charge of helping place Evenk students in educational institutions such as the Herzen Pedagogical Institute. He apologized that he was unable to treat me to a full meal because he himself was just passing through town; he gestured to the several sable pelts hanging over a chair and said these were samples that he would demonstrate at a Leningrad auction house. He urged me to visit his family in central Siberia, north of Krasnoiarsk, so I could see the "real" way indigenous Siberians lived.

The encounter in the Leningrad Northern Faculty spurred me to begin thinking about how native peoples have been influenced by the extensive system of government education and the Soviet period overall as they continue to formulate their identities as indigenous Siberians. In my studies in graduate school, I focused on questions about identity in a multiethnic Soviet Union that by the winter of 1991 came to be called the former Soviet Union. Ultimately, my ethnographic fieldwork stretching throughout the 1990s brought me face-to-face with various indigenous Siberians, but especially Evenki from the Evenk District in central Siberia. Many of the people whom I came to know recounted their own experiences of traversing the educational system in Leningrad and returning home to teach their native languages, become Communist Party leaders, or head up indigenous rights movements. While most people understood that my research would not significantly improve their lives, many were eager to have more information about their contemporary lives made available to a global readership. A stint of fieldwork never went by without someone inquiring if "the book" was published yet.

Many scholars would concur that ethnography is a tightrope walk between recognizing the limits of one's own analysis and perspectives and seeking to portray elements of lived realities for the community or group under study. As Renato Rosaldo writes, ethnography is strengthened by dispensing the "myth of detachment" that often "conceals the dominant class position" of an author (1992: 204). In debunking a myth of detachment, it is worth remembering that there are many social underpinnings to the inherently subjective act of writing ethnography.

For me, Russia was never just a field site for testing out a hypothesis or an interesting place to spend a few years of my life. My political sympathies were very much rooted in my childhood experiences in communes in New England. In this setting the capitalist system's underlying principle of financial gain for a limited few was regularly criticized and the idealized North American domestic social organization—a nuclear household—was implicitly suspect. With this background, from an early age I was sympathetic to the ideals of socialism and during the Reagan years looked to the Soviet Union as a society in which resources were perhaps more equitably distributed than in the United States.

As a college student in the mid-1980s, I joined with a friend who had recently immigrated from the Philippines to found a "socialist club." We set about organizing talks by faculty, including one on the tensions between socialism and feminism; we also formed a student reading group to discuss texts informed by socialist ideals, including more contemporary examples of liberation theology. This was the era of Marcos's fall and Aquino's rise to power in the Philippines, as well as the era of the "nuclear-free," "sanctuary," and "divestment" movements. We spent our time outside of class at gatherings of Democratic Socialists and at meetings with people working with Salvadoran refugees. On a daily basis in 1985 and 1986, we were drawn into the campus protests of the college's investments in South Africa; we felt that we were contributing to a movement that would eventually bring about a more just world. This was a time of hope, and it naturally fit with the era of Perestroika ("restructuring," Soviet style) and Glasnost ("openness") that Gorbachev ushered in as I was beginning my college studies in 1985. The 1986 Chernobyl nuclear disaster was further evidence that the world had to change. From the perspective of many with whom I came into contact, the faltering Cold War reigned over by Reagan and Andropov/Gromyko in the 1980s could be swept aside in a new decade of possibility for citizen movements and social transformation.

In 1988–89, I had the opportunity to study and work in the Soviet Union, just as cultural exchanges were beginning to flourish between the United States and the USSR. In this time of crisis when the policies of Perestroika were taking hold, staples such as soap, butter, and meat were rationed; one day my detergent was swiped while I was waiting for a bus. I learned about living on the margins in urban Russia; I became friends with migrants from outlying towns who were forced to be squatters because they lacked official identity papers and there was a government housing shortage. I also saw how permissible expressions of different types of belonging in Soviet society were emerging in a myriad of ways; I frequented a Hare Krishna café that opened in 1988, attended rock and jazz clubs where young hippies and intelligentsia congregated, and took part (albeit as an observer) in a growing number of opposition political rallies and public forums.

My curiosity about this society undergoing a massive transformation became much more than an avocation, and I sought out a means of understanding what I was experiencing. In particular, I wanted to learn what made people feel Soviet and how this was changing as the very definitions of the society were in flux in a way they had not been since World War II. In the urban setting of Leningrad, I had not been able to ascertain much about how non-Russians or those living outside metropolitan areas were incorporated into this society or about how they were making sense of the changes brought about by Perestroika and Glasnost'. The field of anthropology seemed to offer a way of examining the theoretical and real tensions imbedded in socialism as a system of social organization and as a cultural framework defining the lives of millions of people.

As I was to learn, the field of anthropology was being critically assessed from a number of perspectives beginning in the 1970s, but especially in the 1980s and 1990s. In particular, authors point to the colonial heritage privileging the practice of anthropologists studying the "Other" (see Harrison 1991; Marcus 1986; Asad 1973). Today dynamics of fieldwork continue to be contested as practitioners and communities negotiate the relative benefits gained from ethnographic research (Smith 1999; Rothenberg 1999; Biolsi and Zimmerman 1997). In my initial efforts at ethnography as a white, middle-class anthropologist from the United States, I sensed that I could easily be viewed as reenacting a scenario from the past when earlier ethnologists and explorers of European extraction traversed Siberia in search of a world they found exotic. With this in mind, I sought to establish grounds for a relationship with consultants and members of the central Siberian community that would not be merely academic but would also allow me to address issues that many community members found compelling. These turned out to be issues of identity in the context of disintegrating and reformulating social structures in the former Soviet Union of the early 1990s.

Writing is inherently an activity that feels solitary, but it involves careful choices about social relationships that extend over time and through space. In an effort to respect the privacy of those who so generously included me in their lives, I have used pseudonyms throughout this book, except when a person was speaking in a public capacity. I have also thought carefully about the use of tense in this book. I do not want the reader to think of the Evenki as timeless, unchanging, and lacking the historicity inherent to all human societies, a perspective easily invoked through the use of the present tense, trapping subjects in an eternal "ethnographic present." Likewise, I do not want to position my discussion of Evenki and their social practices as if they no longer exist, something that could be implied by settling on the use of the past tense. In reflecting on these issues, I have chosen to shift between past and present tenses where appropriate and also locate the text in a specific year. The dilemma of tense is, however, only recognized, not resolved, and remains a challenge for ethnographic writing (see Rethmann 2001: xviii).

This book is based on eighteen months of ethnographic fieldwork conducted from 1992 to 1999, primarily in central Siberia in the Evenk District but also in the central Siberian city of Krasnoiarsk (see Figure 1). The core of the fieldwork was carried out in the Evenk District from 1993 to 1994, with shorter stays in 1992, 1995, 1998, and 1999. Funding for the majority of the fieldwork was provided by the International Research and Exchanges Board (1993–94, summer 1998). Additional funding was provided by the University of Pittsburgh Nationalities Room (summer 1992) and the American Council of Teachers of Russian (summer 1995). I owe a debt of gratitude to my mentors over the years—Phillip Kohl, Robert Hayden, Laurel Kendall, Barbara Miller, and particularly, Nicole Constable who taught me to truly appreciate ethnography. A postdoctoral fellowship at the American Museum of Natural History (1997–99) was supported with funding from the Henry Luce Foundation. Teaching release provided by the Faculty of Arts (2000) and by the Peter Wall Institute of Advanced Studies (2002) at the University of British Columbia made revisions for the book possible. I am grateful to the American Museum of Natural History (AMNH) Library Services, for granting me permission to reproduce images for use in the book.

This book could not have been written without the generosity and assistance of many people in the Evenk District including teachers and students at the residential school; Khristina Ivanovna Chardu, former director of the Evenk District Regional History Museum; and a family of local artists—the Borisenkovs—who both warmly welcomed me and helped coordinate initial archival research and final permissions for illustrations. I am also indebted to the Evenk District Regional History Museum for kindly granting me permission to reproduce images from the museum's photographic collection. Members of the Evenk District Association for Peoples of the North, *Arun*, and particularly its first president Zinaida Nikolaevna Pikunova, deserve a separate note of gratitude. From the project's inception in 1992, Zinaida Nikolaevna and her colleagues sponsored me, welcomed me into the community, and patiently taught me about their struggles.

A number of scholars, both in and of the former Soviet Union, deserve thanks for their advice over the years. Igor Krupnik first suggested that I consider Tura as a possible fieldsite; he also read a draft of this project and provided important encouragement. Colleagues at the Institute of Ethnology and Anthropology in Moscow introduced me to the workings of Russian scholarship, sponsored visas for research, and provided opportunities for discussing my findings. Otto Habeck generously shared his comments on an early version of the book manuscript; in particular he prevented me from committing several geographical errors. I am grateful to Olessia Vovina, who, with little advance notice, provided Russian language expertise to fine-tune the manuscript in its final stages.

In my home away from home over the past decade, I was fortunate to make lasting friendships in Tura, Krasnoiarsk, Moscow, and St. Petersburg. In particular the Savoskuls made Russia feel like home in countless ways, providing me with extended hospitality when I first began this project in 1992, and eventually integrating me into their daily lives during many subsequent stays. The Savoskuls did not just take on an extended houseguest but took on the task of engaging me with the pressing issues in their lives, including supply economics and specifically brick procurement in post-Soviet Russia. My archival research in Krasnoiarsk would have been impossible without the warm welcome of the Polonskis and the ever-capable Sergei Levshits. My perceptions of Soviet and post-Soviet society owe much to Elena Kosova's sharp wit, and our discussions over piping hot cups of coffee and cooler cups of other liquids on topics ranging from illicit literature in the late 1980s to humor in the form of jokes (*anekdoty*) as social commentary.

In the late 1980s, prior to this project's inception, Alexander Kozlov introduced me to the intrigues of Soviet youth culture, and in the 1990s Mariia and Vladimir Khomenko, Nikita Kaplan, and Maksim Khromov enthusiastically included me in their rapidly shifting world of central Siberian youth culture. I would also like to thank others in the Evenk District who taught me about their lives and gave so generously of their time over the years; out of respect for their privacy, I have chosen not to name them. This project would have gone unrealized without the formal and informal consultants to this project; some gave interviews, others assisted me in making crucial contacts, and still others provided me with important newspaper clippings, statistics, and citations.

My thinking about this project has benefited from discussions with colleagues, students, family, and friends. In particular, Nina Diamond, Jackie Siapno, and Mrinalini Saran applied their expertise to improve the arguments and readability of the manuscript. Samya Burney provided me with much-needed perspective at a time when the project was faltering, and Yael Lavi and Gideon Shelach prompted me early on to keep a broad readership for my work in mind. Julie Cruikshank's moral support was important in the final stages. Sheryl Clark contributed her enthusiasm for anthropological inquiry as she assisted with the preparation of the index.

Milind Kandlikar has been an intellectual and spiritual anchor over the years that this project has been part of our lives. His multiple readings of the text moved the project along at several critical junctures, and in the final weeks of the manuscript's preparation he made sure that Mira's early months of life were not overwhelmed by the project. Milind's joie de vive and commitment to nurturing ties with friends and family have been a sustaining force. My parents, John Bloch and Rebecca Sheppard, live their lives deeply engaged with issues of social justice and education—the seeds they planted early on were responsible for this book in no small measure. I am also grateful to Rebecca for proofreading the manuscript in its very final stages. The adventurous spirit of my mother, Sue Dwelle, possessed me to take on this project, while the years we shared living in a Vermont commune instilled in me an interest in alternative social systems.

It is hard to imagine that this project could have come to its completion without the generous support of the many people named above. As the author of these pages, however, I carry the sole responsibility for the ultimate form and content of the book.

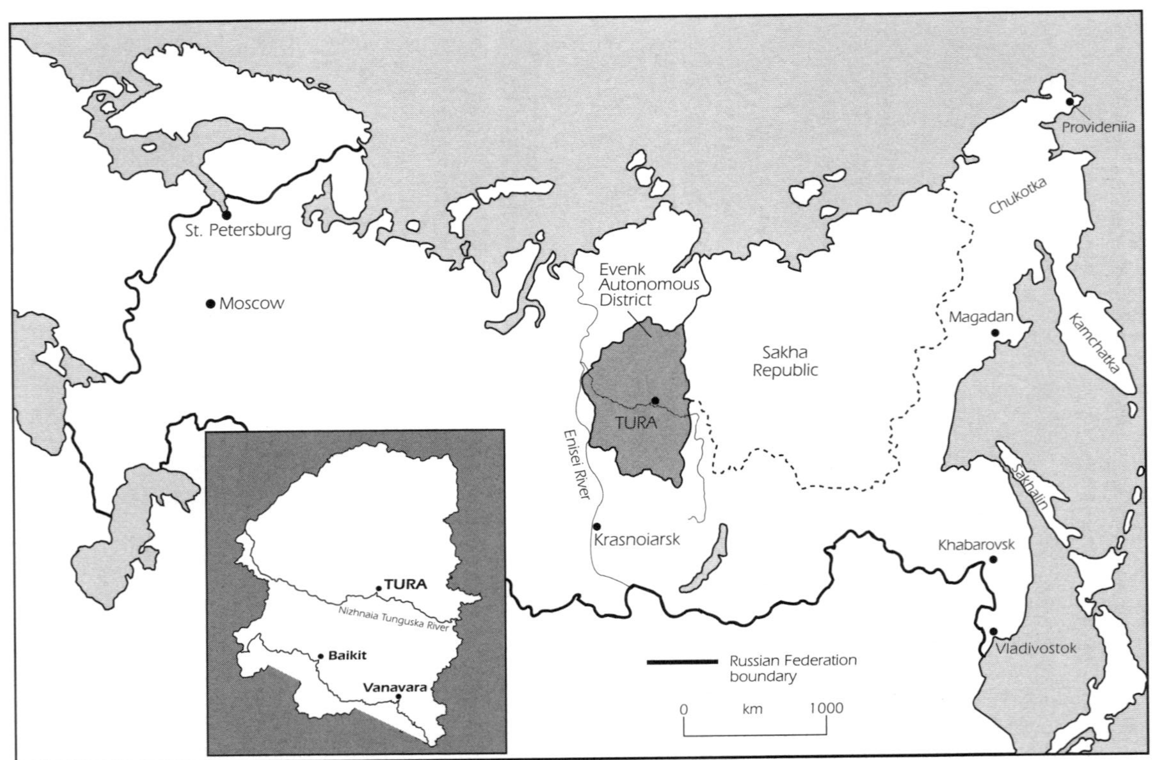

Figure 1. Russian Federation with Evenk Autonomous District inset. Created by Bridget Thomas, Department of Anthropology, American Museum of Natural History.

Introduction
Fieldwork, Socialism in Crisis, and Identities in the Making

> For years political concerns covered up the real history of the people of our country. While it was proclaimed that the history of the USSR was the same as the history of the people, in fact this official history did not represent the people's history. Numerically small ethnic groups especially suffered in this respect. It is not surprising that we do not know our history; customs and traditions are being forgotten, and knowledge of material and spiritual culture is disappearing. Our children are losing a sense of ethnic identity; they do not know the real value of their heritage and culture.
>
> —From the preface to *Evenk Ethnography Program* (Shchapeva 1994: 3)

I arrived to carry out long-term research in the town of Tura in fall 1993, several days following President Yeltsin's decree to disband the Russian Parliament. Following my flights from North America to Moscow and then to Krasnoiarsk, the central Siberian city about 300 miles south of Tura, I sat with friends and watched the live CNN broadcast of the armed crisis back in Moscow. The predominantly Communist members of Parliament refused to abide by the unconstitutional decree to disband Parliament, and in the confrontation that ensued Yeltsin's forces eventually took the building by siege (Khronika smutnogo vremeni 1993). At the time I did not fully appreciate how the political standoff, which continued to unfold and be televised nationwide in the days following as I began my fieldwork, affected my project. In part, President Clinton's support for Yeltsin's violent actions jeopardized my research because Communists in Tura were already seething about U.S. "interventionist" tactics when I arrived in the town. When I accepted a gracious offer to stay in the temporarily vacant apartment belonging to the representative from the Evenk District, I did not realize how much this man was disliked by many anti-Communists and reformers. Only after living in this apartment for nearly a month did I learn that this representative to the People's Congress of the Russian Federation was one of the 100 representatives who barricaded themselves inside the Parliament building for days as Yeltsin's anti-Communist supporters bombarded the building with gunfire.

My fieldwork seemed to be off to an uneasy start, but then this fit with the expected initial phase of ethnographic projects, reified in accounts of fieldwork as a time for "gaining rapport." As many authors have described, anthropological fieldwork is practically defined by a requisite period of gaining the trust of consultants (Kligman 1988: 20; Scheper-Hughes 1979: 11). Nita Kumar has written, "Fieldwork is by its very nature an ambitious, optimistic, very personal effort to woo over indifferent strangers" (1992: 2). Such descriptions of the process of "gaining rapport" appear as a common thread in fieldwork accounts, and ethnographers are increasingly dedicating a portion of their work to considering how their presence in communities intersects with shifting balances of power, heightened social inequalities, and allegiances to be made and, sometimes, lost.

I initiated my research in Tura with a keen interest in the role of education, particularly residential schooling, in defining relationships between indigenous people and the Soviet state. This topic soon came to articulate with broader issues of identity because a major preoccupation of the community revolved around competing ideas about Evenk identities and the future relationship of the state to "small peoples of the North" (*malochislennye narody Severa*). This Soviet government designation encompassed those indigenous groups considered to be numerically "small," with the implied comparison being to the "large" ethnic groups of Russians, Ukrainians, Uzbeks, and others living in the former Soviet Union.[1] Community members frequently discussed the future of government affirmative action policies toward "small peoples of the North." An equally prevalent topic of debate among Evenki revolved around ways to ensure their rights, including access to land for subsistence practices, native language education, and benefits from the privatization of natural resources in the region. The contemporary contest over Evenk identities was tightly related to the rapidly shifting political-economic context in the community. Overall, my research focus on Evenk identities resonated with those with whom I spent hours in conversation, and for those who ultimately had control over my access to archives, statistics, and travel.

As a citizen of the United States, or *Amerikanka* as I was usually referred to, I was not quickly absorbed into the everyday life of Tura. These were the early days of satellite broadcasts of U.S. media, and this incessantly reminded my consultants of the relative wealth and opportunity from which I had only temporarily disengaged. As Roger Lancaster reflects in his work on Nicaragua (1988: 6), given the legacy of anthropology as a discipline often historically allied with government surveillance, it is not surprising that those who become its subjects of study find the projects to be suspect. Furthermore, given my origins as a citizen of the country in most direct opposition to the Soviet Union in the tug-of-war known as the Cold War, it was inevitable that I was perceived as closely related to this global power struggle.

Images of the "West" and Dreams of Consumption

"Gaining rapport" as a North American doing research in a central Siberian town in the 1990s was complicated by the fresh history of the Cold War, which invoked a binary view of geopolitics, with Soviet culture posed in opposition to all things viewed as "Western."[2] After more than sixty years of official open antagonism toward the "West" (*zapad*) and its "decadent bourgeois culture," by the late 1980s, U.S. popular culture was being widely rebroadcast and reimagined throughout Russia.[3] In the 1990s in the Evenk District capital of Tura, youth were especially smitten with Western media images and market glitz, but people of all ages and backgrounds eagerly anticipated weekly television shows such as *Santa Barbara*, *MTV*, and *Dallas*, as well as a Mexican serial *The Rich Also Cry*, depicting the tribulations of contemporary Mexican aristocrats. *Turintsy*, residents of Tura, often spoke in terms of the relative poverty surrounding them in comparison to what they perceived as the wealth of the West.

One reflection of the fascination with the West was an active appreciation for the bright colors and appealing design features of Western packaging. In 1992–93 many apartments in Tura had a shelf displaying boxes or containers with the English labels facing out; some displayed empty cookie boxes, others perfume bottles or candy wrappers. Rural central Siberians were not, however, the only ones smitten with Western products and bright packaging in the early 1990s. In the apartment in Moscow where I briefly stayed, the owners had arranged a wide array of Western packaging, including Folgers coffee cans, Stridex facial wipes, and soap wrappers in a prominent glass-fronted cupboard in the center of the apartment. While the impact of market forces in Moscow and outlying regions differed in degree at this time, irrespective of geography or political affiliation there was a widespread fascination with commodities and the new material possibilities suggested by an expanding consumer culture in Russia.

The array of packaging could be viewed as embodying the aspirations to consume that were burgeoning in the early 1990s in Russia (Humphrey 1995). The packaging was also part of how Turintsy were imagining their new lives in a different political order with open borders; they were able to envision global connections to geographically distant others through foreign consumer goods unavailable in Russia until the early 1990s (see Appadurai 1996). Consumer goods linked a wide range of people to the modernity that many believed had eluded Russia in the late Soviet period. Frequently images of "civilization," *kul'tura,* were invoked in contrast to what was commonly termed as the "backward," *nerazvitaia* or *ostalaia,* life in Russia and in the town of Tura in particular.[4] It was not uncommon for people to display pages torn from Western, English-language magazines on their walls. Among the popular images displayed were advertisements for home furnishings and bath fixtures. In one case an advertisement for Finnish bath fixtures was hung opposite the chamber pot in a water closet that, like most of those in town, lacked running water. The squeaky clean, blond Finnish kids depicted in the immaculate bath chamber seemed to exemplify the view Turintsy tended to have toward the West as a place to envy for its opulence and basic amenities.

As scholars have written about housewares and status elsewhere (Rosenberger 1992), in the early 1990s housewares in Russia increasingly appeared to announce individual aspirations to become more "Western" and thereby increase status levels. The prominent display of wrappers and the aspiration to install a Finnish toilet could both be understood as examples of what Bourdieu (1984) describes in other contexts as the simulation of higher classes' tastes, or cultural capital, by households with insufficient income, or economic capital. In short, throughout Russia in the 1990s consumerism was extensive; some have hypothesized this was the result of an earlier inaccessibility of goods, a sort of thirst created by an earlier dearth of consumer products (Verdery 1996: 26–29). In this area of Russia, consumerism seemed to be at least equally the result of the sudden appearance of advertising on television and sheer curiosity as the result of some sort of flaw in socialist ideology.

An all-pervasive sense of insufficient consuming power was shared by people of diverse ethnic backgrounds in the town of Tura. Russians, Evenki, Ukrainians, Sakha, and the few Azeris and Tadzhiks (displaced by civil war) all tended to share this sense. This was intensified by an insecurity about financial sources and inflation; as soon as much-awaited paychecks were received, Turintsy would seek a means of transforming the cash into the material goods that were available. For those with paychecks funded directly from federal budgets, mostly Russians and Ukrainians working in the local radio and television station or with the local aviation, these were luxury goods such as radios, telephones, and video players. Those subsisting largely on locally issued paychecks or subsidies that were sometimes months late could generally only afford foodstuffs. My presence in the field at a time when such schisms around consumption were beginning to be intensified by television advertising and growing disparities of wealth significantly affected my attempt to "gain rapport."

A Researcher's Cultural Baggage: MTV, Bush's Legs, and the Cold War

As a range of ethnographers (for example, Abu-Lughod 1993; Lancaster 1988; Rosaldo 1989) have attested, the subject position of a researcher is critical to how research is conceived and conducted, and in turn, how communities react to or engage with projects. In my case, "the West" loomed as an icon that often took on far more importance than my stated research project for the people with whom I worked. The legacy of restricted travel both outside Russia and within the country was in part responsible for creating this intense interest but more important was the imagery of binary cultural frameworks established during the Cold War. This historical influence resonates in the lyrics of a late 1980s rock song by the acclaimed Soviet group Nautilius Pompilius. As the chorus of one song laments: "Goodbye America, oooo, where I will never be. Farewell to your faded jeans and your forbidden fruits" ("Goodbye Amerika, ooooo, gde ia nikogda ne budu. Goodbye Amerika, ooooo, proshchai tertye dzhinsy i tvoi zapretnye plody"). The song incorporates a sense of the officially "forbidden" West prior to the onset of Perestroika in the mid-1980s. As in this song, in the popular imagination in central Siberia in the early 1990s, *Amerika,* meaning the West, continued to occupy a central place in a cultural landscape, both figuratively and literally.

The jarring disjuncture between a time when Amerika was a forbidden fruit and a time when its images and products were colonizing the cultural landscape further heightened the attention paid to me as an ethnographer. Various people looked to me as the definitive source of information on the West, and specifically the United States. At one point, for instance, the director of the Office for the Defense of the Family, Children, and Motherhood (Otdel po delam zashchity semei, detei i materinstva), an office established in the early 1990s combining social welfare and housing concerns, asked me to comment on a local community event being termed the "Celebration of the Family." She was interested in what types of activities would be planned for a similar celebration in the United States, but also in how "family" might be construed there. At another point I was asked by students of a local vocational school to give a television interview reflecting on contemporary adolescence and family dynamics. And in the residential school and in several organizations in the town of Tura, I was frequently queried about Alaska. "Do towns there have running water? How much do they get for a sable pelt? Do children there know their native languages? Are there reindeer in Alaska?" and "How much are their [teachers', herders', doctors', etc.] paychecks?"

The knowledge of the United States and its high standard of living relative to the rest of the world was also invoked by Russians and Evenki who sought to align the project of anthropology more with their pressing concerns (compare with Rethmann 1999). In various contexts they questioned my lack of personal complaints regarding the rough living conditions which they faced on a daily basis. Many jokingly inquired if I had been exiled or at least assigned by my academic supervisor to work in the town. While I sometimes grumbled to myself about the unkempt public outhouses or the poor drainage system that sometimes caused spring melt and waste water to flow over the sidewalk and road, for the most part I did not comment on these aspects of daily life; I viewed myself as a guest in Tura.

Following a radio broadcast of an interview in which I was asked how I felt about the town, and specifically about the lack of indoor plumbing, several Turintsy stopped me in the street to talk. These listeners were dissatisfied that I had answered the radio correspondent's question without criticizing the local politicians who had not seen to improving basic amenities. Some people emphasized that as an international researcher I could potentially publicize and perhaps assist in improving social conditions in the region. I took their criticism as a commentary on how anthropology is far too often disengaged from addressing the pain and suffering so widespread in the world. The local sense that research should be tied to direct improvements in social conditions is a reminder to social scientists and echoes Scheper-Hughes's concerns. As she explains, anthropology's "time-honored conventional stance of 'cultural relativity' . . . dedicated to seeing the 'good' in every culture" (1979: 12) is closely linked to a narrow functionalist view of human societies prevalent in the discipline and in need of scrutiny.

Shifting Sites of Power: Political Parties, Spies, and Methods

In the initial stages of fieldwork, I learned that establishing rapport needs to be rethought as not simply an individual's decision to "woo" as Kumar (1992) indicates but as a matter of the complex web of sociopolitical relations into which one enters as a researcher. Furthermore, as I quickly learned, methods of research must be carefully fitted to both research projects and shifting situations in the field. In my effort to use a range of methods, I supplemented semistructured interviews with a household survey. My thinking was that a survey of households would give me a broader sample of perspectives than I could gain in structured interviews. I completed a survey of eighty households, but, ultimately this approach threatened to intensify the dichotomy I had sought to reduce of "us" (social scientists) and "them" (subjects). More importantly, the survey had a detrimental affect on the rapport established with members of the community in the prior months of research. The survey approach was inextricably associated with a strong dichotomy within Russian society between the government (*pravitel'stvo*) and the people (*narod*). As Roger Lancaster found in his work in Nicaragua (1988: 15), the survey approach was associated with an "officiousness" and "social distance" of bureaucrats, or worse, intelligence officers. This misguided attempt to employ such an empiricist method led me both to refocus my efforts on qualitative approaches and to reconsider the dynamics of power in the specific post-Soviet context.

Perhaps the recent break with the Soviet government caused people to be even more suspicious of any official attempts to collect data and quantify their lives, particularly in the privacy of their apartments.[5] The survey emphasized a distancing of researcher from community and reminded Turintsy that the fieldwork was part of a much larger academic enterprise that potentially had little to do with them. Furthermore, the survey reminded Turintsy of the need to "guard" their speech. Other scholars have also noted sharp distinctions between "guarded" and "unguarded" speech in Soviet society resulting from the suspicion that often pervaded social life in the former Soviet Union (Humphrey 1994b: 69). Ultimately, I set aside this method following the completion of a pilot survey; a more extensive survey would have jeopardized the trust of those with whom I sought to consult for more qualitative perspectives. The data collected even in the brief pilot survey has proven useful, however, particularly regarding subsistence practices among Turintsy, and in Chapter 2 I have drawn upon it.

In general, Turintsy welcomed me by inviting me to their homes for meals, taking me out on fishing trips, and introducing me to relatives. Many people eagerly assisted me in my research by introducing me to elderly relatives, loaning me books, sharing photographs, and locating copies of old newspaper clippings. There were some, however, who took umbrage with my project or were at least ambivalent about my presence in the community. For instance, one woman who rented me an apartment for several months—and whose child I tutored in English—quite vehemently announced to me over tea one day that Russia had no need for charity from the United States. This opinion was widely found throughout Russia in the 1990s. Older people especially begrudged the fact that the United States, so recently an official enemy, was now providing what they viewed as charity. This sentiment intensified when spoiled U.S. goods such as sour butter and moldy "Bush's legs" (drumsticks) appeared on the market in 1992–93.[6]

My project met the most resistance from an older generation of both Evenki and Russians who had much to lose in the radical transformations related to the emerging market economy. While the Association of Peoples of the North, a newly established, local indigenous rights organization, had approved my project and invited me to focus my research on residential schooling and youth culture, not everyone was in agreement that I should be present in the town. At several points during my research, old guard Communists accused me of being a CIA agent, despite the fact that from the very outset I described my work as an ethnography project under the aegis of the Russian Academy of Sciences. The presence of an American, who only three years before would not have received a visa to visit the nearest large city, let alone the town of Tura, was both incredible and a direct challenge to local Communists' authority.[7]

These old guard Party members had followed the political and economic changes initiated in Moscow. But, unlike those more powerful urban Communists who had something to gain (for example, positions as CEOs in companies) by quickly acquiescing to the shifting power and opportunities of capitalist mechanisms and appropriating state capital for personal investment, the local Communists were largely isolated from the potential personal benefits of a shift to capitalism. My presence brought them no concrete benefits and merely reminded them of their loss of authority over national policy and cultural production. For instance, in the Soviet period these old guard Communists had wielded considerable authority over deciding what was printed in the newspaper, broadcast over the radio, or advertised in a public space. During my research these spheres became increasingly open and even included notices for previously illegal religious gatherings. The radio and newspaper continued to be government controlled and therefore subject to new restrictions that were no longer defined by local Communist Party leaders.

As has been described for regions of Eastern Europe like Romania, the concept of "centralized accumulation" that operated in the Soviet period allowed a select Communist guard to control the allocation of resources (Kideckel 1993). Through control over everything from access to vacations to housing to freedom of worship, an elaborate hierarchy of Communist Party members and affiliates ensured compliance with cultural norms set by the Central Committee. These "nested hierarchies" of power, as Caroline Humphrey calls them in her examination of former socialist Mongolia (1994b), implicated all levels of society. In the mid-1990s, and especially in 1993 when the Communist Party was briefly outlawed, members of the old Communist guard were acutely aware of their waning authority.

Gendered States

Other segments of the population also felt a loss of power with the shift from state socialism. For instance, women in the former Soviet Union had disproportionately less access than men had to spheres of influence and power. Lapidus (1993) argues that during the Soviet period women were concentrated in the lower levels of organizational and pay hierarchy, and they thus now have less access to the spheres of government being privatized. While across Siberia seventy percent of women were reported to be unemployed in 1994 (Statistika 1994: 1), in Tura there were also large numbers of unemployed male oil-exploration workers.[8] Thus the numbers of unemployed men and women were more equal than elsewhere in Russia. Women in Tura were hard hit by the slashing of government funds supporting the public sector—schooling, medicine, and government stores—in which they formed a majority of those employed. In Tura this trend was evident in the levels and types of unemployment. While all those formerly employed in state organizations and agricultural cooperatives (*sovkhozy*) were in danger of losing their jobs as reorganizations took place, women generally fared worse than men. Men's labor was in demand as the construction of private buildings and housing grew in Tura, while women's labor was widely devalued. Some women with financial resources had the option of seeking additional training as bookkeepers, an emerging sphere of employment as the new federal tax inspection office (*nalogovaia inspektsiia*) began requiring each business or organization to keep careful accounts. The most marginal women resorted to low-paid extra-domestic work of washing floors in town organizations and businesses.

This aspect of restructuring, along with my own gender identity, certainly had implications for my research. First, I became aware of the ways women in particular were often suffering from the shift in political and economic systems, and this led me to focus my research on women's lives, as I discuss further in Chapters 3 and 4. Second, I became acutely conscious of gendered aspects of my interaction with Turintsy. As a number of scholars have suggested (Linnekin 1998; Turner 1996; Back 1993), generational subjectivities and related life course patterns significantly affect research.[9] As I was carrying out my research, there was a striking contrast between my relative lack of responsibility for family and household (or reproductive labor) and the heavy load carried by nearly all young women over sixteen or seventeen years old in Tura. Women were overwhelmingly responsible for childcare, caring for the sick, hauling household water, and shopping for food. The divergence in life courses was not missed by even young girls, who upon first meeting me would invariably ask why I was not married and why I did not have any children.

Like Jean Briggs, who found herself in a daughter role in her fieldwork among the Inuit (1970), as a young woman I was expected by older men and women to conduct myself with what they viewed as proper comportment. The idea of "proper" included both a "feminine" physical appearance—that is, dresses or skirts and make-up—and behaving in culturally appropriate gendered ways, including graciously accepting when men opened doors or insisted on carrying parcels. Moreover, as a young woman with little status from a gendered perspective, my interactions with high status segments of the population, both Evenki and Russians, were less than comfortable because they sometimes demanded what seemed to me to be inordinate amounts of deference. This certainly influenced my decision to interact more with middle and lower status people. In this way practice and theory merged in influencing the direction of my research.

In sharp contrast to the suspicion I sometimes encountered from Communists with firm convictions, most Turintsy welcomed me and were eager to assist me in carrying out my project. As a foreigner I was also assisted by a range of kind Turintsy who worried about my welfare and especially food supplies. I was rarely left without fresh fish or reindeer meat and was regularly invited to social functions. People thoughtfully invited me to their homes for meals and for bathing in their saunas. These occasions were invariably followed by tea with *varen'e,* jam made from local berries, and lively conversation. I was also asked to teach English courses for several hours a week at the residential school. By the end of my fieldwork, I could comfortably shift between interviewing and visiting bureaucrats to interviewing and visiting with the relatively marginalized segments of the population. While this type of role juggling was not always easy, once I established my identity as an ethnographer, someone interested in learning about everyday life, I was able to shift between being the "American representative"—when my presence was requested at official events such as the banquet dinner celebrating the 63rd anniversary of the founding of the Evenk District—and being a less marked member of the community, as when I would join in the residential school outings or help a neighbor pick berries.

Methods in Process

For the first two months of my fieldwork, I observed as many aspects of Tura society as possible while also collecting some basic statistical data. Although I had official letters of introduction from the Russian Academy of Sciences and several key contacts in the town, I felt awkward going through overly official channels each time I wanted to "observe" in a given setting. First of all, in a town such as Tura that exists largely as a bureaucratic center, I was worried that my presence might become too closely allied with official personalities and thereby endanger the trust of "common" people. Second, I was hesitant to impose myself on people merely because their superiors had approved the interaction. Therefore I established my entrée by introducing myself to the immediate superior in a given setting, such as to the head doctor in the pediatric division of the hospital or the head administrator in the orphanage. Occasionally she or he requested to see my letters of introduction, but more often than not, after our brief discussion, he or she simply approved my request to observe on an informal basis. Thereafter, I made individual arrangements to meet with specific people in the organization.

During the early months of my research, I visited day care centers, became acquainted with the schools and divisions of the hospital, shopped and waited in line in small stores and kiosks, attended the first Russian Orthodox church services ever held in Tura,[10] bathed in the public bath house, toured the oil exploration headquarters, attended birthday parties and funerals, dined with new friends, and regularly attended festivals and concerts at the House of Culture (*dom kul'tury*), the Soviet version of a community center. Gradually I began spending increasing amounts of time in the residential school, orphanage, and pediatric/obstetric division of the hospital as I narrowed the focus of my research.

As my research progressed, it centered around informal and structured interviews with people invested in the relationship of the Evenk community to the Soviet and post-Soviet state. I found "casual chat" to be an invaluable research method permitting the speaker to be in more control, for as Humphrey has written, in this way the interviewee "evokes her own attitudes and draws her interlocutor into relationship with them" (1994b: 77). I conducted extensive interviews with activists and local administrators, but the more compelling material that forms the crux of this book was gathered in conversations with ordinary people drawing on and thinking about the place of government structures in their everyday lives. In an attempt to meet a range of people who were interested in thinking about identity and socialization, including ideas about motherhood, family, and schooling, I visited the orphanage, residential school, and pediatric/obstetric division twice a week. In each domain, I engaged in informal conversations, observation, and interviews with parents, staff, and administrators. The residential school and clinic were especially key as places where I was able to meet Evenki from various segments of the population. Evenki from different regions of the Evenk District and, more importantly, Evenki belonging to both high-status and more marginalized social strata frequented these institutions.

In the residential school, I became familiar with the daily routines,the interactions between teachers and students, and the broader place of the institution within the town. The residential school also provided me with an initial identity as a teacher that was comprehensible for the community at large. Most people quickly grasped the purpose of my research in Tura as a social science study. They could not fathom, however, what a young woman without a research team was doing in their town. Although ethnography and sociology are disciplines well understood by the broad public in Russia, the standard conception is that such studies focus on "traditional" culture, like shamanism or reindeer herding, take a few months at most, and are done in teams of researchers.[11] This was the pattern followed by Soviet ethnographers. Although I taught only two English classes a week for a total of one and one-half hours, people in Tura came to think of me as the American who teaches in the residential school.

While the school provided me with a locally meaningful identity, the pediatric clinic was important for expanding my contacts. The clinic was a point of entrée for contacting parents, and predominantly young women, who had attended the residential school recently (in the past ten years or the early 1980s). These parents often had children who were currently attending the school as well. Twenty out of twenty-four women approached agreed to be interviewed in the privacy of a room provided by the clinic, and a few invited me to their homes. The initial structured interviews were conducted in the clinic, on occasion with a tape recorder, but generally women asked that this not be used. In the subsequent open-ended life histories with the six women who chose to take part, they all felt comfortable with the tape-recorder. For these more extensive interviews, we met regularly in each woman's apartment. Usually we met alone, but on occasion the women were joined by family members or friends.

Attending public meetings and social gatherings provided a broader sense of the place of Soviet cultural practice and a sense of the collective in Evenk lives. Through the contacts developed at these gatherings, I was able to collect life histories of older Evenk women. I collected eight extensive life histories of Evenk women aged 65–75. All of them attended residential schools in the Evenk District from the late 1930s to 1940s. Ultimately, these narratives about lives lived over decades of radical change in central Siberia gripped my imagination and propelled me toward writing this book.

Locating the Project in Theoretical Frameworks

Throughout the early and mid-twentieth century, the creation of socialist societies brought about radically new ways of life for populations across the world. In establishing revolutionary governments, socialist nations also radically altered the shape of every day life and the sense of belonging for each and every person. In the case of the Soviet Union, the country was configured out of vastly different regions and the government sought to forge a completely new national identity. Incorporating peoples of different backgrounds and languages, such as indigenous Siberians, was a monumental task facing the Soviet Union when it sought to create a new nation. A painful legacy of collectivization of lands and animal herds, nationalization of private property, and compulsory schooling for indigenous people were all part of this Soviet campaign to sweep the population into a new society and establish the contours of a new nation-state.

The Soviet attempts to create a new society, including altered social hierarchies and imposed structures of learning, were rife with challenges. As a range of authors have documented (Serge 1937; Pika 1989; Conquest 1990; Nove 1993), in the wake of enthusiasm for creating an equitable society, vast injustices took place and political idealism gave way to opportunism. By the late 1930s, millions had lost their lives as the newly entrenched Soviet policies drove apparatchiks and citizens at all levels of the social hierarchy to exercise power against their rivals and those people perceived as endangering the national interest. By the mid-1940s, which brought the devastation of World War II, the country was in ruins, but a nation of "Soviet" people had emerged.

It is a paradox that so many people in the nearly 75 years of Soviet power suffered government-sanctioned injustices of various degrees and yet by the late 1980s relatively few were seeking to jettison their allegiance to the nation. In fact, by the mid-1990s in various regions of Russia only a handful were openly decrying the former Soviet way of life, and more commonly there was widespread support for reinstituting aspects of the Soviet system. This book examines this paradox, specifically asking how a common sense of belonging to a Soviet society took shape in a region of Russia in which indigenous people suffered a specific form of repression—the dispossession of their land, cultural practices, and rights to self-government. Instead of homogenizing indigenous Siberians' experience of Soviet power as one of belonging, this book also considers the ways in which resistances to state power, particularly in schooling contexts, took shape and why resistance was not automatic.

From another perspective the book is an examination of "habitus," the creation of social patterns and structures through the everyday practice of actors (Bourdieu 1977). I am also critical, however, of how the idea of habitus tends to homogenize actors (see Bourdieu et al. 1973). In this book I aim to demonstrate that individuals' actions and beliefs are shaped in society but not in a homogenous way. Specific subject positions influence how individuals transform society, for instance, by mobilizing constituents or by contributing to the smooth workings of institutions such as the residential school. I draw on perspectives of individual indigenous Siberians, specifically central Siberian Evenki, and especially women and men from a range of social strata, to consider the way relations of power are being reconfigured in this post-Soviet Siberian town.

Waning Socialism, Recent Ethnography, and Gendered Lives

The experience of the Evenki, one of the largest indigenous Siberian groups in the Russian Federation today, in many ways exemplifies how the Soviet Union as a socialist state sought to promote its own distinct path of "modernization," including in regard to indigenous peoples.[12] As I argue throughout this book, a focus on one Evenk community in the town of Tura provides insight into the unique ways in which a specific group experienced the Soviet era and continues to understand its identity as a distinct indigenous Siberian group. Set in the post-Soviet era, this book is about consciousness in flux and about the place of indigenous Siberians in broader social movements, both within the Russian Federation and beyond. As Kay Warren has noted, "revitalization" or "ethnic revindication," is an important trend to turn our attention to throughout the world (1991: 103). Warren has cautioned that studies of such new social movements have often short-changed their subjects; they have tended to overlook the internal dynamics of the movements, deemphasize the remaking of culture through activism, overly celebrate "choice" and individuals, and in general gloss over the complexities of people as having multiple identities and allegiances (1991: 103–4). Following Warren, I seek to reflect the internal dynamics and multiple levels of identities in one central Siberian community, while rooting this in a broad sociopolitical context.

It seems impossible to reflect on any group of people within Russia without considering the place of socialist practices in their lives. Purely socialist governments have decreased in number with the fall of the Soviet Union, and some—like Russia, China and Vietnam—have begun to incorporate aspects of market economies. Socialist cultural practices and ideals of egalitarianism (even if not realized in many ways) are recognizable, however, across cultural expanses and continue to play a role in contemporary societies.[13] In the context of Eastern Europe and the former Soviet Union, recent scholarship has addressed a wide range of issues related to these ideals of egalitarianism. First, scholars have focused on negotiations around land reform, primarily in Eastern Europe (Hann 1996; Kaneff 1996; Pine 1996; Lampland 1995; Verdery 1999). Second, scholars have examined gender ideologies under socialism and post-socialism, emphasizing the ways in which women have been marginalized in both eras (Einhorn 1993; Kligman 1998; Gal and Kligman 2000). Most significantly, scholars have indicated that the demise of socialism clears the way for societies in Eastern Europe and the former Soviet Union to move on to establish alternative civic entities (Verdery 1996).

Some scholarship on the former Soviet Union is less eager to point out the inherent flaws of socialist culture as a whole and instead focuses on the ways in which people are interpreting their historical experiences. In Russia, much of this research has been conducted in cities (mostly Moscow and St. Petersburg). It has focused on ethnic identity (Starovoitova 1987), youth culture (Markowitz 2000; Pilkington 1996; Cushman 1995), structures of education (Lempert 1996), and queer culture (Essig 1999). Ries's work (1997) on Muscovite discourses centering around suffering, poverty, and gender politics especially points to widespread contours of cultural practice in the former Soviet Union. Urban Russian intellectual circles have certainly defined a large part of what it means to be Soviet, or now post-Soviet, in a social system that has a tradition of highly centralized media, scholarship, and educational curricula.

Social practices in outlying regions, or the vast majority of Russia that stretches over eleven time zones and is not predominantly urban, have received less attention from Western scholars until recently. Perhaps one of the most important works that has served as a benchmark for studies in dispersed, outlying, or "peripheral" regions has been Humphrey's *Karl Marx Collective* (1983) about a Buriat collective farm. Humphrey's updated and expanded work (1999a) further explores the tensions created by the intersection of an individually oriented market economy and the collectively rooted Buriat society in southern Siberia. Several scholars have also examined the historical development of the intricate historical webs of Russian and Soviet political-economic development projects among indigenous Siberians (Golovnev and Osherenko 1999; Grant 1995a; Slezkine 1994; Vakhtin 1994). In general, this work has tended toward policy and structural analysis, with less emphasis on local experience.

Increasingly scholars are engaging in nuanced ethnographic work in Siberia that reflects the experiential nature of cultural expression in a specific time and place (Rethmann 2001; Kerttula 2000; Anderson 2000; Ssorin-Chaikov 1998). In these works, individual lives take center stage to varying degrees. They remind us that broad-ranging debates in anthropology—regarding tradition, gender roles, emotion, knowledge systems, and relations between periphery and center—are most compelling when they are illustrated not by the policy initiatives of governments but through the practices of people. In a similar manner, in this book I seek to dislodge an image of monolithic Soviet power. My argument revolves around the idea that Soviet power was differentially experienced, depending on the ways in which people were engaging with the state, as people who were urban or rural, men or women, indigenous or Russian. As explored in the narratives at the center of analysis in the book (and particularly in Chapters 2, 3, and 4), the residential school is a setting in which the Soviet structures of power—and the ambivalences around it, the resistances to it, and the accommodations of it—can be vividly examined.

This book integrates perspectives on schooling, Evenk intellectuals, life histories, and the place of material culture and museums in the definition of Evenk identities. Throughout I engage in what Rethmann aptly calls "positioned storytelling" (2000: 2), in an attempt to allow the individual lives of those often overlooked in social science writing on the Russian Federation—women, children, and rural communities, among others—to become central. "Positioned storytelling" is a discursive practice frequently employed by anthropologists (for example, Abu-Lughod 1993; Constable 1997; Wolf 1992); as Rethmann explains, it "disrupts the possibility of reading for certainty and fixed meanings" (2001: 177). Applying this approach to ethnographic writing on post-Soviet contexts is one powerful way of countering a prevalent policy-oriented body of literature that tends to homogenize local experience, leaving out the divergence of views and the ways that people negotiate daily lives.

Contemporary ethnography on Siberia is increasingly turning its attention to gendered experience (Kerttula 2000; Balzer 1993; Chaussonnet 1988). Only Rethmann (2001), however, has made this the crux of her work. As in anthropological writing more broadly, the tendency in writing on Siberia has been toward homogenizing experience as if members of a community or ethnic group share perspectives and social roles irrespective of gender.[14] I aim to demonstrate in different ways throughout this book how Evenk men and women encountered the Soviet state in distinctly gendered ways. Furthermore, I examine gendered experience as it was cross-cut by regional, educational, generational, and emerging class differences in the 1990s.

Here I seek to highlight the ways in which Soviet cultural practice continues as a signpost for many, and perhaps especially for Evenk women, who were both the particular focus of Soviet efforts to transform indigenous social practices, and in some ways the most significant beneficiaries of the social supports offered by the Soviet system. As explored throughout the following chapters, Evenk women's experience of Soviet power structures was distinct from that of men; social mobility within Soviet structures was facilitated for indigenous women through affirmative action and emphasis on women's labor within Soviet systems of knowledge. In contrast, Evenk men easily found employment herding and working close to the land, and while they were not discouraged from avenues of social mobility beginning with higher education, they tended to avoid these.

The following chapters seek to reflect on the differential ties indigenous Siberians had and continue to have to Soviet structures of power such as residential schooling. In this endeavor, however, this book aims to avoid homogenizing "Soviet power," "the Evenki," "the Russians," or "indigenous Siberians." For decades Evenk men's and women's lives were subject to an institution that was quintessentially Soviet and based on ideals of creating an egalitarian society, albeit through rigorous means of assimilation. In paying attention to the experiences of Evenk individuals, we can learn how people negotiate power and interpret and reframe ideologies in their lives.

Schooling, False Consciousness, and Resistance

In my first trip to the Evenk District, in the summer of 1992, the Soviet Union had recently given way (in December 1991) to the Commonwealth of Independent States, a loose consortium of many of the former republics belonging to the Soviet Union, and the Evenk District was now part of the Russian Federation. I spent the summer traveling to various reindeer herding brigades and villages in the Evenk District, meeting with people and listening to them as they began to make sense of the possibilities for political change and restructuring of economic and social life. The legacy of residential schools was one topic widely discussed. In this time of optimism and idealism, some Evenki thought that the schools should be shut down and students should be educated at home. One scholar suggested creating new practices of child socialization rooted in "traditional" family forms (Popov 1993).[15] Others considered returning to the early Soviet practice of a roaming teacher who would visit reindeer herding brigades and small villages periodically; this would allow children to live in the taiga while not missing out on formal education so essential for social mobility (Shebalin 1990: 78).

By 1993, when I returned to conduct long-term fieldwork in the Evenk District, talk of alternatives to the residential school and other radical transformations in the local relationships to the federal structure had diminished. Federal financing for education was severely curtailed, and there was no money for fundamental reorganization. Money that did reach the regions was not going to be released by regional administrations and departments of education for any experimental projects. What could have been a radical departure from Soviet systems of schooling for indigenous peoples was stymied by bureaucratic channels. As examined in the chapters that follow, however, in the mid- to late 1990s, Evenki began renegotiating a relationship to the nation-state and turned to transforming existing structures such as the residential school to meet their needs.

Around the world, schooling has served as a critical element in state-building and molding citizens (Reed-Danahay 1996; Stambach 1996; Chatty 1996).[16] Indigenous peoples in particular have been subjected to mass education as a key instrument of colonial domination and nation-state consolidation. In North America, Australia, Canada, and New Zealand, a system of state-run boarding schools operated from the 1920s until at least the 1970s and sometimes the 1980s; numerous accounts exist detailing the pain of detachment from families and the trials of forced assimilation (Simon 1990; Haig-Brown 1991; Lomawaima 1994; Child 1998; Kelm 1996). In the case of western and southern Africa, a widespread system of boarding schools continues to operate as the legacy of colonial pedagogy is widely absorbed and transformed in the context of post-colonial administration (Stambach 1996; Bledsoe 1992). In the Middle East, and specifically Oman, compulsory schooling for many groups that were nomadic until recent decades only became established in the 1970s as oil profits expanded and the government sought to link nomadic populations into the world economy (Chatty 1996). Across the world, however, not only governments are involved in designing schooling. Indigenous groups are also becoming involved in designing systems of education to meet the needs of their communities and to replace old models of education that were tools for state hegemony (Battiste 1999; Regnier 1999; Thies 1987; Cojtí Cuxil 1996).

In the extensive literature on the anthropology of schooling, the portion of work addressing dynamics of power and concepts of difference within school settings is especially instructive in thinking about residential schooling in central Siberia (see Giroux 1981; Ogbu 1991; Gibson 1988; Wax et al. 1989). The discussion about types of consciousness, resistance to institutional structures, and the social reproduction of educational behaviors is particularly relevant. For instance, Ogbu's work (1991) provides a compelling critique of the idea that educational "failures" of children in school contexts can be viewed as the result of a deficit in knowledge about the system, cultural capital, or language use. Ogbu writes about the types of cultural difference at stake in schooling and how cultural difference, along with active strategies, determines educational success.[17] In this way, Ogbu's work suggests that focusing attention on schooling as an instrument of the state also requires us to pay attention to the role cultural difference plays in the strategies families employ for interacting with school institutions.

In contrast to Ogbu's focus on cultural difference and active family strategies, Willis's work (1977) emphasizes how class structures are reproduced in schooling. Willis's study, focusing on working-class boys in a British school, dissects the broad social relations of power maintained by and reproduced in school settings. While this ethnography of schooling remains unparalleled in its intricate detail of the social reproduction of class among young men, it denies the dynamism of cultural practices and appears deterministic. From Willis's perspective, schooling is an instrument of dominant class sensibilities and the "false consciousness" of the "lads" prevents them from veering from the preordained confines of class.

This central concern in educational anthropology about the degree of agency people have in educational settings and in transforming their life worlds more broadly is at the crux of this book as well. The concept of "false consciousness" sits uneasily in a context in which the state is in crisis and people are engaged in rethinking structures of state power, such as schooling. While people do not necessarily redirect dominant power structures, they are not the mere cogs of preordained social systems. Tsianina Lomawaima (1994) makes a similar point about agency in her work with Lakota Sioux oral histories focused on residential schooling. She argues that while residential schooling for her consultants was generally a painful period when they were separated for extended periods from family and friends and subjected to the disciplinary and civilizing forces of missionary schools, these students were not merely oppressed. Lomawaima shows how these experiences did not preclude a range of effective resistances to the system; these efforts ranged from girls' avoiding wearing the bloomers required by the school dress code to some students running away from the schools. Furthermore, Lomawaima demonstrates that there was a range of interpretations of the system, with some students who excelled in academics and sports recalling their time in the schools fondly. Lomawaima does not invoke "false consciousness" to explain this range of experience but instead concludes that the system imposed its grip unevenly, with some people in positions to accommodate it consciously or even resist it, while others were subsumed and transformed by it. In particular, Lomawaima suggests that girls in the residential schools were "domesticated," while boys did not fall as severely under the purview of the institution.

Parallel to Lomawaima's findings, the experience of indigenous Siberians suggests that the degree of interaction with the institution of the residential school is gendered. In the case of indigenous Siberians, it is widely recognized that girls tend toward success in secondary education while boys have more difficulty succeeding. For the Evenki, this pattern appears to be related to the ways in which the state transformed subsistence practices and instituted residential schooling. As is discussed further in Chapter 3, in the Soviet era women's labor in reindeer herding was devalued while men's remained more constant. The Soviet state's ideology of emancipation of women, inspired by Friedrich Engels's *The Origin of the Family, Private Property and the State* (1972), attached social value to women as wage laborers employed outside the household; and in the context of the Evenk District, this Eurocentric valuation significantly shaped the gendered contours of Soviet structures of power. In the 1990s, girls were expected to complete twelve grades and go on for higher education, while it was socially acceptable, and even respectable for boys to leave school after grade nine and return to villages and herding. As discussed in Chapters 1 and 3, these collectives of herders were generally comprised of family members, but there was only one paid position for a woman as the "tentworker" in charge of domestic responsibilities; in effect the state's reorganization of herding that was established in the Soviet period edged women out of the taiga.

Much of the literature on the anthropology of education focuses on the school contexts and glosses over community, and particularly family interactions with schools. As Reed-Danahay (1996: 37) writes, school ethnography tends to "[work] either exclusively within the school or [look] from the school outward." This book seeks to depict men and women's relationship to schooling as an instrument of the state. In the context of post-Soviet Siberia, the reach of the state is not viewed in the same way, however, that it is in Reed-Danahay's analysis set in rural France. In the 1990s, more often the state was chastised for its lack of involvement than for its overinvolvement in Evenk lives. A simple equation of power and resistance to it, even in Foucault's "mobile and transitory" forms (1990: 96) cannot describe the relationship when, as discussed further in Chapter 5, there is a prevalent sense of the state abdicating responsibility, including for funding schooling.

The following chapters seek to provide a portrait of power dynamics in a Siberian community in the 1990s and the myriad ways that people were renegotiating relationships with the state and within their communities with the transformation of the former Soviet Union. Drawing on these sources, I do not seek to create an exact representation of an enclosed community but instead to provide a dynamic portrait of a community with internal contradictions, individuals with a range of allegiances, and alliances in transformation. Evenki themselves have recently written their own versions of contemporary life and local history (Amosov 1998; Monakhova 1999; Shchapeva 1994), and prominent Evenk author Alitet Nemtushkin has depicted Evenk lives in literature for decades.[18] While I have chosen to write about identities in flux, this is just one of many ethnographies that could have been written based on the complex and vibrant lives of central Siberian Evenki in the 1990s.

Chapter 1 carries the reader through analyses of "identity" as a concept and the ways Evenk identities have taken shape historically. Chapter 2 moves to an overview of Tura as a central Siberian town crosscut by a range of social divisions, particularly illustrated through the portraits of five households. Evenk women's narratives on residential schooling form the crux of Chapter 3, laying the foundation for understanding the way in which Soviet collective culture has informed Evenk identities and resulted in distinct understandings of power among women. In this chapter, I also examine dynamics of power and resistance through the prism of residential schooling accounts. Chapter 4 builds around the narratives of young Evenk women who recently completed their education in the residential school. This chapter considers how generational differences are significant in discussing relationships to the residential school and how the context of emerging market relations influences the place of residential schooling in women's lives. Chapters 5 and 6 shift to the residential school itself, with Chapter 5 focusing on daily life in the school and Chapter 6 shifting to Evenk intellectuals' efforts to transform the institution. Chapter 7 looks toward another important institution in the landscape of Soviet and post-Soviet social life, the museum, to reflect on intergenerational tensions around the way material culture is invoked to represent Evenk identities. The last and concluding chapter revisits ideas about Soviet and post-Soviet collective identities and about shifting hierarchies of power in this central Siberian town.

Chapter 1
Central Peripheries and Peripheral Centers: Evenki Crafting Identities over Time

Rossiia
. . .
K grudi ty nas, Rossiia,
prizhimala,
Kogda zloi dukh vsiu zemliu
szhech' khotel.

I ot bedy soboiu prikryvala.
Takov uzh, vidno, materi udel.

Zemlia moia!
Prizhmus' k tebe shchekoiu.
Ia zdravitsu tebe provozglashu.
Ia—rossiianin!
Zvanie takoe,
Kak vse v Rossii, gordo ia noshu.

Russia
. . .
Russia, you held us tight
to your breast,
When an evil spirit
wanted to scorch
the land,
You shielded us yourself.
Such was the
motherland's destiny.
My homeland!
I press my cheek to yours.
I call you my friend.
I—am a *rossiianin*!
A title that
Like all in Russia, I proudly
answer to.

—Nikolai Oegir, Evenk poet, *Paths Leading to the Spring: Poems*

I was first drawn into the lives of Evenki in the summer of 1992, when I arrived in Tura after a journey of nearly three days by train into central Siberia, from Moscow to Krasnoiarsk, followed by a two-hour flight to Tura. On the flight north, I was fortunate to be accompanied by a local storyteller and teacher who had been introduced to me while she was visiting her sister back in Moscow, four time zones away. As we exited the plane, I followed her instructions to throw a coin into the first body of water we encountered, a stream. This gesture "for the spirits" (*dukham*) would ensure that I was welcomed in Evenkiia, as people living there commonly refer to the Evenk District. After just a few days in the capital of Tura, I had barely oriented myself when I was whisked off in an entourage of young men and women who were flying by helicopter to the town of Baikit.[1] Their folk dance troupe, *Osiktakan* ("Stars"), was scheduled to perform as the highlight of the biannual Evenk folk festival, Evenkiiskie Zori (Evenkiiskie Dawns).

When we arrived in Baikit and piled out of the massive orange and blue helicopter, the festivities began. There were several reindeer tethered near the makeshift outdoor stage, and children took turns sitting on these. It turned out these reindeer had been flown in from a nearby herding brigade that I was to visit in the coming weeks. Several women set up tables to display and sell their handiwork—an array of sable hats, wolverine slippers, and fine reindeer-skin boots with beadwork edging. The festival was orchestrated by the director of the local House of Culture, an institution that played an important role in the social lives of many Soviet citizens, but especially those living in rural areas. After three days of festivities, we waited at the edge of town for our helicopter home to Tura and listened to Bob Marley's "No Woman, No Cry" blaring from the speakers into the recently outfitted discotheque. On the flight home, the head of the Evenk Department of Culture praised the members of *Osiktakan* for their part in making the festival a success.

My research in this region coincided with a wide effort to reaffirm Evenk identity and to simultaneously make sense of additional components of identities—Soviet, Siberian, *rossiianin* [citizen of Russia], Russian, aboriginal and others—for individuals, households, and even folk dance troupes. From my very first days in Evenkiia, I became aware that Evenk identity was not something fixed or understood singularly by the array of people calling themselves Evenki. I also learned that this entity of "Evenk identity" was something very much contested and variously mobilized in the post-Soviet setting. In this chapter I consider broad issues of identity both historically and in the contemporary period in order to explore some of the themes that are invoked as Evenki reimagine what the contours of their community will be in the post-Soviet era. The first section focuses on theoretical reflections on "identity" and "ethnic identity." In the second section, I consider the origins of the Evenki as a group and their history of migration to what is today the Evenk District. In the final section, I consider some of the ways identities were being reconfigured in the Evenk District in the 1990s as some Evenki sought to guarantee educational opportunity or looked to new or rejuvenated ritual practices.

Identities in Theory and Practice

The complexity of allegiances that any individual or even household could have in Tura in the 1990s is illustrated in the hybridity of cultural practices reflected in the Evenk folk festival in Baikit described in the opening pages of this chapter. Despite these elements of hybridity in contemporary Evenk social practices, indigenous intellectuals often consider identity as something fixed or simply rooted in the past. Considering identity as fluid and in constant negotiation is not a politically strategic stand for groups seeking to lay claim to contested resources or power in various forms. For instance, like Evenk intellectuals, Maya intellectuals are struggling to gain control over the representation of their daily lives and history, and they also invoke an essentialist analytic style in their discourse (Fischer and McKenna Brown 1996: 3). These efforts on the part of indigenous intellectuals are in striking contrast to the predominant contemporary approach among social scientists thinking about issues of identity. Siberian studies has encountered a tension similar to that in Maya studies, where the trend for "foreign" academics has been to avoid essentializing identities, and to instead emphasize multivocality and the various and shifting dynamics of power over time (Anderson 2000; Bloch 2001; Grant 1995a; Rethmann 2001).[2]

While popular conceptions of identity sometimes homogenize and freeze it as an unchanging element, contemporary social science theories tend to concur that identity is more accurately theorized as ever-changing. In Comaroff and Comaroff's terms, identity is "both a set of relations and a mode of consciousness" (1992: 54). This concept of identity combines an understanding of how large-scale historical processes of power and situational perspectives mold identities, but it is certainly not the only view of how identity works.

The anthropological research into the formation of identity, and particularly ethnicity, has been widespread since the 1960s (see Eriksen 1993; R. Cohen 1978). Scholars have viewed ethnicity in a range of ways, but there have been two dominant directions of thought: the primordialist and the instrumentalist. Primordialist theorists emphasize the idea of ethnic categories as rooted in a common past or shared heritage and as remaining intact despite cultural contacts (Geertz 1973; Gurvich 1980; Gumilev 1990). While this approach to ethnicity has been sharply criticized by many (see R. Cohen 1978), understanding primordialist concepts of ethnicity can potentially provide important means of understanding consciousness and what one scholar calls the "nature of the stuff on which groups feed" (Eriksen 1993: 55). This is especially the case for indigenous groups worldwide that are increasingly calling upon primordialist theories of identity as they compete with multinational interests over scarce resources (Conklin 1997; Fischer and McKenna Brown 1996).

In contrast to the primordialist approach, the instrumentalist approach, with Abner Cohen (1974) and Fredrik Barth (1969) at the forefront, emphasizes the political aims served by and justifying the maintenance of ethnicity. While Barth focuses on ethnic boundaries and considers them as categorical ascriptions that determine a "most general identity" (1969: 13) and Cohen focuses on ethnic identity as a political tool for securing resources (1974), they both center their analyses on the synchronic nature of ethnic identity. The broader historical and hegemonic processes influencing identity are not central to their discussions.

While thinking of ethnicity as a political tool is particularly useful in situations of "social change" such as the Evenki are experiencing, it is important to understand how and why ethnic identity gets mobilized and reproduced. If one assumes that "ethnicity" is not a primordial category, then how does one explain how it remains salient to a group of people and situationally more or less pertinent in times of social change? As illustrated in the setting of the Evenk folk festival described above, this is a critical question.

Many anthropologists today agree that it is important to avoid an either/or approach to ethnic identity because this disregards important factors potentially influencing the formation of identities (see Bentley 1981). Some research has moved away from an either/or way of thinking about ethnicity and instead looks to situational explanations (see Okamura 1981). By adopting this approach instead of just instrumentalist or primordialist explanations for ethnic identity, research is less restricted by a preconceived model of how ethnicity operates. Adopting a situational perspective can also result, however, in too little attention to the sociostructural aspects of identity. Keyes (1981: 10), for instance, emphasizes the multiple sources for identities and notes that ethnic identity becomes a personal identity only after an individual takes it up from a "public display" or "traffic in symbols."

A recent trend in scholarship related to ethnicity emphasizes that ethnicity is just one of the factors feeding into the formation of identities. Moving from studying ethnicity to studying identity allows for the examination of the ambiguities of identity; the world is not accurately reflected by attempting to divide fixed groups by the rigid boundaries that are often raised in the study of ethnicity. Several authors instead root their analyses of identity in both the concrete historical and contemporary social forces impinging upon identity (Constable 1997; Rosaldo 1980; Gilroy 1987; di Leonardo 1993). These analyses highlight the multiple social forces such as economic position, racial categories, gender, and geography that influence identities, while recognizing the role collective and individual resistance can play in the process of identity formation. Social identities are rarely firmly bounded and more frequently exist in flux, with blurred bounds reflecting hybridity and global cultural transformations (see Bhabha 1994; Appadurai 1996; Ong 1999). From this perspective, identities are not just situational and a matter of "choice" for an individual (see Worsley 1984: 246). Identities are part of larger processes, but they are not just subject to these megaprocesses with humans playing little or no active part.

This approach to thinking about how identities take shape is informed by the important work on post-colonial concepts of nation and power. Much of this work examines how a sense of "nation" is created in contexts in which the frameworks of colonial eras continue to operate in one way or another (see Chatterjee 1993; Mamdani 1996). This work is strongly influenced by "subaltern studies," a direction in scholarship that has particularly focused on South Asia and sought to write historiography from the perspective of those who have been colonized. Perhaps because of its emphasis on critiquing structural aspects of colonial legacies, this influential school of thought has tended to exclude considerations of the disparate experiences of individuals caught up in nation-building.[3] The emphasis on close examinations of groups and a type of sociological homogenizing, with little attention to the interpretations and narratives of individuals who comprise these groups, points to an alternative approach that can be taken to the study of power.

Recent work suggests that how transformations of power are experienced, including during processes of nation-building and "modernity," depends very much on subject position (Rofel 1999; Lancaster 1988; Abelmann 1997). This subject position is constituted through a range of factors such as ethnicity, generation, class affiliation, profession, and gender, and these factors interweave in various ways to influence how people interpret histories and how they depict their lives. In presenting a discussion of both contemporary designations of identity and the historical roots of Evenk identities, the following sections create frameworks for understanding historical consciousness of individual Evenki who together are reconfiguring what it means to be part of this community.

Local, Newcomer, and Native

Like three-quarters of indigenous Siberians in Russia, the indigenous Siberian population in the Evenk District has been concentrated in rural areas until quite recently (Fondahl 1998: 83; Savoskul 1971). As government support for state sable and fox farms lagged beginning in 1993, the primary means for making a living in this area disappeared. The desperate material circumstances in rural areas resulted in substantial migration to regional centers. Small regional centers such as Tura continued, however, to be populated predominantly by Russians and Ukrainians, as well as a small number of refugees, like those from the civil war in Tadzhikistan.

Figure 2. The Udygir family in an Evenk District village. Photo by the author, 1998.

Over the 1990s, this web of people in the Evenk District made up a population ranging from 20,000 to 26,000 inhabitants in an area more than twice the size of California (see Chapter 2 for a discussion of the drop in population over the 1990s). The population included about 4,000 Evenki and 1,000 other indigenous Siberians such as Sakha, a group with its own neighboring titular district.[4] In 1999 the Evenk District capital town of Tura had a population of about 6,000 people, of whom about 900 identified as Evenki. As discussed below, however, this was a rapidly changing population. While Tura was not very large, by the late 1990s it had nearly one-third of the total Evenk District population, with a wide range of designations of identities shaped by migration histories, economic standing, and political affiliations.

Terms referring specifically to indigenous Siberians ranged from "aboriginal" (*aborigen*) to "native"/"indigenous" (*korennoi*) to "Tungus" (*tungus*) to more derogatory terms used by both outsiders and Evenki themselves (in self-deprecating moments), such as "dark/dense" (*temnyi*). Evenki could be included in other categories as well. Each term carried different types of significance depending on context. For instance, few townspeople used the word "aboriginal" in referring to Evenk collective interests unless they were actively involved in indigenous rights politics; this term tended to mark the speaker as engaged with international discourse and having affiliations reaching beyond the town or region. A more common collective term referring to Evenki was "native" (*korennoi*); this term was a familiar one for most people because it was widely used in Soviet parlance. In official communication and in popular speech, the terms "aboriginal" and "native" could both be used narrowly to indicate just the Evenk population or more broadly to include the Sakha or Kety, the other indigenous groups concentrated in the area.[5] For instance, in reporting the levels of literacy in the community, the number of children entering preschool, or other numerical facts, the given source would invariably distinguish between the population as a whole and the numbers for the native population.

Among the Evenki in Tura, there are distinctions based on geography and social status. In particular the Katanga Evenki are recognized as having roots outside the Evenk District. The Katanga Evenki arrived from the Katanga region, an area bordering the southeastern present-day Evenk District and the Sakha Republic—several hundred kilometers down the Nizhniaia Tunguska River—in order to assist in administering the fledgling Soviet town in the early 1930s. As the result of the Katanga Evenki's history of sedentarization and colonial contact, which extended at least fifty years earlier than that of the Illimpei Evenki in the region of Tura, in 1917 the Katanga region already had a small cadre of literate Evenki (Sirina 1995). Historical ties of close affiliation between Katanga

Evenki and Soviet structures of power resonate in a number of ways throughout this book, but particularly in women's narratives in Chapters 3 and 4.

There are also distinctions between Baikit and Illimpei Evenki. In the 1920s when Soviet linguists were creating writing systems for a number of indigenous Siberians, they often chose between several dialects of a language to designate which one would become the official dialect for adoption in textbooks and other written materials.[6] In creating an alphabet for the Evenki in the Evenk District, linguists chose the Baikit dialect, a dialect of Evenk historically spoken by Evenki from the southern area of the Evenk District, south of the Podkamennaia River in the Baikit region (Boitseva 1971: 146; Nedjalkov 1997). This has had long-lasting effects in terms of social stratification among Evenki in the Evenk District because those with the more southern, Baikit, "Sha-type" dialect were able to study the language in their own dialect, while those with the northern, Illimpei, "Kha-type" dialect could not. In favoring the Baikit dialect, Soviet linguists created an internal hierarchy of dialects among Evenki. In the late 1990s, Evenk intellectuals in Tura frequently discussed the problem of "literary" Evenk being considered more prestigious than the local dialect found in the Illimpei region surrounding Tura (Pikunova 1999).

Throughout the 1990s the term "Russian" (*russkii*) was used colloquially by both Evenki and others to refer to non-indigenous Siberians—whether Russian, Ukrainian, Belorussian, or Estonian—who were considered sufficiently European in origin. Furthermore, to be "Russian" indicated that one belonged to a social category associated with patterns of privilege; to be Russian was not to belong to the indigenous community. Within the category of Russian, a number of distinctions were also made, depending on multiple factors. For example, those Russians whose ancestors had lived for several generations in Siberia could also be referred to as "Siberians," *sibiriaki*; historically *sibiriaki* are known for an "attitude of tolerance" (Czaplicka 1926: 490–92). In contrast, the term "newcomers" (*priezzhii*) was used to refer to those Russians who were induced by high pay and benefits to come to the area and planned to stay only for a few years.[7] Throughout this book the term "Russian" is used to refer to the European population in the area; I use the term "Russian" in order to reflect the widespread use of this term as a collective noun in the Evenk District. Where appropriate the other, more specific designations of identity are noted.[8]

Aside from binary distinctions between Russians and natives, there were several other categories of belonging in Tura in the 1990s. Azeri and Tadzhik refugees, who totaled about one hundred people in 1998, were excluded from the category "Russian," and instead they were often collectively referred to as "blacks" (*chernye*). This terminology was adopted from urban areas of Russia, where in the 1990s members of the dominant Russian population frequently derisively referred to people of non-European origin, and particularly those from Central Asia, as "blacks" (Lemon 1995). The few Tatars in Tura were also usually separated from the Russians semantically and simply called *Tatary*.

There were also inclusive terms invoked by community members. For instance, those recognized as rooted in the community were often termed simply "locals" (*mestnye*) or "ours" (*nash*). In the common situation in which passengers were patiently waiting for days at the Krasnoiarsk airport for a flight home, people from the region would gather together as the *Evenkiitsy*, or "Evenk District people"; it was also common for people from Tura to identify each other as Turintsy. Yet another term that was less widely used, but growing in usage, was *rossiianin*, meaning "a citizen of Russia" (see Balzer 1999: xiv).[9] This inclusive term was most often used in formal civic settings, such as in newspapers or public addresses. Others would also invoke it, however, especially in seeking a way to represent collective needs or desires. For instance, the Evenk poet Nikolai Oegir writes in the poem cited in the epigraph to this chapter: "I—am a *rossiianin*! A title that like all in Russia, I proudly answer to" (1989: 26).

As was the case across the North in Russia in the 1990s (see Kerttula 2000; Rethmann 2001; Fondahl 1993), the Tura community was divided (or combined) along a number of lines. Local, newcomer, native, Russian, and black could intersect in various ways. For instance, you could theoretically be referred to in one situation as "black," and yet in another be considered "local." Newcomers would not be referred to as "locals," but they could be considered as *Evenkiitsy*, or from Evenkiia. As will be further discussed in this and subsequent chapters, these categories were activated in relational terms and were invoked in shifting ways, depending on circumstances and who was talking to whom.

Evenki Past and Present

As historically nomadic reindeer herders, the Evenki were not always concentrated in government-designated regions like the Evenk District. The Evenki are thought to have originated in the steppes of present-day Mongolia; in fact, today there are nearly as many Evenki in China and Mongolia combined as in the Russian Federation. In Russia the Evenki comprise one of the larger indigenous Siberian groups; the Evenk population consists of about 30,000 people and stretches from the banks of the Enisei River in central Siberia to the Amur River region in the Russian Far East, an area encompassing nearly five time zones.[10] Along with this extensive settlement, at least three distinct dialects of Evenk, a

Tunguso-Manchurian branch of the Ural-Altaic family of languages, have evolved over time (Nedjalkov 1997).

For decades scholars have debated the origins of the Evenki, as defined by a set of ethnological, physical, and linguistic traits. Sergei Shirokogoroff, probably the most renowned Siberianist in the twentieth century, argued that some time in the end of the second-century B.C. ancestors of the Chinese displaced the Evenki into present-day Russia from the Yellow and Blue River Basins in China (1919). Other scholars have drawn on evidence of similarities in dwelling types, clothing, and artistic styles to support an interpretation that Evenki have closer ties to the ancient Neolithic population of the Baikal region than to populations in second-century-B.C. China (Vasilevich and Smoliak 1964: 623). Scholars do agree that the Evenk language reflects connections with both Turkic and Mongolian languages; very likely the Evenki as a distinct ethnic group emerged out of the mixing of Turkic-related groups from the north of Siberia with groups that formed in more southern regions.

Between the twelfth and thirteenth centuries, some Evenki began to migrate north to occupy regions such as what is today the Evenk Autonomous District. Few other groups sought to live in the relatively harsh climate, where snow is on the ground from early September to late May and winter temperatures average –40 to –50 degrees Celsius for four

Figure 3. Father and children herding in the Russian Far East, circa 1901. Image #1589, AMNH, Department of Library Services.

months of the year. Evenki were drawn, however, to a habitat that offered ample opportunity for hunting and fishing and was ideal for reindeer, which could feed off the plentiful lichen found in the tundra and taiga. Today Evenk populations can be found throughout the areas that they historically occupied—from the shores of the Enisei River to Lake Baikal and beyond to the Amur River, in addition to northern Mongolia. As was the case prior to the first Russian incursions into central and eastern Siberia in the seventeenth century, the Evenki continue to share this vast area of nearly two million square miles with many other groups, including the Eveny, Kety, Sakha, and Buriat Mongols.[11]

Russian and Soviet government ethnic designations have had a significant impact on the configuration of Evenk identities in the twentieth century. In the pre-Soviet period ethnographers often classified the Evenki along with the Eveny as belonging to the "Tungus" people (Shirokogoroff 1933; Habeck 1997).[12] In the seventeenth century, the Tungus were counted as possibly numbering as many as 36,000 people (Dolgikh 1960: 617). The 1897 Russian census counted 64,500 Tungus; more than one half of them (33,500) were living in the southern Siberian area near Lake Baikal and were engaged in agriculture (Vasilevich and Smoliak 1964: 621). By 1928 those peoples who had been referred to collectively as Tungus began to be referred to by Soviet authors specifically as "Evenki" and "Eveny," that is, according to the ethnonyms supposedly recognized by each group. Based on his extensive research in a herding community in the Taimyr, north of the Evenk District, David Anderson argues (2000: 98–109) that these categories are, in fact, quite fluid. The way in which these groups, as well as other native groups, were officially renamed by the Soviet state indicates how naming is part of administrative prerogatives. These are more closely linked to state methods of categorizing and controlling than necessarily to local realities at a given point in time.[13]

Kinship, Leadership, Ownership

A brief overview of the historical social organization of the Evenki provides a foundation for considering the influence Russian and Soviet systems of knowledge had on Evenk cultural practices. The Evenki historically practiced clan exogamy, and generally one herding group, or band, consisting of one or two extended family groups belonging to the same clan, herded 50–100 reindeer (Shirokogoroff 1933: 246). Each family group tended to consist of a man, a woman, several children, older relatives—usually the man's parents—and occasionally young couples. Thus a typical family group comprised those sharing a reindeer skin tent, or *chum*, and generally consisted of three generations (Monakhova

1999).[14] Members of a given family group slept in one tent; meals were shared between family groups, and herding activities were undertaken as a band. Men generally hunted, trapped, and oversaw reindeer herding and breeding. Children were expected to take part in all these activities, but full responsibilities only came with adulthood (Strakach 1962). Women generally cared for young children, prepared meals, sewed, tended young reindeer, and milked does. Some women, however, also took part in hunting and herding. Among Evenki living in the area north of Lake Baikal, women dominated herding activities, while men were largely occupied with hunting (Fondahl 1998: 28). In the area of the present-day Evenk District, women typically were responsible for cooking, sewing, and other household activities, in addition to hunting, fishing, trapping, and managing the reindeer herding and responsibilities of relocating camp when men were off hunting (Monakhova 1999: 35–36).

Reindeer herding was central to the Evenk way of life. Reindeer were held as common property of the band, but individuals sometimes also owned select reindeer (Vasilevich and Smoliak 1964: 646–47). In contrast to many other reindeer herding peoples, the Evenki had completely domesticated reindeer. The reindeer milk that women collected was an important dietary supplement, and in the winter they stored frozen blocks of milk in the ground for extended periods. Men generally hunted wild reindeer and used the domesticated ones for transportation by riding the reindeer itself with a saddle. In the early twentieth century, Evenki began using reindeer sledges, but earlier they only used sledges pulled by people.

Although the Evenki had no permanent political leaders, there was a clan assembly (*sagdagul*), generally consisting of grown men, and sometimes women, who were heads of households (Vasilevich and Smoliak 1964: 644). This assembly dealt with socioeconomic issues such as the adoption of children, territorial disputes, and punishments for infringements of proper conduct. Evenk oral tradition also relates that as influential members of the community, shamans sometimes acted as leaders in times of intergroup conflict.

"Shaman" is a term widely used in north Asian languages to indicate healers with varying degrees of spiritual abilities and leadership power (Humphrey 1994c: 206). The term itself may have evolved from the Sanskrit word *sramana*, a common designation for a Buddhist monk in ancient sacred texts (Mironov and Shirokogoroff 1924).[15] The Russian language incorporated the term "shaman" from the Tungusic speaking peoples in the seventeenth century. In the Evenk version of shamanism, shamans interact with the spiritual world, which the Evenki believe to be composed of three elements: the middle earth, where people live; the upper world of the supreme god and other gods; and the underworld, where the spirits of the dead reside (Forsyth 1992: 54). It is possible that at one time the Evenki had, as Caroline Humphrey describes for the "inner Asian hinterland"—southern Siberia and northern Mongolia—two types of shamanism that differed according to how they represented social reproduction (1994c: 198–99). Humphrey terms one type "patriarchal" because she views it as focused on the continuation of patrilineal clans through shamanic influence over the symbolic reproduction of the patrilineal lineage. Humphrey calls the other type "transformational" because it was involved in all the forces in the world—natural phenomenon, humans, animals, and manufactured things. This second type of shaman manifested his or her power through the trance, while the first type would conduct sacred rites and was a diviner but could not master spirits or enter a trance.

Among the Evenki, the powers of the shaman could be inherited by men and women, but they were more commonly found among men. Shamans were recognized as arbiters between the spirit, animal, and human worlds; they were given the task of performing sacrifices of the unusual white-colored reindeer at ritual events such as weddings and funerals and the advent of the hunting season. Because the ability to smith iron was associated with the spirit world, shamans often adorned their skin clothing with animal representations of the spirit world made from iron. Then, as today, however, people were connected to the spirit and animal worlds through daily practices, not just through the medium of a shaman. In maintaining reciprocal relationships with spirit and animal worlds, a balance was maintained. These relationships continue to include feeding the hearth fire morsels of fat or a splash of vodka, killing animals at prescribed times, and respecting certain animals—like bears—thought to be closely related to humans. Many Evenki believe that these prescribed interactions with spirit and animal worlds ensure today, as in the past, that one's household will be safe and healthy and that disregarding these relationships can, and historically could, mean dire consequences for individuals or whole clans (Anisimov 1950).

According to ethnographic accounts dating from the nineteenth century and more recently (Mordvinov 1860; Kytmanov 1927; Shirokogoroff 1933; Dolgikh 1960; Vasilevich and Smoliak 1964; Karlov 1982), the clan as the basic unit of Evenk social organization underwent various changes even before the radical reorganization implemented by the Soviets in the 1930s (as discussed later in this chapter). Although there is no written record prior to the seventeenth century, oral tradition holds that for most of the year Evenki lived in small bands consisting of two or three families that belonged to one or two interrelated clans (Tugolukov 1988: 525). In summer several bands would gather in camps of about a dozen tents and engage in exchange of trade goods such as tobacco and pelts. At this time parents also arranged marriages for their children, an arrangement that usually involved an exchange of reindeer between the families.

Vasilevich and Smoliak argue (1964: 645) that by the seventeenth century ownership of reindeer among the Evenki was delineated by individual families, and that these were "economically speaking" considerably separate from clans. These individual families accrued varying numbers of reindeer and apparently fought with one another over territory. In the same period, the development of trade relations with Russians, the depletion of the sable population, and the rapid Russian occupation of land contributed to the breakdown of former Evenk clan relationships. Evenki moved about as they lost control of land they had formerly used for subsistence activities, and this movement resulted in the creation of new communities consisting both of Evenki from different clans and of various other ethnic groups, including Kety and Sakha. Vasilevich and Smoliak (1964: 645) write that until the Russian Revolution these new communities engaged in collective labor instead of labor being based on the former framework within the joint family or clan.

Whether or not this ideal communal arrangement depicted by Vasilevich and Smoliak existed, there is evidence that in the eighteenth, nineteenth, and early twentieth centuries the increasing role of trade and taxation was causing internal strife among Evenki and between Evenki and other groups. From the seventeenth century onward, tsarist policy engaged Cossacks in collecting taxes, or *iasak*, in the form of furs from indigenous Siberians throughout Russia (Slezkine 1994: 13). As early as 1614, one group of Cossacks known as the Mangazeia imposed a fur tax on Evenki living in central Siberia near the Nizhniaia Tunguska River, and by 1623 nearly all the Evenki living near the Enisei River were paying tax in furs (Vasilevich and Smoliak 1964: 623). In the eighteenth and nineteenth centuries tsarist policies moved more toward trade and Christianization among the Evenki.

The Russian Orthodox Church and Shifting Relations of Control

While prior to the Soviet era most interaction between indigenous peoples and Europeans was connected to trade, even as early as the seventeenth century missionaries sought out converts among indigenous Siberians. Russian Orthodox Church schools were also expanding their efforts in Siberia by the eighteenth century, but they attracted few indigenous Siberian students (Bazanov 1936). One of the largest church efforts resulted in twenty elementary schools being set up in Kamchatka and the Kurile Islands in the mid-1700s; these lasted until the 1780s (Sgibnev,

3–4, cited in Forsyth 1992: 142). These schools largely served a Russian settler population, however, and did not actively seek to incorporate indigenous Siberians.

As for many other indigenous Siberians, the establishment of Russian Orthodox missions had little impact on the daily lives of the Evenki in central Siberia. In 1754 a Russian Orthodox mission was established on the banks of the Enisei River in Turukhansk, a town about 360 miles downstream from present-day Tura along the Nizhniaia Tunguska River. It appears that for years the mission took little interest in the surrounding populations of indigenous Siberians in the region. By the mid-nineteenth century, however, the church was becoming involved in the budding systems of surveillance and control of indigenous Siberian populations that were to become fully developed in the Soviet era. From 1862 to 1915, the central Siberian region fell under the Enisei diocese (*Eniseiskii dukhovnyi konsistorii*), and those Orthodox missionaries working in Turukhansk Territory were instructed to keep records ranging from their daily activities to a registry of births, deaths, and baptisms (Anderson and Orekhova 2002: 97). One document in the Evenk District archive collection dated December 1855 lists the Tungus newcomers to the area and a count of those who were "believers" in Russian Orthodoxy.[16] A September 1855 account notes marriage dates for members of the indigenous population along with information about their trade partners in Turukhansk.[17] Archival documents suggest that relations between clergy and native peoples were often strained because of inordinate charges for ritual services and the clergy's disdain for native ritual practices; there were some exceptions, however (see Anderson and Orekhova 2002). This region served as a point of exile for priests in disfavor with the church hierarchy.[18]

While the church did not avidly promote conversion, it gained some converts through its role as an interlocutor between the Russian government and the indigenous population. Thus by the mid-eighteenth century, tribute requirements for indigenous Siberians were reduced if they converted to Russian Orthodoxy. For instance, in November 1855 a priest sent a request to Irkutsk that tribute not be demanded from a certain "Tungus" for a period of three years because he had converted. Even with this inducement, however, few members of the indigenous population converted.[19]

In 1868 the Russian Orthodox Synod announced the possibility for clergy to receive a medal of "Saint Ann, of the third order" for good works dealing with education in general. In August of that year the Turukhansk church received word from the Enisei diocese that they should open a seminary and a school for indigenous students.[20] In the same period, missionaries were sent out from Turukhansk to outlying regions, including to what are today towns in the Evenk District. In 1892 one of these missions founded Saint Basil's church in Essei, the most northern village in the Evenk District, which is located on the border with the present-day Sakha Republic (see Anderson and Orekhova 2002). Although in 1913 the priest counted 1,562 Evenki and 1,328 Iakuty (Sakha) who lived in the region, few were drawn to attend church or send their children to school there. Although the mission was nearly abandoned by the time the Soviets arrived in the early 1920s, its former presence was recalled by several Evenki and Sakha living in Tura in the early 1990s.[21] One woman recalled that in her childhood her grandparents kept a Rus-sian Orthodox icon beside the shamanic bundles and talismans safeguarded in their *chum* in the taiga.

Evenki and Trade in the Early Twentieth Century

The Russian Orthodox Church briefly located in Essei was strategically established along one of the major routes traversed by Sakha and Evenki in the course of their yearly trade. In the Soviet period, the 1926 *Household Census of the Arctic North* (*Pokhoziaistvennaia perepis' pripoliarnogo Severa*) also took note of the key role that trade played in the life of indigenous Siberians in the region. In particular the census carefully documented the degree to which various indigenous Siberians, including the Evenki, were acquainted with Russian goods. In the early twentieth century, Evenki in this region attended an annual fair where they encountered Russians and traded sable pelts and fish for textiles and beads, metal, guns, and foodstuffs, including tea, sugar, salt, flour, and vodka.[22]

In addition to Russian Orthodox and Russian trader influences, over time the Evenki have had a wide range of cultural contacts. For instance, in the late 1990s collections at the Evenk District Regional History Museum (hereafter Evenk District Museum) reflected the longstanding Evenk trade links with China. Artifacts on exhibit included Evenk garments with buttons and ornamentation made from Chinese coins dating from the eighteenth century. Trade ties with the neighboring Sakha were also evident in the museum's collection of ornate silverwork and iron acquired by Evenki to create buttons, tools, sled details, and icons. The Evenki have a long-standing interaction with the Sakha, historically a sizable seminomadic group living to the north and northeast of Lake Baikal. By the mid-seventeenth century, the Sakha already lived as pastoralists with semipermanent residences. They had considerable knowledge of metal forging, and unlike the Evenki, they could make metal out of iron ore (Forsyth 1992: 56). Since this metal was particularly prized by the Evenki, those living in regions bordering the present-day Sakha

Republic would travel ten to forty days to trade with the Sakha. As one elderly Evenk woman described to me, intermarriage between Sakha and Evenki in these same neighboring regions was also common. In her mother's youth, in the 1940s, people would travel days to arrange marriages between Evenki and Sakha.

For hundreds of years the Evenki have interacted with different groups, including with representatives of established nation-states. Only with the onset of the Soviet era in the North, however, did Evenki begin to experience a radical transformation of their way of life.

"Modernization," Sedentarization, and Sovietization

Evenk lives within Russia today have significantly changed from how they were lived even fifty years ago. Forced sedentarization began in the 1930s when Soviet cadres fundamentally reorganized production among indigenous Siberian groups. As among other indigenous Siberian groups like the Nivkhi (Grant 1995a: 91), Soviet cadres introduced what were called "simplest hunting units" *arteli* for short, and convinced Evenki to combine their reindeer herds into larger collective groups for "production." This new organization of herding was meant to create joint use of herding equipment and techniques, but it was also meant to diminish the ties of clan-based social organization. One source claims that by 1937 through the "voluntary socialization" of reindeer herding there were thirty-two of these *arteli* in the Evenk District and eighty-six percent of the entire Evenk population was involved (Vasilevich and Smoliak 1964: 652). My interview material suggests that this wide scale collectivization was not particularly voluntary and probably did not encompass as much of the reindeer as officially recorded. One woman said that when Soviet officials targeted her father's herd of 600 reindeer in the early 1930s he first attempted to hide them in another area of the taiga before he finally gave in and relinquished them during the state's wholesale collectivization of reindeer a few years later (see Chapter 3). David Anderson points out that, with their specialized knowledge of the environment of the region and its rugged valleys, herders were able to hide portions of their herds while offering up some for the official count (2000: 47).

Soviet agencies charged with the task of collectivization intensified their efforts in the late 1930s in converting former *arteli* into *kolkhozy* (*kollektivnye khoziaistva*), or collective herding enterprises, in which many of the original Evenk herders remained primarily in charge of their former herds with minimal direction from the state. With the changes in organization, reindeer herding units came to be called "brigades." As discussed further in Chapter 3, by the late 1930s and in a reorganization in the late 1950s to the 1960s, indigenous Siberian men were consolidated in state cooperatives where they continued to herd reindeer, hunt, or fish and turn over the end products to the state. This pattern officially continued until 1992 with the breakup of the Soviet system of state-organized production. In the post-Soviet era, Evenk clans vied for decollectivized land and control over herding and hunting territories, and by 1998 most of these had been predominantly claimed. As David Anderson notes (2000: 160–70), however, in some areas the decollectivization or privatization of state cooperatives has not taken hold because of local circumstances where territory bounded by the earlier Soviet state designations has continued to be politically beneficial for many.

In some cases in the Evenk District, clans have recently established claims to territory that formerly included Soviet villages. In conjunction with collectivization of herding and the restructuring of social relations, in the early 1930s these villages began to be targeted as "lacking prospects" or "inefficient" (*neperspektivnye*); they were gradually shut off from the broader network of Soviet bureaucracy by the 1950s. By the end of World War II, one half of the former settlements established in the Evenk District in the early twentieth century no longer existed. In the Illimpei region alone the small enclaves of Vivi, Amovsk, Agata, and Kochumdeisk were officially closed and lost their doctor's assistants, veterinarians, and trading posts, all frequented by Evenki. In the 1990s, however, many families continued to return seasonally to these areas to fish and hunt.

In restructuring and consolidating the settlements, the Soviets not only streamlined production (and the supply of "producers" with foodstuffs) but also forced indigenous peoples into closer interaction with the central bureaucracies. This effort to consolidate villages and towns and resettle populations was part of a broader trend repeated throughout Russia in the 1960s as *sovkhozy* (*sovetskie khoziaistva*), or state agricultural cooperatives, replaced the *kolkhozy* (Pallot 1989). In the *sovkhozy*, reindeer herds were fully collectivized and became the property of the state, entirely supervised by government-appointed specialists; this contrasted to the former *kolkhozy*, where there was minimal direction from the state.[23] The 1960s resettlement policy, repeated in the 1970s and 1980s in some regions of Siberia, displaced Evenki from traditional areas of herding, hunting, and fishing. It also led to a loss of skilled and administrative positions that Evenki had held in the small enclaves because newcomers occupied many of these jobs in the consolidated towns.[24] While in 1932 Evenki comprised 81.9 percent of the Evenk District population, by the late 1990s they comprised just under 15 percent of the population.[25] The influx of newcomers into the Evenk District followed a trajectory similar to that in other regions of Siberia (Grant 1995a: 120–30; Bogoslovskaia 1993; Habeck 1997).

Identities, Education, and the Politics of Language

The policies noted above led to radical shifts in Evenk social organization and cultural practices from the 1920s to 1990s. A particularly strong reminder of this legacy is the decreasing number of Evenk language speakers at the onset of the twenty-first century. Many Evenk intellectuals argue that language is critical to the revitalization of Evenk cultural knowledge (Monakhova 1999: 44). Recent statistics indicate, however, that today knowledge of Evenk language is not a primary signifier of Evenk identity. For instance, according to the 1989 Soviet census, of the 29,901 people who recognized themselves as Evenki, only 9,075 said they considered Evenk as their native language (Gos. kom. RSFSR po stat. 1991: 141). In the mid-1990s in Tura, it was extremely rare for Evenki under thirty-five to speak Evenk fluently. As inmigration from outlying villages intensified, however, this situation shifted somewhat in the late 1990s.[26] Aside from language, there is a wide range of factors that continues to shape Evenk identities. The line between "Russian" and "Evenk," for instance, is delineated in part as a strategy for pursuing resources available to members of each group. In everyday life, however, there are myriad ways in which these spheres are fused and intertwined, and language is one of these.

As Humphrey notes in her insightful work on ethnic identity and "chat" among the Buriat (1994b), everyday speech reflects borrowings between spheres; this is certainly the case with Russian and Evenk language usage. The Soviet era especially left its imprint in terms of technical and bureaucratic vocabulary borrowed from Russian. For example, in the Evenk sentence "*Sobraniela upakt sagdyl kolkhoznikil eimeicheityn*" ("All the adult *kolkhoz* members came to the meeting" or "*Na sobranie prishli vse vzroslye kolkhozniki*" in Russian), the word for "*kolkhoz* members" would be expressed in Evenk using a Russian root *kolkhoznik*, with an Evenk suffix, *-il*. There is also borrowing in the other direction, from Evenk into Russian, and this is most common for terms specifically associated with traditional Evenk subsistence practices or clothing. For instance, the Evenk word for tall boots sewn out of reindeer hide and sinew, *untal*, is used by Russian speakers and supplemented with Russian suffixes to produce, for example, *unty*.[27] These small, but illustrative linguistic examples reflect the widespread cultural hybridity that continues in many forms in the North.

While it did not necessarily preclude affiliation with a range of identities, knowledge of Evenk language was a definite indicator of Evenk identity in the 1990s; it was quite unusual for those without at least one Evenk parent to take an interest in Evenk language.[28] While those who knew Evenk were viewed as "true" (*nastoiashchie*) Evenki, many younger Evenki considered themselves to be Evenki but did not know the language. As discussed in Chapter 2, while some households had a type of primordial perspective on their alliance with either Russian or Evenk spheres of symbolic capital, many had complex kinship and social ties rooting them in both spheres. The Evenki in Tura employed a sort of "prospiospect," to borrow a phrase from Ward Goodenough (see Wolcott 1989), a stance of shifting identities in the context of multiple influences.[29] Each person had a prospiospect that was not just "Evenk" or "Russian" but an amalgamation of a range of experience. Particularly in instances of social mobility, such as education, individuals drew on a sense of identity as fluid and as something that could be transformed for instrumental purposes.

Given that possibilities for pursuing education were expanded if one was considered "indigenous," in the realm of education identities tended to be especially fluid. In the 1990s entitlements for "indigenous peoples" (*korennye narody*) seeking higher education continued to exist at a number of levels. While places in Russia's elite institutions—the Moscow State University, the Peoples' Friendship University of the Russian Federation, and the Leningrad State University—were the most sought after, there were slots reserved in regional institutions as well.[30] Slots were generally reserved for a set number of students from specific administrative areas, including the Evenk District, and were available for students majoring in humanities and increasingly in social sciences and medicine.

In 1993 the elastic nature of identities in the Evenk District was underscored when students in Tura were applying for university. In the first instance, a young woman, usually self-identifying as Russian, was accepted to study at a major university in Moscow at the expense of the Russian government. Given that the Russian government allotted the Evenk District five slots in Moscow universities for "peoples of the North" (that is, indigenous Siberians), this hopeful student successfully emphasized her previously downplayed Evenk heritage—her grandmother was "pure" (*chistaia*) Evenki and her mother considered herself one-half Evenki. Although neither the student nor her mother spoke Evenk, they mobilized this aspect of their multidimensional identities to secure educational opportunity. In a second instance, a member of one of the few remaining "German" households, in which both parents were of German descent, was admitted to study in a university in Moscow in one of the slots reserved for peoples of the North.

Typically degrees of authentic ethnic identity were not the deciding factor in granting opportunities for higher education. The real focus was on the likelihood that the young people who were given this opportunity would return to these regions that suffered from the loss of highly trained newcomers. Those considered sufficiently local, not newcomers that is, became "peoples of the North" for the purposes of sending students for academic training that could later result in fortifying local professional ranks. Thus regional administrations selecting students for scholarships chose to reinterpret central government affirmative action policies to suit local needs.

In the cases where Evenk families moved out of the district, usually to the southern city of Krasnoiarsk, students would often return to the Evenk District to take qualifying exams for the university. Sometimes the students had never attended elementary or high school in the district but would arrive for the exams in early summer. By taking entrance exams in the Evenk District as "peoples of the North," students were automatically considered for the reserved slots in the institutions of higher learning. They could take the exams in the southern cities, their primary residences, but then they would not be able to vie for the reserved slots. Only in rare cases did students choose to study in disciplines or institutions in which there were no special allotments for indigenous Siberians.

What it means to be Evenki has transformed significantly over the past fifty years as Evenki have come under the purview of the state and now find themselves in a post-Soviet state with new configurations of power. Evenk identities have not just been defined, however, in a top-down manner; Evenki have also been active participants in negotiating situational identities. In addition to these renegotiations around ethnic identity, in the Soviet and post-Soviet era other aspects of identity have also been significant. As the next section discusses, Soviet identity was "performed" in contexts like the House of Culture. For many, the House of Culture was a site embodying Soviet cultural practice, and in the 1990s it was also the site for government-sponsored cultural revitalization programs and a meeting place for the new religious organizations taking root in Tura.

The House of Culture and Ritual Life Reassessed

State-sponsored "cultural work" (*kul'turnaia rabota*) was central to the Soviet project extending throughout Siberia (Bloch and Kendall 2004). These state-supported cultural revitalization efforts often are reminiscent of similar efforts across the world in which invoking tradition is closely linked to legitimating state or regional power (Handler 1988; Watson 1995; Kaplan 1994). In the context of an indigenous community in the 1990s, however, state-sponsored cultural revitalization, or "cultural invention" (Linnekin 1991; Conklin 1997), was not simply the Soviet state's construction of a distinct indigenous identity as something to be contained in museums, performed, and studied as part of the past. As I also explore in Chapter 7, the Evenki I knew who were involved in performing tradition in the form of dance, song, and handicrafts did not see these acts as "inventing" culture. Being part of a folk dance troupe, singing, or sewing warm fur clothing was instead part of daily life and sociality. The state created institutions and funded organizations, but the revitalization of Evenk cultural practices that was busily taking place when I first arrived in Tura in 1992 and continued in various ways throughout the 1990s involved people who themselves breathed life into these sites and found meaning in them. In the 1990s, Turintsy continued to value Soviet institutions such as the House of Culture, but many also began to look to new or renewed forms of sociality such as organized religion and healing practices.

In Tura, as in other Soviet towns and villages, the "House of Culture" (*Dom kul'tury* or "De Ka" as young people called it) was the primary center of organized social life for much of the Soviet period. While in cities these social centers were sometimes called "Palaces of Culture" and in fact were housed in former tsarist-era palaces, in Tura the House of Culture was a cavernous, rather unappealing two-story structure of grey concrete built in the 1980s in the town center. This institution sponsored events throughout the year to mark holidays such as the "Day of the October Revolution," New Year's Eve, and "the End of Winter." It also housed various clubs such as a chess club, a sports club, a rock music group, and the Evenk folk dance group (*Osiktakan*), and hosted a weekly discotheque for teenagers. Moreover, the House of Culture served as the site for civic events. It was a polling site for the election of local and federal representatives and was used for public send-offs for young men entering the army. In the post-Soviet era indigenous groups in some parts of Siberia established separate cultural centers they viewed as distinct from the more orthodox, state-sanctioned House of Culture (see Gray 1998: 297; Khelol 1997). Throughout the 1990s, however, the Evenki in this region had not created such alternatives, and in fact, in Tura many Evenki, as well as other town residents, continued to frequent the House of Culture as an important gathering place, both for civic events and for entertainment.

Most significantly for Evenki, in conjunction with the residential school, the House of Culture was a place where Evenk identities were bolstered through state-financed means. The various clubs housed within the House of Culture and the holiday events celebrated there focused around reproducing what were referred to as "traditional" (*traditsionnye*) Evenk songs, dance, and clothing. For instance, in 1993–94 the House of Culture had an Evenk folk music ensemble consisting mostly of elderly women who sang songs in Evenk and Russian; the songs featured lyrics about life in the taiga. The Evenk folk dance ensemble also performed a number of choreographed pieces that invoked shamanic practices and were accompanied by the steady beat of a hide drum. In the 1980s and early 1990s, this was a popular group for youth to belong to; the troupe traveled extensively in the Soviet Union, as well as abroad, and it was also considered a source of employment for those principal dancers who were paid by the Department of Culture. In the 1990s, in addition to the dance and music groups, the House of Culture also housed a "methodological center," where three women were employed in crafting the details of traditional, material culture for set design, costumes, and ritual events. By the late 1990s the growing demands of the Evenk District Sakha community for greater government recognition and a corresponding allocation of resources were also evident in the House of Culture, where a Sakha drama group was briefly established.

The majority of educated Evenki in the Evenk District in the early 1990s were employed in the sphere of "culture" as "cultural workers" (*kul'turnye rabotniki*) in institutions such as the residential school and the House of Culture. The concentration of Evenki in these spheres ensured that they were steeped in this enterprise of producing officially designated versions of tradition (Bloch 2001). When the Ministry of Culture lost much of its financing from the central government in 1993, however, the House of Culture became a less focal aspect of Tura social life. Many of the cultural workers—musicians, artists, and choreographers—were compelled to seek employment in more lucrative spheres. One artist who had been trained as an architect joined the town planning office. A musician employed at the House of Culture admitted to me with a note of shame that he had decided to leave his job to shovel coal in one of the town boilers. His new position would pay four times more than what the House of Culture could offer him.[31] The deterioration of this institution represented the demise of a broader system that had played a critical role in placing Evenk identities within a structured, shared, Soviet context.

Priests, Shamans, and Consciousness in Flux

The rapid demise and public denigration of formal Soviet ritual left a gaping ideational hole for many people in the Russian Federation. In the Evenk District in the 1990s, youth often openly derided symbols of the Soviet era, carving disparaging graffiti in public outhouses and exchanging anecdotes parodying socialist policies and Soviet leaders. Older people and Evenk intellectuals, however, often found this disrespect for Soviet cultural practice and ideology disconcerting. They spent decades taking part in a common Soviet consciousness and often proudly proclaimed themselves as Soviet citizens (*sovetskie grazhdane*). Such was the case of one retired reindeer herder who described himself to me as a "Soviet person" (*sovetskii chelovek*) in our conversations in 1993. One afternoon he proudly exhibited the medals he had won for fighting on the Western Front during World War II and for leading a successful herding brigade for a number of years.

One reflection of the widespread sense of belonging to a Soviet society was the ongoing salience of Soviet holidays. Many of these did not just disappear from the landscape with the creation of the Russian Federation. Some Soviet holidays such as May 9, Victory Day (*Den' Pobedy*), commemorating the end of World War II for the Soviet Union, or November 7, October Revolution Day (Den' Oktiabr'skoi Revoliutsii), commemorating the Russian Revolution, continued to be widely celebrated. These days were marked by concerts organized at the House of Culture and private parties. These were also occasions when Evenki living in southern cities made an effort to travel home.

Lenin's birthday, April 22, while not widely celebrated in Tura in the 1990s and significantly not marked by an event at the House of Culture, was inscribed in local consciousness. The holiday was designated as "Labor Day" (Den' Truda), at a time when the Communist Party was briefly outlawed in 1993–94. One "Labor Day" event in Tura in 1994 particularly illustrates how Soviet ritual practice remained pertinent for an older generation in the 1990s. Lenin's birthday began with the daily 7:30 A.M. Evenk District radio broadcast. The feature program was a medley of former tributes to Lenin that concluded with the commentator's note of relief that the days of requisite odes to Lenin had come to an end. That afternoon I learned from the young commentator that she had been personally threatened by a group of people identifying themselves as members of the Communist Party. Soon after the program they barged into her office and began to berate her for her views; they emphasized that without Soviet power and Lenin's vision the Evenki would not be at the "level of development" that they were today. She was warned to avoid such disparaging remarks or else her job would be in danger.

Some people in the Evenk District, however, were not finding comfort in the structures and ideologies of Soviet cultural practices; they were looking for new ways to make sense of their world, and organized religion became one of these. Prior to 1993 there had never been an organized religious group in Tura, although there had been occasional missionary outposts in the region in the late nineteenth and early twentieth centuries, as mentioned earlier in this chapter. In the summer of 1993, Russian Baptists and Dutch Evangelical missionaries made their way north from Krasnoiarsk to bring the word to the people of Tura and to several surrounding villages. While there was no church in which these groups could gather, they erected tarps on the residential school grounds and began giving sermons. The group of Evangelists from the Netherlands made a particularly strong impression upon one young

Evenk man who had grown up in Tura. He recounted how they gave out free Bibles printed in Russian and how everyone was extremely friendly. An Evenk educator also remarked that she was impressed that the missionaries took an interest in translating the Bible into Evenk; the Evangelists even approached her about possibly working on this project.[32]

In the fall of 1993, people continued to discuss the missionaries' summer visits, but by November the focus turned to a small group of Turintsy who decided to form a Russian Orthodox community. Although the local administration had not granted a permit for the group to meet, about forty interested people gathered in the House of Culture on one chilly evening in November. The majority of the group were Russian women, although there were a few elderly men and Evenk women. Most attendees sat dressed in fur hats and boots, shivering in the freezing, cavernous cement building. A radio correspondent taped the discussion about establishing the first church ever to exist in Tura. The primary organizer of the gathering requested ten names of people for a petition that would provide justification for the Russian Orthodox Archdiocese in Krasnoiarsk to support the fledgling group. The evening concluded with a conflict between the organizers and the director of the House of Culture. The director became concerned about repercussions from the town administration and claimed that a nongovernmental organization, the church group, could not legally meet in a government building. Despite this tension, the group continued to meet once a week and even held Easter services in the town administration's office building.[33] By the spring of 1994, there was also a Baptist group meeting weekly in a Tura apartment.

By the summer of 1995, both religious organizations had established their own permanent sites of worship in Tura. While most in the town knew of these two groups, neither attracted large numbers. On average, as the Evenk boy who assisted in the services told me, there were ten to fifteen people at the Russian Orthodox Sunday service. (The few times I attended, however, I was the only person present.) The Baptists attracted more followers, with twenty to twenty-five people frequently taking part in services and the popular social hours held each week; several women told me they liked the Baptists' strict rules about abstention from alcohol. During the summer of 1995, both churches attracted only Russians as regular attendees, except for one elderly woman with mixed Sakha-Evenk heritage. Neither church had permanent leaders; the Baptist church operated with an itinerant Ukrainian minister who traveled between parishes being established in small towns extending from Krasnoiarsk to Tura, and the Russian Orthodox Church was presided over by a Russian lay priest, or *batiushka.*

Many Evenki and Russians readily discussed their belief in some type of "god" (*bog*). Unlike Russians in town, who by 1995 often wore wooden or metal crosses as pendants, Evenki did not conspicuously demonstrate these beliefs. Some elderly Evenki scoffed at the idea of a "God"; as one elderly women explained to me, "we see life in all living things—the sky, the ground, animals—how could there be a single god?" Some younger Evenk women, however, were curious enough to attend at least one service "just to find out about it." One young woman, whose infant daughter had died in an accident in the mid-1990s, told me she had sought solace by attending a service at the Baptist church. She found the proscriptions against watching television, drinking, and even dancing too stifling, however, and decided to visit the Russian Orthodox Church. While she did not become a regular churchgoer, she did find the Russian Orthodox Church more to her liking because it did not ask believers to abide by the restrictions imposed by the Baptists. She called on the *batiushka* to consecrate the burial of her daughter in the town cemetery.

While by 1999 religious groups in Tura were freely gathering and had managed to avoid any substantive intimidation, in Russia as a whole there was growing opposition to institutional religion. Generally, there was more opposition to foreign groups than to the Russian Orthodox Church. In some cases foreign Baptist missionaries were openly intimidated and beaten by thugs, as in Magadan. In Provideniia, Chukotka, a town on the Bering Strait, there were mysterious fires in the Russian Orthodox Church building that were believed to have been caused by arson (Bloch and Kendall 2004). In early 1999 a major case was brought before a Russian court in which Jehovah's Witnesses were accused of breaking up families and seducing young people to join the church; they were charged with bringing undue harm to Russian citizens and were temporarily prohibited from proselytizing (National Public Radio broadcast, February 8, 1998).

An event in the summer of 1995 underscores the extent to which ritual practice in the Evenk District was being reconfigured. I was invited to attend the funeral services for a middle-aged Evenk man from a respected family. He was one of the young entrepreneurs or "shuttle traders" (see Stanley 1996) who imported goods from China, India, Turkey, and Saudi Arabia for resale in Krasnoiarsk and Tura. He died in Krasnoiarsk under circumstances that people spoke about with lowered voices; apparently the man had alienated many who considered him a dishonest businessman and a possible drug addict. His mother, a highly respected retired teacher, was unable to pay for the funeral expenses and the more distant relatives were unwilling to contribute. Because the mother was a venerated teacher and the deceased had taken part in the organizing committee of the local Association of Peoples of the North, *Arun*, this organization stepped in to take charge of the event.

Planning for the event took several days because transporting the corpse back from Krasnoiarsk was complicated and funerals, like weddings, were usually elaborately commemorated. The indigenous rights activists persistently made phone calls to the local administration to guarantee free passage for the corpse on the next freight flight from Krasnoiarsk. They also had to arrange for the practical and ritual elements of the funeral, as well as the banquet (*pominka*) to follow the funeral. These arrangements included ordering from Krasnoiarsk wreaths with bright plastic ornamental flowers to lay upon the grave, locating a gravedigger, obtaining a sheet for the morgue's use, commissioning an artist to write well-wishings on the long, wide, black ribbons that were draped over the grave, and arranging for a priest.[34] All these careful details reflect standard elements of funeral preparation in Russia today; they are the stuff of a shared Soviet (and pre-Soviet) cultural practice carried over into the present. (There are also burial practices and beliefs about the afterlife that continue to be specific to indigenous Siberians, although in this case Evenk traditional practices were not being publicly invoked.)[35]

The preparations were done with the dedicated care of an organization that was fully aware of its role in orchestrating tradition. Although none of the organizers claimed to be particularly fond of the deceased, the purpose of *Arun*'s involvement was clearly intended to reap social clout specifically among the Evenk community. Members of *Arun* were, however, unsure of the appropriate way to conduct a funeral in this era of shifting rituals. At the last minute, members decided to invite the *batiushka* and thereby introduced grounds for conflict over ritual practice within the community. Given that many Evenk elite were critical of organized religion and some were Communists, the *batiushka*'s participation in the funeral highlighted that this period of time was one in which ritual was truly contested for Evenki. At the actual funeral, those opposing the Russian Orthodox proceedings stood as far as possible from the lay priest, who consecrated the body and sang prayers for over one hour. Several of those in this group snickered openly as the priest blessed the soul of the deceased and prepared the body for transport to the nearby cemetery.

At the actual burial site, it was the *batiushka*'s turn to feel uncomfortable; he refused to take part when the mourners who had gathered engaged in the graveside ritual of passing around a glass for taking shots of vodka and "feeding" a shot to the soul of the deceased or to the lingering spirits. To the ardent, newly converted *batiushka*, this must have appeared as a breach of Russian Orthodox burial protocol and a "pagan" act. Throughout my research, I found that many Evenki and Russians in the region would feed the spirits in a similar manner before drinking at home or around a campfire or after arriving in a new place. This type of recognition of the spirits at the graveside ensured a safe, untroubled passage to the other world; in daily life, feeding spirits ensured that they remained appeased and that they would not become restless. Aside from the *batiushka* no one else seemed to be bothered by the syncretic ritual practice at the graveside.

In addition to organized religion, an equally significant element in competition for influence in Evenk ritual life was the growing belief in the supernatural or spiritual realm, or at least a more open discussion about it. While such beliefs were spreading throughout Russia in the late Soviet period, the historic role of shamanism in this region defined the shape this was taking. Unlike in the Sakha Republic (Balzer 1996) or in the Republic of Tuva (Drobizheva 1996: 253–54), no local shamans had emerged in the Evenk District by 1998.[36] Healers had begun, however, to travel regularly throughout the region. In 1993 and 1994, one healer from Ulan Ude, Buriatiia, spent two months in Tura doing what some called "amazing" acupressure; others considered him a charlatan. In the winter of 1994, another healer came from the northern part of the Sakha Republic and traveled to Evenk villages primarily treating alcoholism through hypnosis. As one Evenk woman who sought treatment explained to me, "This is what our people have lost. We no longer have our own shamans." Public health officials sometimes became alarmed by the influence that healers were wielding, and in at least one case in 1999 a healer who was thought to be Chinese was deported for operating without a license.[37]

While former Communist Evenki sometimes scoffed at discussions of spiritual life, by the mid-1990s shamanism had widespread cachet in the Evenk District. One example of this was a permanent exhibit dedicated to local shamanism that opened in the Evenk District Museum in 1995. Although for decades the museum had solicited donations of shamans' clothing, amulets, and drums from known descendants of shamans, the items had only been displayed as part of the exhibit declaring the victory of Sovietization over "backward" practices. The 1995 exhibit shifted to a sympathetic portrayal of Evenk shamanism and the systems of knowledge enmeshed in it. Along with a painted backdrop of the Nizhniaia Tunguska River in the winter, the exhibit featured a shaman's spirit helpers—carvings of birds elevated on wooden poles. As the director explained to me, in an effort to remove the authoritative voice of former exhibits condemning shamanic practices, there was no text accompanying the exhibit. (Chapter 7 examines the Evenk District Museum and its ties to historical consciousness in the region more extensively.)

In the late 1990s, hereditary ties to shamans were often quietly disclosed to interested parties such as ethnographers, even if actual shamanic practitioners were widely considered to have disappeared. For instance, I was studying photographs in the Evenk District Museum collection one afternoon when a researcher from a museum in the southern Siberian city of Komsomolsk-on-the-Amur arrived hoping to meet shamans in the area and work with the pertinent museum collections. While the researcher did not meet shamans, she did hear from those she met about extensive kinship ties to former practitioners. Tugolukov (1980) estimates that there were about thirty shamans in the region prior to 1938, and several elderly Evenki I met during my research claimed to have grandparents who were shamans. Making claims to shamanic heritage is not the same as claiming shamanic powers, but it was significant that in the mid-1990s older Evenki sought to quietly trace their lineages to a shamanic tradition that only became officially permissible in post-Soviet Russia.

This rejuvenation or reaffirmation of Evenk cultural practices was also apparent in naming. For the past several decades in Tura, Evenki have tended to give children Russian names. Names like Ivan, Sergei, Grigorii, Vladimir, and Andrei were widespread for boys; common names for girls were Vera, Galina, Alexandra, Tanya, and Mariia. In rare cases other names were given to children, but these were not Evenk or Russian names; these usually resulted from intermarriage between an ethnically non-Russian man (such as Tadzhik or Tatar) and an Evenk woman.[38] In a departure from naming practices of the 1970s and 1980s, several girls born in the region of Tura during 1993–95 were given the name "Sinilga." In a vivid example of the "reinvention of tradition" (see Hobsbawm and Ranger 1990), the name Sinilga invokes a tie to shamanism. The unusual name is that of a powerful shaman woman in the book *Ugrium reka,* a novel that enjoyed popularity throughout Siberia in the late Soviet period and into the 1990s.[39]

As Evenki continue to remake their identities in the twenty-first century, there is much to be negotiated, including issues regarding ritual practice, land use priorities, and educational ideals. In several regions of Siberia, shamanic and other non-secular ritual practices have resurged as part of daily life (Balzer 1996; Zhukovskaia 1995; Rethmann 2001: 158–69).[40] Given the place of shamanic practice in contemporary efforts to envision Siberian histories and the widespread reception of non-biomedical forms of healing, shamanism could re-emerge as integral to Evenk systems of knowledge. As this chapter has explored from a range of perspectives, Evenk identities are not, and never have, been static. As opportunities for higher education and social benefits become increasingly less accessible, however, it is possible that the flexible nature of what it is to be Evenki will become more rigid.

The next chapter moves from these broad spheres of history and ritual practice in which Evenk identities are constituted to consider the lives of people in specific households. Set within the context of the town of Tura, these households are variously negotiating their material well-being and also their alliances with post-Soviet structures of power like the residential school.

Chapter 2
A Siberian Town in the 1990s: Balancing Privatization and Collectivist Values

> This letter is a cry from the soul of desperate people. Why do you, leaders of the district who are invested with the full authority of the government, allow such chaos . . . [in] the distribution and procurement of apartments. . . . So it turns out that it's our fault that we are not *apparatchiki* [bureaucrats] but simple people from the periphery, that we lived our whole lives in the taiga and in villages. . . . Where is your acclaimed "politics of assistance and rejuvenation for indigenous Siberians"? Name even one of us who has a decent apartment. . . . What monies are being used to build these *kottedzhi* for high district and regional officials?
>
> —Letter to the editor from three Evenk women, *Evenkiiskaia zhizn'* (1996)

> Andrei asked me what struck me as changed in Tura since 1994. . . . When I said that there seemed to be many more private houses, he reacted saying that was just for the people with means. He elaborated: "We are simple workers. People like us cannot afford this type of thing. Everything has been *embezzled/privatized*" ("My prostye rabochie; eto nedostupno nam; vse *privatizirovali*" [his emphasis]).
>
> —Author's fieldnotes, June 1998

Anxiety over *privatizatsiia*, literally "privatization," was discussed by people at all levels of society during my time in central Siberia. While the term appears to describe the transition to a market economy in a detached, objective manner, in fact *privatizatsiia* is a process that was most widely understood in terms of its implications. People across the former Soviet Union and Eastern Europe often opposed what they saw as embezzlement of collectively owned government property (Hann 1996: 45; Kaneff 1996; Pine 1996: 136; Lampland 1995). Judging from this response and her own work in Buriatiia, Humphrey has suggested that socialist practices created specific collectivist values (1999a: 478). The process of selling off state-owned assets such as factories, collective farms, reindeer herds, and machinery was and continues to be highly charged in moral terms; privatizing is not a mere change in management, but a radical shift away from state mandates to deemphasize social stratification. This "involution of the state," as Bourdieu describes parallel processes throughout Europe in the late twentieth century (1996: 34), results in the failure to provide long-guaranteed social services such as education, health care, child care, and housing. Fundamentally, when the state no longer ensures these basic needs, the onus falls back on the household.[1]

This chapter introduces the context of the central Siberian town of Tura in the 1990s, with an emphasis on the implications of market reforms for the social ties between people and the broader sense of community. In the first section, I briefly situate the town before turning to aspects of the social stratification emerging there in the 1990s. In the second section, I discuss how specific households viewed the breakdown of long-term, communal foundations for social bonds. As discussed earlier, schooling is one of the central issues being negotiated by households as they seek to redefine relationships with the state.

The Setting

In 1924, just seven years after the Russian Revolution, the Committee of the North sent a cadre of Soviet personnel to what is today Tura, to establish an administrative and cultural outpost, or so-called "culture base" (*kul'turnaia baza*). This site, which juts out slightly into the intersection of the wide Nizhniaia Tunguska River and the Kochachum tributary, had been a seasonal trading post for years prior to the Soviet arrival. In the 1990s, Evenki continued to travel to Tura from villages to trade, seek out social benefits, attend school or make arrangements to fly on to other cities. These journeys between centers of trade and administration were a significant part of daily life and daily negotiation. In the late twentieth and early twenty-first centuries these journeys most often began with access to aviation.

During one of my early trips to Tura in 1992, it was impressed upon me just how crucial the air connections had become for people in Evenkiia. Arriving at the city of Krasnoiarsk after a lengthy train journey from Moscow, I set off for the airport. At the Cheremshanka (Wild Garlic) Airport, I managed to fit into a flight that was said to be full. I boarded the plane along with the other passengers carrying their own duffel bags, suitcases, and hefty bundles of merchandise, and we stowed our luggage on the designated rack at the back of the plane. There were surprisingly few passengers. Half the seats in the 40-passenger plane had been folded aside, and sacks of onions were stacked in their place. Early in the flight my eyes began to burn as the onions emitted a pungent odor and onion skins breezed about in the cabin. The stewardesses stopped serving mineral water and hurried to cover the onions with numerous cloth napkins in an attempt to prevent the strong odor from fully permeating the cabin.

While this was one of the most memorable trips I took between Krasnoiarsk and Tura, by the early 1990s it was quite common for people to be packed into planes along with freight such as onions, a relative luxury good treasured in the winter for its vitamin C. In many cases, those transporting the foodstuffs chartered the flights and provided a few passengers with an additional opportunity for flying between the two points. In the late Soviet era, the flights scheduled several times a week between Krasnoiarsk and Tura made it possible for government-run stores in the town to be supplied with perishable foodstuffs such as vegetables, fruits, eggs, and milk throughout the long winter months. By the early 1990s, however, flights became infrequent and expensive. Private companies transported these luxury goods to the private stores in which a small portion of Turintsy shopped.

The vast distances and expansive landscape, combined with the government financial crisis of the 1990s, created in the Evenk District a widespread sense of being detached from the rest of Russia. In fact, the regions in Russia to the south of the Evenk District, but especially the industrial centers closer to Western Europe, were referred to as the *materik*, or "the continent," as if the Evenk District was an island of sorts. This terminology was most often used by newcomers, for whom the term invoked a sense of longing. As Keith Basso eloquently writes, "Landscapes and the places that fill them become tools for the imagination, expressive means for accomplishing verbal deeds, and also, of course, eminently portable possessions to which individuals can maintain deep and abiding attachments, regardless of where they travel" (1996: 75). In retaining an image of the *materik* as a separate place, a place that was in part elevated in imaginations as ideal, as a place to return to and a place to long for, these newcomers in the Evenk District detached themselves from the rural surroundings and associated themselves with an urban, European-defined identity. For newcomers, a distinct sense of place was evoked through reference to the imaginary "continent," and this set the newcomers apart from indigenous inhabitants and their own more local sense of place.[2]

The relatively complicated and expensive means of travel between the *materik* and the Evenk District heightened these distinctions, but so did the social interactions that were specific to travel to the Evenk District in the 1990s. Passengers flying to Tura frequently gathered together in the Cheremshanka Airport waiting for upcoming flights or providing moral support for fellow *Evenkiitsy* when flights were delayed for hours or days as a result of bad weather. The "Yak-40," so-named because of its 40-person seating capacity, was the standard plane used for transportation between Tura and the metropolitan center of Krasnoiarsk, and passengers loaded and unloaded their own baggage into the tail of the plane. These flights were like cross-sections of Tura—with cheerful young men returning from their two years compulsory army service, young women students dressed in the latest city fashions with black platform boots, bureaucrats and politicians traveling back from Moscow and Krasnoiarsk, elderly men and women returning home after treatment in city hospitals, and no-nonsense women entrepreneurs carefully shepherding their wares bundled into gigantic parcels for resale in Tura. With this range of people, mostly familiar with one another, flights to and from Tura provided ideal opportunities to catch up on town events. Few passengers paid attention to the landscape below.

As one flies north toward Tura, the stunted evergreens and vast patches of green and off-white and orange lichen stretch on into the distance without interruption, except for the few abrupt beeline swaths cut into the taiga carpet by geophysical expeditions. Herds of reindeer are occasionally visible against the backdrop of the low, thin vegetation of the rolling plateaus and shallow valleys. The reindeer, which until the early 1970s formed the backbone of the Evenk subsistence economy, are lost in the details of the taiga as the plane descends. The terrain is brought into focus with small patches of dwarfed larch, evergreen, and birch trees becoming visible.

This is the Central Siberian Plateau that covers much of the Evenk District's land mass. Tura is located in an area that is considered taiga but has the additional predominant feature of larch trees. The taiga surrounding Tura is also characterized by stunted evergreens and some birch trees, few more than 15 to 20 feet tall, and these clusters of trees are interspersed by stretches of high plateau covered only with lichen. The treeless area, or tundra, between the ice cap and the tree line of Arctic regions, is located considerably to the north of Tura. The area around Tura includes some features of the tundra, however, namely permafrost and low-growing vegetation such as lichens, mosses, and stunted shrubs.

Throughout the 1990s the town of Tura continued to be difficult to access by land. There were no roads extending beyond the outer boundaries of the airport, which is 14 kilometers west of the town, or beyond the town dump, cemetery, and ecological research station, which are several kilometers to the northwest. The Nizhniaia Tunguska and Kochachum Rivers form the southern and western boundaries of the town and in the 1990s they served as important routes for transportation. At the beginning and end of summer, barges delivered tons of supplies to the area, and in the winter months villages along the river depended on the frozen waterways for the gigantic "Ural" trucks to transport goods.

Seasons and Subsistence

In the 1990s the pace of life in the town continued to be tied to the seasons. During winter, transportation was more limited for town-dwelling people. In 1993–94, some relatively well-off households and most hunting cooperatives had snowmobiles that they used on the trails in the surrounding taiga from mid-October to early May. When there was sufficient snow, from early December to late April, snowmobiles were used for transportation around Tura. When road conditions permitted, cars were used as well on the single dirt road stretching from the center of town out to the airport and on several smaller dirt roads connecting residential concentrations of two-story apartment houses and a few private houses. In the early 1990s, there were few cars in Tura; there were, however, quite a number of motorcycles with sidecars attached and these were driven even during the winter months. For those without their own transportation, a town bus made rounds in the morning and evening. In the summer a motorboat provided transport once a week to the closest village of Nidym, located 25 kilometers up the Nizhniaia Tunguska River.

When I arrived for my field research in the fall of 1993, the barges supplying the region had just departed. Annually they brought building materials such as brick, lumber, and glass; fuel in the form of gasoline, crude oil, and coal; and basic housewares and foodstuffs. Basic food items such as flour, salt, carrots, cabbage and potatoes were readily available in the government stores in which foodstuffs continued to be subsidized by the district budget. By this time, nearly two years after the Russian Federation had been established, imported goods such as alcohol, cookies, and cheese and perishable foodstuffs like butter, fruit, and eggs were being sold in the mushrooming privately owned kiosks and stores. Entrepreneurs were not restricted by the seasons or the water level for barges to make the trip along the river; they flew in goods year round. Only the most well-off households could afford, however, to rely solely on these stores for their supply of food. In contrast, most Turintsy were busily engaged in a flurry of activity salting and canning cabbage and carrots and storing potatoes as the winter months neared.

One day in early winter when I stopped by to visit a friend at his studio located above one of the town's coal-fired generators, I learned of the place of ice in the local imagination. As the coal generator clanged away, my friend was completing a painting featuring a view of the frozen Nizhniaia Tunguska River as seen from the studio window; this would be incorporated into the exhibit on shamanism being installed in the Evenk District Museum. Beside the work bench, a long series of dates was penciled in on a beam. This was a record of the ice break-up (*ledokhod*) for previous years. Each year toward the end of May, people eagerly wait for the ice to break on the river, the sign that spring is finally arriving after eight long months. This incredible event begins with the ice flowing in a sheet and then becoming separate blocks before it eventually melts into the swollen river.

The first time I encountered the *ledokhod*, in late May 1994, the powerful mass of ice-covered water forcing its way between the banks of the Kochachum River reminded me of toothpaste being squeezed from a tube. The friction of the icy surface sheets being propelled along the riverbank created a "shshshshshshshsh" sound, a phenomenon called *shuga* by locals. This eerie background sound, something like white noise, lasted only for about 24 hours before the river flowed more freely. The *shuga* had broken up and separate smaller blocks of ice had formed; the waterways created on either side of the ice flows now acted as buffers preventing the friction of the *shuga* against the banks. Each year the ice melt, which extends for several weeks into June, creates dangerously powerful currents and flood waters that threaten towns and villages along the rivers. By the time the yearly flood waters subside in mid-June, many Turintsy are planting their hearty crops of potatoes in the plots assigned by the town council.

For decades, a convoy of barges, *karavan*, arrived to supply Tura twice a year, in the fall and spring. The vessels were commissioned and stocked in Krasnoiarsk with financing from the district administration. These were high-spirited times when the gigantic barges could safely traverse the river, timing their travel with the few weeks of high water during spring melt-off and fall rains. By 1992, however, the steady departure of barges packed with freight began to invert the emotions evoked by this seasonal structuring of life in Tura. The yard of each apartment block was cluttered with the sturdy steel storage containers that would be filled with furniture and other belongings to be sent south to Krasnoiarsk as freight. As salaries went unpaid and nearly one thousand people were laid off from work in the oil exploration outfits, a steady stream of people mostly identifying as Russian began to pack up and move from the town where they had lived for five, ten, or twenty years. Instead of a collective relief being associated with the arrival of barges and the replenishing of foodstuffs, building material, and fuel, the departures of the barges piled with steel containers came to mark a further breakdown of the Soviet infrastructure.

Again in August 1998 the *karavan* was associated with turmoil in post-Soviet Russia. When Russia was unable to pay the interest on its loans from the International Monetary Fund the economic crisis destabilized the country. In one week the ruble fell from 6 rubles to $1 U.S. to 18 rubles to $1 U.S. Throughout the North there was a real threat of people going without food and fuel for the winter. Regions left without the usual federal government subsidies were unable to pay for the critical barge shipments, and at the same time the reserves of food and fuel stockpiled in the Soviet era were exhausted. Ultimately, some relief came with last minute central government allocations and international aid contributions.

No matter what the political-economic situation was, the short summer was relished by Turintsy. In the six weeks or so of summer and into the autumn, before the first snowfall in late September, women of all ages from nearly every household actively collected seasonal berries such as cloudberries (*moroshka*), bilberries (*golubika*), wild cranberries (*brusnika*), and red and black currents (*smorodina*). Russians were particularly fond of collecting mushrooms such as chanterelles, "slippery jack" (*masliata*), and one called literally "eat raw" (*syroezhka*). The mushrooms were dried or canned for winter consumption. After work each day in late summer, Turintsy were often found walking along the town roads toward the forests with a pail in hand for collecting the berries or mushrooms. While Evenki historically avoided mushrooms, berry-picking is a time-old subsistence practice (Sviridova 1995: 61–62). A special berry scoop (*sovok*), historically made from birch bark, was swiped along bushes to dislodge and collect berries. Birch bark scoops had been widely displaced by plastic and aluminum versions in Tura by the early 1990s, but there has recently been renewed interest in the birch bark version among town Evenki who are involved in reviving material culture, as I discuss further in Chapters 6 and 7 (Sviridova 1995).

In the 1990s, while berries and mushrooms served as an important source of vitamins, the local diet revolved around reindeer meat and fish. Evenk and Russian residents of the town relied heavily for subsistence needs on hunting and fishing, resorting reluctantly to store-bought, packaged sources of protein. More than two-thirds of the eighty households polled either procured fresh meat and fish themselves or arranged for these food products through friends and relatives living in villages. Nearly all the households polled gathered berries and mushrooms themselves. If meat or fish was absent from a meal, people did not consider themselves fed.

The way Turintsy incorporated subsistence practices into their lives reveals something about how they imagined themselves. In her work on

Muscovite narratives, Ries writes in regard to subsistence gardens and berry gathering that Muscovites engaged in these in large part for the "symbolic value and identity they derived from these practices" (1997: 135). She argues that during Perestroika (late 1980s and early 1990s) among other practices, subsistence gardening/gathering functioned symbolically to mark practitioners as *narod*, or belonging to the Russian people, in contrast to being associated with those in power or with access to wealth and connections. Unlike in urban Russia, in Tura in the 1990s the class divisions had not yet transformed a widespread local reliance on subsistence gathering; even those who had relatively more access to power and wealth directly drew on the local resources to supplement their diets. Unlike the primarily symbolic weight Ries ascribes to subsistence practices for urban Russians, in Tura gathering berries and mushrooms, as well as fishing and hunting, were a critical source of nutrition for all segments of the population. This common reliance on the local environment bound residents together in a common identity as *Evenkiitsy*, to be distinguished from those dwelling in the *materik*.

In the 1990s, luxury food consumption did, however, begin to indicate growing schisms based on wealth within the town and Evenk District. Most households relied heavily on potatoes as a staple; in the most hard-up households, fried potatoes were the main dish for every meal, with an occasional addition of fish or canned meat, and tea with canned, evaporated milk (*sgushchenka*). The more prosperous Evenk households, which tended to have ties back to their villages of origin, had a steady diet of fish and reindeer meat, while Russian households tended to consume more imported meats, including chicken, the Russian version of hotdogs (*sosiski*), and keilbasa or salami. In 1993–94 about one-third of households in Tura grew their own potatoes and harvested them in the fall of each year. Those who did not grow potatoes bought them in the government stores. By 1998 when government stores were nearly empty, the prevalence of potato planting had increased; nearly everyone sought to plant a small plot or share land with a neighbor who had rented it for a five-year term from the town. Land left fallow for more than one season was subject to reappropriation by the town administration for reassignment to someone else, so if someone could not use a plot, she or he often tried to find a friend or relative who temporarily could.

Some foods deemed "traditional" also served as markers of identity and carried significance as prestige foods and sometimes comfort foods. On one occasion when I visited a herding camp located several hours by helicopter from Tura, the grandmother was so taken with meeting me, the first foreigner she had ever encountered, that she offered me a foot-long reindeer tongue as a gift. I did not fully appreciate the import of this, but when I returned to Tura and a friend eagerly unwrapped the tongue to prepare it to boil up for a meal, she explained that this was a very unusual gift. Reindeer tongue, prized in the herders' camps as a delicacy, was rarely found in Tura and my friend had not had the chance to eat this for years.

Other traditional foods were more frequently encountered in Tura. "Evenk chocolate" (*evenkiiskii shokolad*; *khakin*), or frozen reindeer liver, was offered to me with tea on many occasions, with the instruction to let it slip down my throat and to have another piece to build up my strength. Lightly seared chunks of reindeer (*chukin*) were a common dish served for lunch or dinner. And fish, either in long, thin, frozen strips (*stroganina*) or in splayed, dried form (*iukola*), were common snack food. On special occasions like birthdays or holidays or during fishing trips beside a campfire, orange caviar (*ikra*) was often eaten. The types of fish and the ways of preparing the fish seemed endless.[3]

These foods were savored by many in Tura, and perhaps most by Evenki, who often spoke of them in connection to their lives growing up in the taiga. Russians who felt rooted in the region, either through intermarriage or through a connection to subsistence practices, also appreciated the traditional delicacies. However, as Kerttula (2000: 113) writes regarding traditional foodstuffs among the Chukchi and Yup'ik in Chukotka in eastern Siberia, newcomers in Tura were likely to point to these foods as a means of distinguishing themselves from indigenous inhabitants. Through disdain for such foodstuffs, some newcomers sought to identify themselves as being somehow more "civilized" (*kul'turnye*), more connected to an industrial economy, and more integrated into the new market economy.

From the early to late 1990s, the increasing social stratification in Russia overall was reflected by food practices in Tura. As private stores were established, food staples for wealthier segments of the population began to include more packaged goods. Those in positions of relative wealth—entrepreneurs, pilots, and people like radio and television employees working in the well-financed government organizations—increasingly dined on expensive Ramen (instant) noodles and Campbell's soup. When salaries were going unpaid for months in the early 1990s, Turintsy used a barter system to purchase such foodstuffs (Anderson 1998). Organizations would receive food (or other items) from those who were in debt to them, and in turn the organizations would pay employees in kind.[4] This system was widespread in Russia throughout the 1990s and into the present. It had less impact, however, on those who were unemployed and on rural migrants to Tura, who often did not have a place in the organizations tendering the goods. Those finding themselves increasingly impoverished—such as pensioners, single mothers, and the unemployed—were relying less on expensive purchased items and more on subsistence plots, fishing and hunting, and reindeer meat sent along by relatives in villages. Some also made use of the limited social welfare support in the form of modest payments and occasional foodstuffs such as tea, sugar or butter issued to those deemed in need.

Making a Living and Migration

In the late 1990s, the local government continued to be the primary employer in the spheres of administration, health, education, public culture (for example, the House of Culture and museum), and communication (for example, radio, newspaper, telegraph, and post office). In the Soviet era, there was no official private commerce, and all Tura residents worked for the state. In addition to the administrative and social service positions, there were positions in the oil exploration outfits, the quartz extraction outfits, and state agricultural cooperatives, or *sovkhozy*, like the town fur-processing cooperative and the lumbermill. The *sovkhozy* operated on the principal of "centralized accumulation" that was practiced widely throughout the former USSR and in many other socialist countries (Kideckel 1993). According to this system, Tura was both "center" and "periphery," depending on whether it was seen in relation to district villages or to Krasnoiarsk or Moscow.

In the case of Evenkiia, the practice of "centralized accumulation" dates back to 1930 when hunting and fishing, as the fundamental modes of production were organized so that each person filled a contract for the state herding, hunting, or fishing cooperative. The collective provided transportation and ammunition or tackle. Pay depended on fulfilling the contract, and bonuses were paid when the hunting cooperative as a whole fulfilled the plan. Sable and fox pelts, fish, and reindeer products like antlers and hides were transported to Tura, where they went through initial processing before being sent on to major cities for final processing and packaging. For instance, sable pelts made their way from the *sovkhoz* contract trappers through an intricate web of middlemen to be sold in a Leningrad auction house.

With the onset of market relations, these state cooperatives nearly shut down. In 1994 in the Illimpei region, which includes Tura, only two of the former ten *sovkhozy* continued to sign contracts with sable trappers and with fishermen. The rising cost of supplies—gasoline and ammunition—and helicopter transportation made the venture unprofitable, and the Russian government was no longer underwriting the costs or providing the means for marketing the resulting products. Near Tura, access to hunting grounds even just for subsistence needs was increasingly competitive, so hunters were compelled to fly to more remote areas. This was difficult to arrange for several reasons. In general, former herding and hunting territories were claimed by different clans when land was decollectivized in the mid-1990s. Access was no longer negotiated through the state cooperatives, but through personal or family connections, as discussed in the second section of this chapter. Furthermore, for those who could negotiate access, many could not afford the cost of the helicopter and so were foregoing the hunting season. As one old-time hunter told me, "If I can find transportation I'll just go this year out of habit; I won't get anything for it." Besides the general dissolution of the Soviet infrastructure, the plummeting value of sable on the world market in the 1990s was also severely affecting local trappers.

As a market economy emerged in the mid-1990s and government jobs became an increasingly less reliable source of income, many people turned to doing additional part-time work, termed *shabashnichat'* by locals. Beginning in 1993, government paychecks distributed through the Tura post office were often four to five months late. Bartering and day labor became common. These alternate means of support did not, however, provide a solution to the insufficient funds available in the local bank because some services did not lend themselves to barter. For instance, in August of 1995 government organizations received funds channeled through Krasnoiarsk for vacation pay and regular paychecks that had been held up since May 1995. The timing of this hold-up of paychecks caused extreme consternation for Tura residents who planned to take their yearly vacation in June or July. Many had to spend their vacations at home because they could not pay for flights. For years residents of the North had relied on paid (*l'gotnye*) vacations, for which the government covered roundtrip transportation, meals, and accommodation every other year. Less than one-half of these benefits were eventually paid in 1995. The erosion of benefits was just one more reminder that the Soviet social system was unraveling.[5]

As newcomers failed to receive the entitlements such as significant pay differentials and vacations that the Soviet system used to lure them to live and work in the North, they departed for their cities of origin. As part of this trend, in addition to a plummeting birthrate, between 1992 and 1993 the population of the Evenk District fell rapidly from just over 26,000 people (with 3,973 Evenki) to just over 25,000 people (with 4,050 Evenki); by 1998 it was estimated to be 20,033 (with 2,805 Evenki).[6] The situation in Tura (see Table 1) was similar. For nearly a decade prior to 1991, the numbers of people arriving and departing in Tura every year were about equal, about 420 people. In 1991, however, there was a sudden change, with more than twice as many people migrating out of the town as were moving there. By 1992 the outmigration for the calendar year was severe, with nearly five times more people departing from the town than were arriving.[7] The outmigration continued in 1993, and by the end of the 1990s the total population of the Evenk District was twenty percent less than it had been just under a decade earlier.

The severe drop in the number of Evenki in the district between 1993 and 1998 (from over 4,000 to under 3,000) was largely caused by an alarming increase in mortality across Russia in the 1990s, and especially in the North among indigenous Siberians. Between 1989 and 1999, the average longevity of Russian men fell by nearly ten years to under sixty years of age, while the average longevity of indigenous Siberian men fell by more than ten years from fifty-five to under forty-five years of age (East West Institute report 1999: 1). The statistics on Evenki in the district also failed to reflect migrations that were increasingly taking place without being registered in the town centers.[8]

Beginning in 1993, the intense outmigration of newcomers from Evenkiia and inmigration of Evenki to Tura was leading to a shuffle of housing. With the privatization of housing in 1991, housing stock went from being entirely government-owned to belonging increasingly to individuals. People planning to leave Tura privatized their apartments and usually sold them to individuals, but sometimes to the town administration. The fee for privatization was minimal and, in fact, most of the housing was privatized at no cost.[9] By 1995 the outmigration of newcomers had slowed considerably, but the Tura mayor's office still reported buying 42 apartments for distribution to those Turintsy deemed most in need (S bol'noi golovy na zdorovuiu 1996).

By 1995, Evenki were migrating in significant numbers from villages into the regional centers. As day cares, schools, and cultural clubs closed in outlying villages, flights were also severely cut back, and daily needs such as bread, sugar, and tea became scarce. Village Evenki were increasingly establishing households in Tura in hopes of improving their circumstances. Those who were able to do so bought apartments in Tura, while retaining their houses in the villages. Those who could not afford to buy apartments, such as the women who authored the letter to the editor cited at the outset of this chapter, appealed to the Tura administration to become eligible for housing provided by the town. Many lived temporarily with relatives while they waited to resolve their housing problems. Unofficially, this migration of Evenki from villages to the town

TABLE 1. Population Shifts in the Evenk Autonomous District (EAO), 1964–98

Population	*1964*	*1984*	*1992*	*1993*	*1998*
EAO Total	11,830	21,430	26,062	25,056	20,033
Evenki	4,000	3,503	3,973	4,050	2,805*

Source: Okruzhnoi otdel statistiki EAO (1965, 1985, 1993, 1998).
* This figure is from a report published by the EastWest Institute (1999: 1).

of Tura was estimated to have resulted in Evenk comprising nearly 900 people in Tura by 1999, and all indications were that the outmigration from villages would continue as long as material conditions remained desperate in outlying villages.

Housing and Social Stratification

Tension over housing reflected the increasing social stratification in Tura and the interwoven politics of identity. Evenki newly arrived in Tura often had difficulty finding affordable housing. While technically they could appeal to the mayor's office to be included on the list for government-financed housing, they were not readily considered equal residents of Tura. For instance, the mayor of Tura wrote in response to the letter cited at the beginning of this chapter, "Why should the Tura population suffer just because people from the villages vie for housing in the district center?" (S bol'noi golovy na zdorovuiu 1996). Unlike Evenki recently arrived from villages, young professionals such as English teachers and doctors were offered apartments upon arrival. In other parts of Russia, these people might have waited for years or simply had to save to purchase an apartment.

In the 1990s most Turintsy lived in housing originally built by the government because few could afford the luxury of building their own houses and few had the necessary connections for leasing land. Some newly arrived Evenki and most longtime Turintsy lived in two-story, prefabricated apartment buildings constructed in the 1960s and 1970s. The standard plan for these long, sloping, weathered wooden buildings had three entryways with four apartments leading off of each of the two landings. The apartments were generally one or two rooms with a small kitchen and a water closet where residents kept pails for waste water, because there was no running water. The water closet was rarely isolated as a separate toilet space and more commonly also served as storage space for manual washing machines, skis, conserves, canned mushrooms, and winter clothing. All buildings in Tura were heated by means of centrally located coal furnaces and generators that pumped hot water throughout the town to radiate in apartments, stores, and municipal buildings. Many apartments also had stuccoed brick stoves for additional heat and cooking. Electricity for the town was provided by oil-powered generators.

When I arrived in Tura in 1992, my Evenk hosts drove the large "Ural" truck through the town center, and my attention was drawn to the newly constructed buildings along the main thoroughfare. I wondered out loud what the solid wooden buildings with neat blue trim framing the windows might be, and the curt reply was *portovskie doma*, "airport houses." In 1992 these few rows of two-story apartment buildings erected in the late 1980s stood out in the town as the ones most recently constructed but also as the ones most often inhabited by *ukraintsy*, connoting families of Ukrainian pilots and airport technical staff.[10] While the airport personnel were not all Ukrainian, a popular perception associated this privileged housing with the best-positioned social group in town, the pilots. Most of the aviation personnel—pilots, mechanics, traffic controllers—were from Ukraine, where they had been trained in prominent aviation facilities. In short, this portion of the population had access to a specialized education, and therefore employment, that few Evenki could aspire to attain. Throughout my research the airport houses continued to act as reminders of the class divisions in the town.[11]

It was not just who generally inhabited these airport houses that signified class difference but also the physical structures themselves. In the early 1990s, these houses were the only ones with plumbing (*kanalizatsiia*). Built by the airport to house its senior staff and pilots and their families, these apartments were known to have a convenient water provision, sometimes even flushable toilets. Unlike the weekly municipal water delivery system for most inhabitants of Tura—whereby each apartment dweller lugged his or her water from a barrel located on the street—the airport service bureau delivered water and workers piped it directly into large containers located inside each apartment. This was a significant difference in amenities; especially when it was -40 and -50 degrees Celsius those scooping water from a barrel and heaving a full bucket up a flight of stairs had no doubt about the gradations of privilege in the town.

In addition to the few airport personnel, the well established administrators and former Party personnel enjoyed high status housing in contrast to the majority living in dilapidated apartment complexes. These administrators and political personnel tended to live in what locals called *kottedzhi*, or semiprivate houses. These *kottedzhi* were constructed as one house divided by a single wall into two dwellings. Some *kottedzhi* were built in the early 1980s under the direction of the district administration, but the ones constructed more recently (since 1993) were built by individual organizations such as the residential school, hospital, or police department. This housing was then distributed to well placed employees in the respective organizations. With the shifting social stratification of the town, local entrepreneurs also constructed detached private houses with their accrued capital; these were also called *kottedzhi* by local Turintsy. In either case, these dwellings had their own backyards, outhouses, and saunas.

The public discourse around housing significantly indicated the shape of emerging social stratification in this region. The shared semantics in regard to housing in Tura, including the use of the term *kottedzhi* for housing occupied by both the former Soviet Party elite and the emerging business class, reflects how new social hierarchies developing throughout Russia were overlapping with preexisting structures of privilege. The second section of this chapter turns to considering how households in Tura in the 1990s were positioning themselves in a time of jarring social change and growing social stratification.

Households, Private Property, and the State

The growing schism between those with and without access to wealth was one of the most striking features of daily life in Tura in the 1990s and into the present, and by extension, in Russia overall. This section focuses on households as I examine daily decisions made by individuals within the constraints of their circumstances. In this way, my approach follows that of at least one Russian social scientist who emphasizes that social science should be written to depict the unique, holistic nature of specific locales, not to fit within the paradigms of large mechanisms, be they government programs or academic exercises (Panarin 1997: 149). The portraits of Evenk households in this section provide a framework for discussing how Evenki in different social positions make use of social networks and institutions. I have grouped the household portraits according to degrees of access to economic capital, including education, housing, and income. Relationships with former Soviet institutions such as the residential school and ties to relatives in villages are prevalent themes in the daily narratives on identity politics in these households.

As Humphrey writes about southeastern Siberia (1999a: 469–71), kinship and forms of sponsorship in general are proving to be increasingly important in central Siberia as former state structures of support weaken. A focus on households provides one way of examining shifting relationships. The intention here, however, is to take a critical stance toward the concept of "household" and use it only in order to encapsulate fluid domains of domestic life. The following portraits are rooted in households, but, similar to feminist scholarship reflecting on household analyses (Stack 1974: 31; Yanagisako 1979), they also extend to broader networks of social life.

In examining the heterogeneous nature of Evenk households, this section also breaks apart the monolithic concept of "community." The social stratification depicted here within Evenki as a group points to the fact that people have various allegiances and an ethnic allegiance is not always primary. Also, there are significant gender differences in the ways that Evenki interact with community structures. The critical role of women in household decisions suggests, as Stack (1974) does in her work, that economic disparity patterns household roles and community relationships. Women's roles in households are central to the households' survival; even in cases where men are present, women are often still the primary decision makers. Paying attention to agency within these households means recognizing this crucial fact of the decision making around household concerns such as sending children to residential school or negotiating instrumental allegiances to Evenk symbolic capital.

In considering five households, this section seeks to illustrate the way that households, and often the household heads—women—have negotiated relationships with state structures such as schooling. The five household portraits are meant to illustrate three broad groupings of households as "prosperous," "transitional," and "marginal." The first two portraits concern households that prospered in the post-Soviet period because of access to either economic or political capital. The second two "transitional" portraits consider households that continue to struggle with the deterioration of the Soviet infrastructure. One reindeer herding household has been displaced from its primary life in the taiga, and another town-based household has suffered from unemployment brought on by the failure of the government-sponsored oil exploration. The last portrait of a "marginal household," examines the situation of a town-based household with few kin ties; households like this one, headed up by a single parent, usually a mother, were most desperate in the 1990s. The extreme poverty of these households underscores the critical role of kin ties for maintaining a household when the state abdicates responsibility and financial support for those in need. For each of these portraits, I consider the degree to which households drew upon Evenk identities as a resource for securing their well-being in the 1990s and the way in which the residential school was involved in the strategies engaged by households.

Prosperous Households—Economic Capital and Political Connections

In the early 1990s, there were few households that could be viewed as prosperous in Tura, and they were almost exclusively newcomers like the Ukraintsy discussed above. By 1999, however, it was evident that some Evenki had prospered significantly more than others with the onset of market transformations. These prosperous households could be thought of as falling into two groups, those that benefited from their access to economic capital and entrepreneurial savvy and those that were politically connected. They shared a common trait of relative power gained in the 1990s, as the well-being of households became more obviously differentiated in Tura. While no single household was necessarily composed of both politically connected people and entrepreneurs, often these households had close kin connections with people in each of these spheres.

Figure 4. Berrypicking along the Nizhniaia Tunguska River. Photo by the author, 1998.

The households with economic capital usually included older members who had acquired higher education, so these households served as a clearinghouse for Evenk community material needs and also for information. In the shifting context of market transformation, these households fared relatively well as they generated capital through control over former state property and natural resources. A brief sketch of the property belonging to such households would include a car, a motor boat, a motorcycle, a snowmobile, and at least one house constructed since the early 1990s. However, since land could not be owned in the Evenk District even in the late 1990s, these households leased it.[12]

The Polgogir household was typical of the very few households one could characterize as "prosperous." In 1995 it was composed of four residences, although when I first met the Polgogirs in 1993 they were living in just two apartments. The oldest member of the household was Nadezhda Sergeevna, who taught at the town residential school.[13] She was also a renowned storyteller and artisan, or *masteritsa*.[14] While Nadezhda Sergeevna was completely bilingual in Evenk and Russian, her three children spoke only Russian as a native language and understood just select phrases in Evenk. All three of the children (in their mid-30s and early 40s in 1996) had attended the residential school. Because their mother lived in Tura while they were of school age, however, they could have attended the town school, where newcomers and other Turintsy studied.

Like most Evenki of her generation, Nadezhda Sergeevna Polgogir grew up in the residential school system. She was one of twelve children, and in 1938, at the age of nine, she was sent from her parent's reindeer herding clan to study in the Evenk District town of Baikit. After graduation she went to study in a college for teacher training in the city of Igarka, located near the Arctic Circle. In Igarka, Nadezhda Sergeevna met her future husband, a Ukrainian who worked for the railroad in Norilsk. When they married, she began working in a day-care center associated with the rail company. After a few years, they moved back to Evenkiia to the town of Baikit, where Nadezhda Sergeevna taught in elementary schools and her husband worked in the local administration. In this period the Polgogirs had three children. After about ten years, their marriage broke up and Nadezhda Sergeevna moved with the children to several different Evenk District villages to teach before she eventually settled in Tura. She taught decorative arts in the residential school and began to write and publish songs in Evenk. Nadezhda Sergeevna's husband died soon after they broke up, and so Nadezhda Sergeevna raised the children with assistance from her siblings.

Eight of Nadezhda Sergeevna's brothers and sisters died in the taiga before reaching adulthood, and her parents died while she was in high school. Like Nadezhda Sergeevna, the other three surviving siblings, all girls, also attended the residential school, and two of them went on to receive higher education. In the mid-1990s one sister was teaching Russian literature in the residential school; the other sister, who has a doctorate in linguistics, was working in an educational research institute in Moscow, where she lived with her family.

The eldest of the four siblings, Nina, dropped out of the Baikit residential school after the third grade and returned to live with her parents' clan in the taiga. Of the four sisters, only Nina continued to subsist by hunting and fishing until the time of her death in 1998. When I first met Nina in 1992, she recounted one instance of her extreme marginality as we crouched together smoking her heavy filterless cigarettes. She told me of her recent difficulty in receiving entitlements such as her pension. Because she had lived most of her life in the taiga, she had never been issued an internal passport. Like others remaining outside the confines of villages, Nina had managed to be excluded from this form of standard Soviet bureaucratization and categorization that the majority of Evenki encountered by the 1970s.[15] Like other remaining taiga dwellers, hunters and reindeer herders often relied on family support for negotiating town bureaucracy and for supplies such as tea, cigarettes, flour, and bullets. Nina's family, and especially her nieces and nephews—Nadezhda Sergeevna's children—had taken this role seriously.

In 1995 Nadezhda Sergeevna's three children all lived in Tura and made a living doing business. The two younger children, Mikhail and Tamara (in their thirties), were both single and made their living running small import businesses. (As discussed in Chapter 4, Tamara worked as a teacher for ten years prior to going into business in 1993; Mikhail had been involved in trade most of his adult life, but only beginning in 1990 was he able to conduct this officially, given the Soviet restriction on private business.) In addition to their regular trips to Krasnoiarsk in search of goods for resale in Tura, like many other young former Soviet entrepreneurs, each of them had traveled to China, Saudi Arabia, and Turkey looking for merchandise for resale (see Stanley 1996). Trips were dedicated to buying goods—mostly clothing, but also electronics, foodstuffs, and jewelry. In the context of a failing Soviet infrastructure, this access to material goods and foreign travel became vital for maintaining the few remaining taiga households. It also solidified the Tura community's perception of the Polgogirs as members of the nouveau riche. (Only since 1990 were non-Party members able to travel to non-socialist countries.)[16]

Nadezhda Sergeevna's eldest son, Viktor, was considered particularly wealthy by local standards. In his former position as director of the state lumber cooperative, he had managed to transfer significant capital (machinery and lumber) into his direct control. Beginning in 1993, he took over the town's only sawmill, a construction firm, a pig farm, and several other small businesses. By 1995 the three siblings had their own incomes and residences, but the younger siblings often appealed to their older brother to finance a new business venture, such as a new discotheque in town, or to support continuing education at the university in Krasnoiarsk. Unlike the eldest sibling, the younger ones regularly took meals at Nadezhda Sergeevna's apartment. Nadezhda Sergeevna in turn relied on the eldest son for her material needs, such as buying groceries and procuring expensive medicines.

As the most entrepreneurial member of the Polgogir household, Viktor was the community icon for success. Like other prospering Turintsy, Viktor built a *kottedzh* in 1993; he and his wife and four children lived in one half, while Nadezhda Sergeevna occupied the other side. The most prominent symbol of Viktor's business success that marked the social distance from the rest of the Evenk community was his black Jeep Cherokee; it was the only one in Tura in 1995.

While this prosperity trickled down to Nadezhda Sergeevna's sister in the taiga to some degree, the relative entrepreneurial zeal of the Polgogir children certainly distanced them from many Evenki who continued to rely on subsistence reindeer herding, hunting, and fishing. In fact, in 1992 when I traveled with Nadezhda Sergeevna's daughter Tamara to reindeer herding brigades, it turned out that the trip was her first experience in the taiga among reindeer herders. One afternoon visit we made to a brigade was especially poignant. I was dressed in sneakers, jeans, and a dark, long-sleeve shirt to ward off the mosquitoes, while Tamara made no concessions to the rough, muddy conditions. She chose to emphasize her identity as an urban entrepreneur by donning a flashy white acetate running suit.

Despite the efforts of young Evenk entrepreneurs to distance themselves symbolically from Evenki living in the taiga, they were still very connected to the family there. The Polgogir social position derived as much from their extended family ties rooted in a pre-socialist past as from Nadezhda Sergeevna's long-standing membership in the Communist Party. By the mid-1990s, the government was no longer subsidizing food and transportation to villages, and kin ties between the villages and Tura became even more important. Those living in Tura came to rely on the meat and fish sent to Tura by relatives in villages. In turn, for villagers, Tura was an increasingly important center as the village infrastructure comprised of schools, state agricultural cooperatives, nursing units, and cultural centers closed down by the late 1990s. Villagers often stayed with relatives in Tura who provided temporary housing, food, and childcare.

One example from the spring of 1998 highlights this critical aspect of transregional kin ties. On one of my many visits to Nadezhda

Sergeevna's, I arrived at her second-floor apartment, where fish soup or reindeer stew was often simmering away on the stove, to find her tending a ten-month-old child. He turned out to be a second cousin's child from the village of Surinda, where Nadezhda Sergeevna had prominent relatives. The child scooted across the floor, and Nadezhda Sergeevna ably followed him. As we spoke, Nadezhda Sergeevna offered me and the child small chunks of frozen reindeer liver (*khakin*), a true delicacy. The mother and her child were staying with Nadezhda Sergeevna for a few weeks so the young woman could take care of some social welfare documents and also have a vacation from her small village.

While kin ties were increasingly critical in the 1990s, positions as local powerbrokers in the Soviet era continued to translate into economic opportunity. For instance, in 1995 Nadezhda Sergeevna's long-standing membership in the Communist Party positioned her to have access to renting out prime land and obtaining low-interest loans, while her children had access to privatized state property. This situation whereby former Communist Party membership translated into the post-Soviet nouveau riche status parallels trends throughout the former Soviet Union and Eastern Europe (Nagengast 1993; Wanner 1998).

While the multigenerational character of most Tura households confounds attempts to make clear correlations between degree of economic well-being and identity politics, it is noteworthy that Nadezhda Sergeevna's grandchildren did not attend the residential school. Nadezhda Sergeevna's son Viktor and his Russian wife Sonia decided to send their children to the town school, where there were few Evenk students; as they explained, at the town school their children could "mix with many different children." This seemingly innocent choice between two schools located in one town highlights a significant aspect of increasing social stratification in Tura. In this simple moment of social reproduction, class concerns took precedence over ethnic identity. Despite Nadezhda Sergeevna's venerated role as an Evenk artisan and songwriter, the town school was chosen for the grandchildren. This school choice reflected a wider trend. As a key location in the growing Evenk revitalization movement (as discussed in Chapter 6), the residential school tended to be viewed negatively by the Evenki who had been successful in the market economy.

Politically Connected Households

Some households with less tangible wealth also benefited from the market changes. In contrast to those households with more economic capital, politically connected households could be distinguished by their relative social position despite such conspicuous wealth. Household members typically had higher education and were active in local politics. Throughout the 1990s, household members were employed in a wide range of politically important positions. Women tended to work as administrators, school principals, or local politicians, and men worked as veterinarians, game wardens, or police officers. Like the households more involved in private enterprise, these households often maintained strong ties with extended family living in outlying villages. They tended to act as conduits for essential goods and services for those households, including housing children who were attending the residential school. In return, these households often received fresh reindeer meat and fish.

Although these households were not as well-off economically as those involved in private enterprise, they enjoyed a relatively high degree of material comfort. In terms of material goods, in 1998 it was rare to see cars in these households, but they did have motorboats, motorcycles, and sometimes snowmobiles. Although they were not able to build houses, they did have relatively spacious apartments, and they tended to have land contiguous to their apartments on which they could grow hardy crops. Their small land holdings also allowed them to build private outhouses, saunas, and greenhouses. These resources were increasingly prized as the town's financing for sanitation and bathhouses decreased, and as store-bought vegetables became impossible for most to afford after 1993.

The Labinko household serves as a typical example of a household that was well positioned with the shift toward a market economy. In 1998 the household consisted of two parents (Nadia and Ivan), three boys—aged ten, sixteen, and nineteen—and a grandmother, Galina Petrovna. Galina Petrovna, who was a retired film projectionist and worked part-time in a fur-processing organization, lived separately but often shared meals and the burden of housework (see Chapter 3). Nadia worked as a bookkeeper and manager in the Association of Peoples of the North, Arun. Her husband, Ivan, worked as an assistant fish and game warden. Their apartment was considered relatively spacious with three rooms and a kitchen for the family of five. Additionally, they had a separate yard where they had built a sauna, outhouse, and several greenhouses for growing tomatoes, cabbage, and squash. They also had a summer kitchen with a wood stove arranged in the yard. For several weeks each summer their flowerbeds were overflowing with blossoming impatiens, marigolds, and poppies.

Nadia's parents were born into families that still practiced reindeer herding, hunting, and fishing as a way of life. When Nadia's mother, Galina Petrovna, was nine she was sent to the residential school in Tura from Ekonda, a village two hours by helicopter to the northeast of Tura. Upon completing school, she went to Krasnoiarsk and studied to be a projectionist. After graduating, Galina Petrovna returned to Ekonda, where she met and married Nadia's father. He died before Nadia entered school, so her paternal grandfather in Ekonda, who was a widower, took primary care of Nadia while her mother traveled around Evenk villages with the agitprop to show films.[17]

By the time Nadia was in school, Ekonda had a school system extending to the fifth grade, so Nadia only left for Tura's residential school when she was eleven. By this time she spoke Evenk and Russian fluently. Upon completing residential school she spent ten years working as a Party assistant in the village of Surinda. There she met and married her Tatar husband Ivan. (He came from a southern Siberian region to take advantage of the opportunities for young skilled workers. With his training as a biologist, he easily found work in the fish and game division.)

After they had waited for several years, in 1992 the Tura administration granted the Labinkos a relatively spacious apartment in Tura when the newcomer Ukranian family that had occupied it abruptly left town. Ivan moved to a position in the central Tura fish and game office, and Nadia found work as a bookkeeper. Nadia explained, "Right after we moved in people would come by and harass us! They said we did not deserve the apartment, but we came by it completely fairly since this is a family with many children (*mnogodetnaia sem'ia*). Besides this is my land!"[18]

Nadia had an especially strong tie to what she viewed as "my land," meaning that as an Evenk she thought she should have priority in access to the social and natural resources of the district. This strong feeling partly grew out of her continuing close ties with the village of Ekonda, where she spent her early childhood years, but it was also tied to her work in *Arun*. As discussed further in Chapters 5 and 6, throughout the 1990s *Arun* was actively promoting cultural revitalization in the educational system and was also becoming involved in negotiations about indigenous versus newcomer land use.

In 1998, Nadia's 102-year-old paternal grandfather still lived in Ekonda, and despite the infrequent flights, she was able to see him periodically because of her work with *Arun*. She traveled there to assist villagers with new tax laws, claims on land, and emergency needs such as obtaining food and medicines. She also accompanied several foreigners to meet with her grandfather. Nikolai Mikhailovich was an important link to Evenk cultural knowledge of an earlier era for both Nadia and for the Association of Peoples of the North in Tura.

In 1998, I accompanied Nadia on a visit to Nikolai Mikhailovich. She brought medicine for an ailing aunt; oranges, bananas and onions for a cousin; three bottles of vodka, including one for her grandfather; and a new flannel shirt for him. Aside from looking into her grandfather's well-being, Nadia also conferred with village women about the health of preschoolers who were spending the summer living with relatives in Ekonda, "to get away from the filth of Tura," as she explained, and she discussed arrangements for sending other children to Ekonda for the remainder of the summer. As we waited for the helicopter, she also advised three women on how to organize their bookkeeping for newly established clan organizations (*rodovye obshchiny*) in such a way that they would not be heavily taxed. Boarding the helicopter we were loaded up with a bucket of fresh fish to pass on to a cousin's cousin, a burlap bag full of reindeer meat to pass on to another relative, and a parcel of fresh fish for Nadia's household in Tura.

While the links between town and remaining villagers were increasingly crucial, in contrast to more entrepreneurial households like the Polgogirs', the Labinko household also had a more self-conscious approach to its Evenk identity. Although Nadia's husband was Tatar, and had been raised in a milieu with Muslim cultural practices, he had also adopted many Evenk practices. He had lived in an Evenk village for nearly a decade, and his work as a fish and game warden was closely tied to the local subsistence economy. He also understood some Evenk language. The three boys in the household knew very little Evenk, but their mother actively sought to ally the household with an Evenk identity. She sent all three boys to study at the residential school, where she hoped they would learn more about their heritage as Evenki. (One of her sons was also active in a school club that performed Evenk folk songs.) Nadia explained to me that one son had attempted to study at the town school but had been incessantly taunted about his ethnicity.

In many ways this emphasis on Evenk identity can be understood from a situational perspective. As a household with few economic resources but aspirations for social mobility, an Evenk allegiance was important. It would facilitate opportunities for higher education, future employment in the area, and better housing options for the children as they formed their own households. Notably, in 1998 one of Nadia's sons had recently begun studying Arabic and had decided to apply to law school in the southern Siberia region where his father had grown up. Once again situational, multiple identities played themselves out in a context of scarce resources, this time as a young man of Evenk-Tatar background looked to the University of Tatarstan for a scholarship in his chosen field of study.

Transitional Households—Herders and Displaced Laborers

The vast majority of households did not prosper with the political-economic transformation and even struggled against poverty conditions. In contrast to more prosperous households, transitional households lacked significant economic and political capital. Beginning in the early 1990s with the breakup of state cooperatives and state oil exploration outfits, many households were forced to actively seek out new means of surviving. Those with ties to the herding operations sometimes sought to herd and hunt as private households or clans and market their products in town. Those more firmly rooted to a town cash economy and infrastructure had fewer options.

Some Evenk households with ties to the former state-run herding operations began to maintain at least two abodes; this allowed them to take advantage of the possibilities in both locations. This dual household base meant that people were still rooted in the traditional subsistence economy. This type of household was rare prior to the breakup of the Soviet Union, but in 1992 it became increasingly common as *sovkhozy* that had been in charge of organizing reindeer herding and fishing collapsed and other forms of economic organization took shape. Some Evenki applied for government start-up grants available for establishing private hunting and herding organizations (*rodovye obshchiny*). With this start-up capital, they usually bought snowmobiles, traps, fencing (to regulate reindeer movement), and foodstuffs, such as tea, sugar, and flour for the herding and hunting base. They also used these grants to buy apartments from newcomers who moved out of Tura in large numbers between 1991 and 1993. These new Evenki households were the least well established in Tura, and therefore they were often not registered with the town passport bureau.

The primary role of the town half of these households was to serve as a site for directing resources back toward kin in the villages and taiga. They provided a place for children to live while they attended residential school, the medical training college, or the vocational school. They were also important for household members who needed to be in Tura for extended medical care or other official business. These town households were not considered the primary ones, and different members of the extended household were constantly moving between Tura and the given village or reindeer herding camp.

The members of these households did not generally have formal university degrees, but the adults often had some vocational training that gave them skills as veterinary assistants, nurses' aides, or bookkeepers. In contrast to other village households, these households had a relatively high degree of economic capital in their home villages; they sometimes sought to buy apartments in Tura. (Because their primary residences were outside Tura, they were not automatically eligible to receive apartments through the Tura administration waiting list.) As one woman related, in Tura she and her family lived "poorly," but back "home" in the village they had a big apartment, a snowmobile, and all the furnishings that were missing in Tura. A family's household in Tura was often maintained at a minimal level, with barely any furniture, just a couple of beds for five or more people, and a television set. The capital for buying a one-room apartment in Tura (about $200 U.S. in 1993 and $600 U.S. by 1995) was usually garnered by the sale of recently privatized herding operations.

The Yoldogir household was typical of the transitional herding households. One of the Yoldogir children with whom I had become acquainted through events at the House of Culture introduced me to his family. It was late May, and the ice had just broken on the river, so when we met on the street the Yoldogirs were returning home from the river with an ice supply for melting down into drinking water.

In 1993, Stepa and Anna Yoldogir bought their one-room apartment in Tura, which served as the base for their household, for 1,000,000 rubles from a departing Ukrainian pilot.[19] They explained that when they learned that Anna had a medical problem and that she would need prolonged treatment, they traveled from Ekonda and decided to buy the apartment. It appeared, however, that their reasons were far more complex. In addition to Anna and Stepa, in 1995 the immediate household consisted of five people—three boys (aged five, eighteen, and twenty-two) and two girls (aged fourteen and sixteen). The household also included four other people: an older daughter (aged twenty-three) living in Ekonda in their four-room apartment and two older sons (aged twenty-four and twenty-seven) who, along with their grandmother, maintained a brigade of 100 reindeer near Ekonda. The Tura household arranged and channeled resources for the family generally, including for the three children who were in residential school and for the reindeer herding component of their family. During one of my visits to their apartment in 1998, Anna and Stepa were busily collecting supplies to send out to their sons and grandmother in the taiga on a helicopter that was due to depart shortly; the supply list included bulk noodles, matches, vodka, cigarettes, and canned meat.

The Yoldogirs received private ownership of their reindeer in the winter of 1993, through the recently issued policy of "clan lands," *rodovye zemli.* The phrase came about after 1990 as indigenous people throughout Siberia sought to establish their rights to natural resources before they lost access to them through the impending process of privatization (Osherenko 1995). The criteria for a clan, or *rod,* that had herded continuously throughout the Soviet period was initially introduced by the Ministry of the North to establish who was qualified to lay claim to a herding territory (Mikheeva et al. 1993). According to a local Evenk District decree, families that could prove that their ancestors had historically herded in a given region were eligible for receiving funds to reestablish clan-based reindeer herding in that region. While theoretically all Evenk families were eligible for these funds, the majority of those who established clan organizations had held high positions in the state hunting or herding cooperatives. Thus those who were in the best positions to consolidate and administer *sovkhoz* capital were the same ones who applied for the government start-up grants. In 1993 about forty Evenk and Sakha clans were granted rights to territory on which they could herd reindeer. Many times this was the territory on which they had herded as members of the state cooperatives; according to the Yoldogirs, they did not even have to fill out any papers.[20]

Stepa's membership in the newly formed "Farmers' Association" (*Assotsiatsiia fermerskogo khoziaistva*), to which forty or so reindeer herders belonged in 1995, also required his presence in Tura. The so-called "farming cooperatives" (*fermerskie khoziaistva*) that operated at bases located throughout the taiga were primarily involved in herding reindeer, trapping sable, and attracting a few wealthy tourists wanting to hunt and fish. These enterprises were formed in 1991 when state agricultural cooperatives were formally disbanded and federal monies became available through several Russian government ministries—including the Department of the North and the Ministry of Agriculture—for small business enterprises initiated by indigenous Siberian populations (Mikheeva et al. 1993: 13). The district administration, in conjunction with the Association of Peoples of the North, initially dispersed these start-up funds for small "traditional" enterprises involving hunting, reindeer herding, and fishing. Funds were available to those deemed "native," a category that technically included just indigenous Siberians, but like the educational slots reserved for "peoples of the North" discussed in Chapter 1, sometimes got stretched to include Russians who were native to the region, especially if they were working in partnership with an indigenous person in their new enterprise.

In Tura, Stepa represented the interests of Ekonda "farmers" as the association discussed how to distribute and market its members' products—reindeer meat, antlers, sable, fox, and fish—and provide for their material needs.[21] This Farmers' Association also lobbied the local administration for subsidies, tax breaks, and funds to buy snowmobiles, chainsaws, additional reindeer, and foodstuffs for the hunters and herders. The growing importance of the association became clear to me in 1995 when Stepa explained that it was just beginning to institute membership fees in order to pay for the bookkeeping and administration costs.[22]

Aside from economic reasons for being in Tura, education also played some role in the Yoldigirs' decision to maintain a second household. The Yoldogirs had sent all their older children to the residential school. Until 1993 they had resided in Ekonda, where the school only extended to the fourth grade. Even though Anna and Stepa Yoldogir had lived in Tura since 1993, their children continued to attend the residential school, with their youngest son still being enrolled there in 2002. It was convenient for the children to attend the residential school because the Tura apartment had only two beds and generally little space. In contrast to the other Tura households sending children to study at the residential school, the Yoldogir children spent most of their time at the school. They not only ate most of their meals there, but they spent many nights in the dormitory. When their parents were in town, however, the children stopped by to visit and to catch up on news from Ekonda.

For the Yoldogir household, the residential school was a functional aspect of post-Soviet society. Unlike the Lapinkos, the Yoldogirs were not especially concerned with cultural preservation or language issues. Both parents were Evenki, and they had always spoken Evenk with their children. Furthermore, their direct involvement with reindeer herding, hunting, and fishing through their clan land ensured that the household remained firmly rooted in the subsistence elements of an Evenk way of life. For the Yoldogirs, the residential school had little symbolic value as a nexus of Evenk cultural practices, but it did provide some essential education and nurturing for their children.

Displaced Laborers

The majority of households located in the town of Tura struggled with poverty as the market conditions tightened around them. Like the herders maintaining two or more households, other households relying more on town-based wage labor experienced the jarring impact of economic restructuring in the 1990s. These households, which were by far the most common, differed from the more prosperous ones in that they lacked any economic capital and had relatively little political power. Unlike the displaced reindeer herders, their members were actively seeking to reestablish or formulate new sources of income because they had recently lost other sources. Women often had some two-year vocational training and worked in the sphere of social services as nurses' aides or day care providers. A significant portion of these households included men who were formerly working for the oil exploration outfit in town. After they were laid off in the early 1990s, these men combined seasonal hunting and fishing with the part-time, pick-up jobs that, when available, often paid eight to ten times more than the regularly salaried social service positions women frequently held.

Prior to 1991 the state agricultural cooperatives employed at least half of the town from October to April, and the government oil exploration and quartz processing outfit employed another 2,000 people. In contrast to the town's *sovkhozy*, which largely employed Evenk and Russian men and women with only secondary education, the state oil and quartz exploration outfits employed primarily male newcomers with specialized education. By 1992 nearly 90 percent (about 900 positions) of the jobs in the oil exploration outfits and an equal number in the quartz exploration were curtailed, leaving a significant portion of the newcomers unemployed.[23] These people were trained in geology and geophysics and generally came to Tura in the 1970s and 1980s to seek their fortunes; thus they were not inclined to stay in the town when the central government curtailed the financing of mineral and oil exploration. Those who still remained in Tura by 1993 tended to be married to Evenk women and were generally the less highly qualified staff employed in oil exploration such as the shaft borers.

Evenk kin ties played a prominent role for these households, but they also relied on pensions and the institutional support available in social service agencies. The unemployment that plagued these households affected their well-being most directly in terms of alcoholism, most often among the men but also among the women. The weight of household subsistence was often carried by women, who sometimes worked two jobs to make up for the loss of men's steady employment. Unlike the more prosperous households, these households did not have the means of transportation—cars and motorcycles—that eased the daily burden of grocery shopping for which women were primarily responsible. In households with male partners present, the men often owned motorboats, but with the rising cost of gasoline, by 1994 and 1995 they could rarely afford to use them and instead fished from the riverbank.

The housing situation for these families also contrasted to that of the more prosperous households; they did not own their housing. These households generally lived in the town-owned, two-story prefabricated apartment buildings found throughout Russian towns that were constructed with great speed in the 1970s and early 1980s. (In Tura these were meant to provide shelter for the rapid population influx that arrived to staff the oil exploration operations.) These households lacked land on which to grow crops, and they shared an outhouse for each eight units. While a few households had built saunas on nearby town property, most people lacked the resources to do this and also feared losing their lumber if the town declared their endeavor to be illegal. The muddy or dusty area, depending on the season, surrounding the clusters of five or six apartment buildings had little or no landscaping or even wild grass.

The Zubov household was typical of a town-based "transitional" household characterized by displaced labor and basic housing conditions. The Zubovs lived in an apartment in a nonprivatized town-owned building. Svetlana Zubova was introduced to me in 1992 through her cousin, Tamara Polgogir, and as we became better acquainted Svetlana often invited me to drink tea with her at her place of work at the hospital. Breaks for tea were often shared with the whole work collective, not just with two or three people as coffee or tea often is in North America. Our discussions over tea, first at work and then at home, covered a range of topics, but inevitably provided perspectives on gender, workplace dynamics, and town politics. In this context Svetlana recounted something of her life to me.

Svetlana recounted how she lost her mother at a young age and was raised by an aunt in Ekonda. When Svetlana came to Tura she was already in high school, but as she explained, not a very good student. After leaving school at age fifteen, she soon became pregnant. She refused to get an abortion, but given her youth, her older sister insisted on taking the child to raise him where she lived in a central Siberian city. Svetlana agreed on the condition that upon marriage she would have the child back. Meanwhile, Svetlana enrolled at the medical training school in Tura.

Within two years Svetlana was married to Fedor, a young shaft borer from the Russian Far East. As promised, Svetlana's sister returned her son to her. Meanwhile, the couple tried unsuccessfully to have their own child. Finally, they adopted a child from the town orphanage, and shortly thereafter their own child was born. Thus, in 1993 they had three children—two girls aged five and eight and a boy aged thirteen.

By 1993, Svetlana had worked for nearly thirteen years as a nurse. Her husband's work in the oil drilling industry was in danger of being curtailed. The fish and meat channeled through village relatives were less commonly found in this household because Fedor's family was not in the area and Svetlana's village kin were somewhat distant. The diet consisted primarily of potatoes, occasional fish—which Fedor caught in the Nizhniaia Tunguska or Kochachum Rivers—tea, sugar, and bread. In the fall and winter months, mushrooms and some berries supplemented the diet.

By 1995, Svetlana was employed again at the town clinic after spending one year working in the newly opened home for the elderly. When the home for the elderly moved to Baikit in 1994, she went back to her lower-paying position in the clinic. Meanwhile Svetlana's husband was suddenly out of work in 1994 when the oil operations were completely cut back. He was reduced to moving from job to job without much hope for constant work, and he began spending more time on the riverbank fishing and more hours drinking. Earlier the household had never planted a plot to supplement their food sources, but in 1995, with the rising cost of potatoes and other foodstuffs, they began to consider renting a plot from the town.

In these tough material circumstances, Svetlana's decision to send her two school-age children to the residential school made sense. Even though the town school was somewhat closer to their apartment—the residential school was nearly a mile walk—the residential school provided more services. In a material sense, the residential school provided the extra support that Svetlana needed. She was comforted to know that her children could always get something extra to eat during the day and they had a place to stay the night if she was called to travel on health inspections to the surrounding villages.

Like the more prosperous households, households like the Zubovs also relied on kinship ties to make ends meet. For instance, the Zubov household did not have access to any sizable segment of land, but Svetlana could rely on her Polgogir cousins to assist her financially. Svetlana was well aware of the complexities of identity politics and the need for multiple sources of both material and symbolic capital. She noted that since her husband was not Evenk, but a newcomer, she needed to make sure her alliances with the Evenk community were beyond a doubt. Otherwise, not only her financial stability would be tenuous, but also the opportunities for her children to continue their education beyond Tura. Svetlana was hoping that along with her own official identity as Evenk, the symbolic capital of the residential school could help propel her children into some of the few slots in top institutions of higher education reserved for indigenous Siberian groups such as the Evenki.

Single Mothers and Marginality

Marginality is not something created overnight. For some the breakdown of important kin ties among the Evenki began with the imposition of collectivized herding, and it was exacerbated by the ruthless market economy that took shape in the early 1990s. This final household portrait illustrates the importance of kinship ties and education for social mobility and the ways in which some Evenki suffered when their kinship ties were weak. Single women heads of households, especially those who lacked education beyond the residential school, were even more limited in professional options and a means of making a living. In the highly professionally segregated Russian system in which one gained position in direct correlation to years of schooling, they were employed in unskilled positions such as security guards and janitors.

Like most Evenk households in Tura, these households lacked many of the material comforts that the more prosperous households enjoyed. For instance, the households in this group generally lived in nonprivatized housing that did not have private saunas or outhouses. For most Turintsy, attending the sauna and having a bath was a weekly event usually occurring on Saturday or Sunday. There was a public bathhouse on the banks of the Nizhniaia Tunguska River, and this was where many people bathed until 1991, when a flood destroyed the bathhouse. For nearly four years, people without their own saunas crammed into the much smaller facility that had served those engaged in oil expeditions. The regularity and type of bathing were signifiers of nascent class schisms for Tura's residents, because those with running water and private saunas were not restricted to bathing once a week.

These marginalized households also lacked other material goods that more prosperous households had access to, such as motor vehicles, boats, or private plots for cultivating potatoes and other vegetables. Instead, they got by with mutual assistance through neighbors in similar social positions and with some support from social services. Sometimes the households were in dire straits, with women checking into the hospital for medical treatment or alcohol detoxification while preteen children looked after themselves at home. While marginalized households frequently consisted of single mothers, single mothers were not necessarily stigmatized. In fact, it was rare for indigenous women to be childless after age 25, with a certain stigma surrounding those women who remained childless. This appears to be a pattern in the North. For instance, in her fascinating analysis of family configurations in a Chukotkan community, Kerttula (2000) discusses how single motherhood is not stigmatized because having a child is considered an essential, defining feature of being a woman, and extended family support is usually a given.

Not all single mother households in Tura were equally marginalized. Many single mothers managed households that thrived on their ability to safeguard economic capital and nurture instrumental kin and broader social ties (see Chapter 4). Unfortunately, this was not the case for all single-mother households, some of which were unable to establish a stable existence in the rough conditions of an emerging market economy. The example of Dunia Kislova, a single mother of four children—two boys aged five and eight and two girls aged fourteen and ten in 1998—illustrates the situation for these particularly marginalized households.

When I first met Dunia in 1992, she lived with her three children in an apartment she had just received through the Office for the Defense of Family, Children, and Motherhood. In the tiny one-room office, families could find clothing for their children, obtain a small loan, seek housing, or get chits for emergency food. One evening after she finished her double shift as a watchperson at the nearby day care center, Dunia proudly showed me around the dark, three-room, first-floor apartment and discussed plans for redoing the wallpaper, fixing the gouged woodwork, and insulating the leaky windows with cotton and caulking.

Dunia had left her husband a few months earlier because of his drinking, and she related how relieved she was to be more in control of her children's social circumstances. Her husband had returned to his parents' household in the Ukraine, and Dunia was not expecting to receive any child support. Although her financial circumstances were difficult, she had some social support from a friend who was also a single mother raising two children. Dunia was hopeful about her financial outlook and planned to enroll that winter in bookkeeping courses at the local vocational school so that she could find better-paying employment.

Dunia had spent her early childhood in a nearby village, just twenty-five kilometers west of Tura along the Nizhniaia Tunguska River. After first grade she left her family to study in the Tura residential school. She recalled these years fondly and contrasted her time in residential school to the summers spent at home, where she and her friends would raid potato fields to supplement their diet. This was especially the case when her parents were on drinking sprees and did not manage to take care of providing meals for their two children. Dunia completed high school and went on to study in Leningrad at the premier Herzen Pedagogical Institute. After failing the first year, she decided to return home. Soon after, she married and became pregnant with her first child.

In 1998, Dunia's social network still involved only a few kin. Instead it revolved around her friends, and especially Zhenia, a young woman who was also raising children by herself (see Chapter 4). Dunia and Zhenia had recently received from the town administration "apartments"—actually small houses—on the outskirts of Tura.[24] They were both eager to escape from the crowded, slumlike living quarters of the two-story apartment buildings where they shared an outhouse with eight other households. On the outskirts of town, they could grow some potatoes and the children would be able to run freely; in the center of Tura they had no yard of their own.

While Dunia's material circumstances were even more severe than those of households like Svetlana Zubova's, she did not look to the residential school as a means of alleviating her stress or banking symbolic capital. In fact, Dunia's material circumstances were largely the reason she was suspicious of the residential school. As a single mother, she was regularly visited by social workers. Dunia said she thought they were trying to take the children away from her. In this context the residential school became an extension of the social forces that Dunia viewed as working against her. Those children who were taken away from their parents (Evenk or Russian) because of rulings that they were neglected or poorly cared for, lived and studied at the residential school. As discussed in Chapter 5, many Evenki living in Tura chose to send children to the residential school—as opposed to the town school—as day students. Some single mothers like Zhenia, Dunia's friend living next door, were also eager to make use of the residential school as a resource for raising their children. Dunia's dislike of the residential school was not shared by the majority of single mothers and was instead tempered by her social position as a Katanga Evenk.

As a Katanga Evenk, Dunia disliked being associated with local Illimpei Evenki, who she viewed as having less social stature. Dunia could potentially have had extensive ties in the Evenk community irrespective of the residential school, but because her relatives did not approve of her most recent marriage, she was estranged from them. As a Katanga Evenk, Dunia viewed the residential school as an institution for local Illimpei Evenki but not for people like herself whose mother had attended Leningrad University. Dunia's multilayered sense of class and regional identities reflects yet another element of the complexity of identity politics in Tura.

Households, Resources, and Identities in a Time of Privatization

These accounts of five Evenk households are meant to convey a sense of the dynamic identity politics in the Evenk community in Tura, and by extension to emphasize broader trends in how senses of identity and belonging are mobilized in rural post-Soviet contexts as communities face the privatization of collective resources. While growing class schisms threaten to weaken Evenk claims to natural resources and the Evenk voting block during local and regional elections, deeply rooted kin ties continue to provide critical support for daily life. As households like the more prosperous Polgogirs and Lapinkos or struggling households like the Yoldogirs, Zubovs, and Kislovs pursue material security, they may not necessarily look to their Evenk identity through the vehicle of the residential school. They may continue, however, to look to kin, sometimes Evenk kin. As reflected in these accounts, this work of identifying ideal affiliations and establishing and maintaining networks is generally women's work among the Evenki in this community. In many cases women strategically decide on how to ally their households to secure optimal well-being, but as reflected in these accounts the "choices" are certainly defined by the structural factors of economic and political resources, as well as educational training.

The significant schisms in this Evenk community reflect growing social stratification that was increasing in the 1990s because of disparate access to resources such as privatized land and government grants. As indicated throughout this chapter, the household groupings employed here are fluid and there is considerable interaction between various households. For instance, the Polgogirs maintained connections with their cousin Svetlana Zubova, and she could count on them to help her out financially. Similarly, the Labinko household had kin ties in the same village as the Yoldogir household, and they had common friends from that village. These household portraits are not meant to be rigid categories, but instead to show the degree to which networks do extend between different social strata, as well as within similar strata. Humphrey (1999a: 492) has identified similar patterns of "horizontal" relations in her work in Buriatiia, while also emphasizing how the socialist vertical patterns of resource control and allocation are perpetuated into the present.

In contrast to the Buriats described by Humphrey, the Evenki do not have a history of elaborate hierarchies embedded in their pre-Soviet social organization. Still, I argue that the sense of the collective, what Humphrey calls "collectivist values engendered by the socialist experience" (1999a: 492), remain critical for many. While there is certainly an element of sheer practicality about this, there is undeniably also a common belonging to a Soviet past. This analysis of households reflects that the import of socialist symbolic capital was, for instance, embodied in the residential school. The school continues to serve both material and symbolic purposes for many Evenki. As indicated especially by the last example, however, the household groupings also reveal a wide range of variation in how households conceive of this socialist, collectivist identity. The example of the Kislov household underscores the fact that material situation alone does not determine a strong allegiance with the residential school as a source of collectivist identity. As discussed further in Chapter 4, many factors played into how households viewed the residential school in the 1990s, and by extension their sense of connection with socialist, or Soviet, collectivist cultural practices.[25]

The households examined here provide portraits of different strata of the Evenk community. As is most vividly demonstrated by the example of the Polgogirs, however, the nature of households as groups of people with various social alliances and generational ties confounds direct correlations between household types and a singular attitude toward socialist cultural practices or Evenk identity politics. For instance, although Nadezhda Sergeevna's eldest son avidly took up his position as nouveau riche, in many ways she was more allied with Evenk intellectuals and their interests in cultural revitalization. Thus Nadezhda Sergeevna's allegiances to the residential school were tied to the symbolic importance of such an institution as a place committed to Evenk interests and Evenk cultural rejuvenation. Her situation reflects the complexity of emerging Evenk identities when many Evenki have parallel and sometimes conflicting personal ties.[26]

Moving from this household level of analysis, the next two chapters consider two generations of women's narratives in regard to the residential school and its place in their lives. Chapter 3 takes up a central paradox raised in thinking about Evenk relationships to the Soviet and post-Soviet nation-state of the Russian Federation. Why is the institution not widely vilified by Evenki? Given the hardship for Evenki in negotiating the Soviet knowledge systems imposed on them, why has there been so much attachment to Soviet cultural practices in the 1990s, particularly among older Evenk women whose attitudes ranged from ambivalence to nostalgia toward residential schooling?

Chapter 3
Red Ties and Residential School: Evenk Women's Narratives and Reconsidering Resistance

> As we rode away from the residential school and out of town, up the rough gravel road toward the cemetery, the rickety bus shifted its passengers from side to side. One older Evenk woman pointed out the window, exclaiming: "Look, that's where the businessmen live, in those new *kottedzhi*! I couldn't live there; I was raised as an *internatskaia*." An elderly Evenk woman seated across from her friend replied, "Yeah, we would be uncomfortable out here all alone away from the center. We were raised as part of the *kollektiv*."
>
> —Author's fieldnotes, Tura, fall 1993

While the last chapter examined the way that households in Tura were negotiating shifting socioeconomic contexts and their relationships to the residential school, or *internat*, this chapter considers the historical significance of the residential school in this central Siberian community, particularly from a gendered perspective.[1] Evenk men and women had differential interactions with the institution, in part shaped by the Soviet state's gender ideologies and in part shaped by what men and women had to gain from the system. The ways people engaged with Soviet social transformations have implications for the ways in which different Evenki imagine communities today. Exchanges such as the one between two Evenk women indicated above suggest that Evenk women's narratives are a significant departure point for thinking about Evenk ideas regarding power, resistance, and community in the post-Soviet era.

Dominant scholarship published in the West on the former Soviet Union and Eastern Europe (for example, Arendt 1966 and Conquest 1990) has overwhelmingly invoked universal "signs" of oppressive state power and automatic resistance to it. Such scholarship has been central in instituting political science as the chosen discipline involved in reflecting on this region of the world.[2] In contrast, ethnography, with its central aim of "decoding signs that disguise themselves as universal and natural" (Comaroff and Comaroff 1992: 10), has proven to be a powerful tool for understanding Evenk perspectives on Soviet structures like the residential school. As Evenki spoke with me about Soviet and post-Soviet society, including residential schooling, I found that binary perspectives on power invoking concepts such as "oppressed" and "oppressor" did not explain the range of relationships many had to Soviet social systems and cultural practices. I encountered only a few individuals who viewed their days in residential school as an oppressive experience. In fact, as discussed in the previous chapter, in the 1990s households often continued to look to the residential school structures for social support or as a means for political mobilization. Many of my conversations with Evenki revolved around the ways in which they proudly felt themselves to be part of Soviet society and the pain, or at least ambivalence, they felt with its downfall.

The conversation between two Evenk women noted above belies a simple model of oppression in thinking about the relationship of indigenous Siberians to the former Soviet nation-state. First, the women's comments reflect widespread criticism of the contemporary reforms and the resulting social stratification and individualism throughout Russia. (The new wealth was perhaps most evident in the 1990s with the mushrooming of private houses built by nouveau riche in the growing residential belts of urban and even rural areas.)[3] People were especially critical in more peripheral areas such as the Evenk District, where, as noted earlier, for the past several decades the population has depended heavily on the government for food, shelter, healthcare, education, and transportation. As former state-controlled natural resources such as oil, gas, and timber are increasingly exploited by a select few in Russia, as well as by multinational companies, the vast majority has seen its standard of living plummet. Many people in Russia in the 1990s were also looking to the Soviet past as an era when times were better. Second, aside from being a commentary on social stratification, the bus conversation also indicates the way these women viewed their lives as being enveloped in Soviet society and in some ways defined by Soviet institutions like the residential school. They felt part of a collective endeavor and literally part of the collective, or *kollektiv,* which was embodied in the residential school.

This chapter examines the way in Evenk women's accounts about the residential school are accounts that can be read to understand better the contours of Soviet and post-Soviet power in indigenous communities. As massive reconfigurations of power take place in the Russian Federation, including at the level of the Evenk District and the town of Tura, indigenous peoples like the Evenki are challenged to interpret their historical experiences and reconfigure allegiances. In thinking about power relationships from a historical perspective in this chapter, I seek to destabilize homogenizing models of power that rest on binary assumptions of oppressed/oppressor. In particular, I argue that social experience and interaction with these structures is gendered. As scholars have emphasized in other contexts (Nelson and Rouse 2000; Mohanty 1991), however, this is not to replace one version of universalizing stance with another. Stating that people make sense of power through gendered experience does not mean that all men or all women have similar experiences and interpretations; gender is a defining feature in men's and women's lives, but other factors such as class, regional identity, and generation are also central to how they encounter power.

As both an institution created in the Soviet period and one that influenced the collective consciousness of Evenki and other indigenous Siberians for decades, the residential school is an ideal site for thinking about relations of power between the Evenki and the Soviet state. The residential school in the 1990s both set Evenki apart from the rest of the community and acted as a symbolic nexus for cultural revival and even political mobilization. Several scholars have explored the unique experience of the "collective" in socialist and post-socialist societies (Verdery 1999; Humphrey 1999a). For instance, Verdery writes of a "collective" sensibility in Romania in which a clash exists between "conditions promoting individual entrepreneurship" and "values of community" (1999: 66). Only a few scholars, however, have examined the ways in which a socialist collective experience was gendered (Berdahl 1999; Husby-Darvas 2001). In ethnography focused on indigenous Siberians the role of gender in the encounter with the Soviet state has attracted little attention, with the noteworthy exception of Rethmann's work (2001). Following scholars who have emphasized the significance of gender in historical experience (Rethmann 2001; di Leonardo 1991; Stacey 1988), this chapter explores how the residential school represents a uniquely gendered historical experience within the layers of power in Soviet society. In this context indigenous peoples, and indigenous women in particular, were singled out by the state as subjects for transformation.

In an effort to understand how indigenous Siberians interpreted this state power, the first section of this chapter turns to considering debates about resistance, accommodation, and "false consciousness." The narratives of older Evenk women form the crux of the second section of the chapter. What drew me to these accounts was a desire to learn how those most targeted by the Soviet system of residential schooling would reflect on the impact of schooling on their lives. In terms of political allegiances, there were clearly gendered patterns. I learned early on, for instance, that all twenty-five of the people continuing to belong to the Communist Party in Tura in 1994, at a time when the Party was briefly outlawed, were elderly women. In this chapter I argue that such a phenomenon can be understood from the perspective that older women, more often than men, saw themselves as part of a collective, as part of a society they had participated in building. They were at the center of an ideology of social transformation, but this positionality was not highly valued in a post-Soviet era. Women had been the icon of Soviet efforts to transform society, and indigenous women in particular represented the "backwardness" that Soviet power sought to control and civilize. Drawing women into socialist relations of labor, the ideology went, would free them from oppressive, patriarchal structures, either of capitalism or tribal societies. In this chapter, I explore the ways in which such an ideology influenced older women's subject positions. I also explore ideas around Foucault's formulation "where there is power there is resistance" (1990: 95). If Foucault is correct, then why did the women's accounts I heard reflect so little resistance to these state structures seeking to impose on them Soviet ideals about women's labor and the ideal structure of a Soviet society?

Gendering Resistance and Power

Building on a rich tradition of scholarship on power relations and subordinates as the subjects of inquiry, in recent years social scientists have turned to thinking about power in a broad spectrum of contexts and configurations.[4] Foucault's wide-ranging and foundational scholarship has been especially central to this enterprise (1980, 1978), and it has been accompanied by a burgeoning interest in "resistance" studies (see, for example, Willis 1981; Guha 1983; Scott 1985). In thinking about Evenk women's accounts, I turn particularly to recent feminist scholarship on resistance. Several authors suggest that by paying attention to the subtle forms women's resistance can take, very different accounts of resistance emerge that do not necessarily feature the social movements or obviously political forms of resistance that are often studied (Raja and Gold 1994; Abu-Lughod 1990).[5] In my research I sought to pay attention to what might be subtle forms of resistance to Soviet structures of power, but I also began to question if there was necessarily resistance to all forms of power. Conversely, I began to ask myself if it was also possible that Evenk women had been so influenced by Soviet structures of power that they were often unaware of them and unconcerned about resisting them. Was it possible that Evenk women were suffering from a "false consciousness," that they had come to believe in the dominant ideologies naturalizing the power of elites?

Early ethnographic works explicitly examining power and its manifestations particularly emphasize the mechanisms of reproducing relations of power (see, for example, Willis 1981). In these works the Marxist concept of "false consciousness" is invoked as the central explanatory force for why those engaged in such systems do not particularly resist them. In contrast, Scott's analysis radically affected studies of resistance to shift them from a focus on the reproduction of power to informal resistance or "everyday forms of resistance" (1985 and 1989). In this work Scott firmly establishes the importance of considering all types of resistance in examining relationships of power, and he emphasizes the ceaseless resistance of subordinates in power relationships.[6] Instead of invoking "false consciousness" to explain the perpetuation of oppressive power relations, Scott emphasizes the ubiquitous nature of resistance as a reflection that peasants (resisters) are perfectly aware of their lot. Scott's challenge to those concerned with issues of oppressive power relationships—not to dismiss the import of the "non-collective," "foot-dragging"—has perhaps had the most widespread impact on resistance scholarship.[7]

In contrast to Scott's analysis, in which resisters and oppressors are clearly distinct, what is most striking about Evenk women's narratives is the apparent overt accommodation of forms of power.[8] Feminist anthropologists have particularly turned attention to such issues and sought to understand how power (and resistance) might be something experienced differentially by men and women (see, for example, Ong 1987; Sharp 1990; Abu-Lughod 1986).[9] Most critically, feminists have sought to disaggregate power and resistance and demonstrate the multiple layers and ambiguities that coexist (Gal 1995; Abu-Lughod 1990). They have sought to examine carefully "power," "resistance," and "false consciousness," and in general they avoid homogenizing concepts and groups of people under study. For instance, in her work on power and resistance among Bedouin women, Abu-Lughod addresses the concept of "false consciousness" (1990: 47) and notes some dilemmas of interpreting such a form of consciousness.[10]

Abu-Lughod's efforts to break apart the monolithic idea of "resistance" by pairing it with issues of consciousness provide a particularly useful means for understanding Evenk women's accounts. I am hesitant to view Evenk women as merely cogs in the machinery of post-Soviet society. Instead, I argue that the accounts that follow can serve as what Abu-Lughod has called a "diagnostic of power" (1990: 41). Instead of reading them as sources for demonstrating relative degrees of resistance to power, they should be read as indications of the forms that power takes and the ways in which people may resist, but are just as likely to accommodate and take part in, structures of power. I examine Evenk women's accounts in this chapter as a means of understanding the positionality of a range of Evenk women. Their relative lack of resistance to power structures turns our attention to the ways that people also accommodate and take part in multiple layers of power in Soviet and post-Soviet society.[11]

Accommodation and Hierarchies of Power

The terms "resistance" and "accommodation" appear widely in works seeking to examine unequal power relationships, but they are not always carefully examined. The term "accommodation" has received less attention from scholars, perhaps because it is particularly slippery.[12] As Scott notes, "Actions such as pilfering, desertion, poaching, and foot dragging do imply, by the very fact that they avoid open confrontations, a certain accommodation with existing power relations" (1989: 22). Scott's examples raise, however, the question of distinguishing between resistance and accommodation. Can "the very fact that they avoid open confrontations" serve as an adequate definition of accommodation? This is not just a matter of semantics because examining accommodation further sheds light on how power is a matter not of a simple dichotomy, but more of a continuum. People in various social strata and positions in society do take part in the configurations of power that exist; they are not simply victims or oppressors. These nested hierarchies of power are found in multiple cultural contexts (see Humphrey 1994a), including in post-Soviet society.

A better understanding of how power, and therefore also "accommodation," operates entails more clearly recognizing the agency of "oppressed" or "resisting" people. Several scholars have demonstrated that those who are in structurally oppressive work relationships still exercise some possibilities for control (Romero 1992; Constable 1997; Gamburd 2000; Ozyegin 2001). Sometimes what first appears as a simple binary relationship between victim and oppressor is more complex and includes opportunities to challenge ingrained patterns of hierarchy in home communities. The idea of women taking "control" of their situations shifts an examination of power relationships from the oppressed/oppressor dichotomy and instead underscores that women also actively engage in power relationships. This literature underscores the need for nuanced concepts of power and resistance and for the infusion of concepts of instrumentalism into analyses of unequal power relations.

Even an instrumentalist approach faces, however, the problem of distinguishing between resistance and accommodation. For instance, in contexts in which women are resisting pressures for higher productivity in work settings (Rofel 1992: 94; Lamphere 1987: 29–30), it often seems to be a matter of perspective whether this should be termed resistance or accommodation.[13] Women could also be seen as accommodating power structures by not quitting their jobs in oppressive work conditions, or they could be seen as reinforcing prevailing beliefs in some spheres where women are viewed as less efficient workers.[14] Instead of primarily viewing the women's actions as allied with reproducing power relationships, one could also argue that the women acted out of "instrumentalist" concerns for personal well-being. Such scholarship underscores the definitional problems of looking for cases of resistance or accommodation, whether in instrumentalist or power-allied forms.

Consider the Evenk women on the bus at the start of this chapter. Are they simply accommodating Soviet power by reflecting on being part of the collective, or could they have resisted it? While concepts of resistance and accommodation can be slippery and are not always distinct, they are still useful. By engaging concepts of differential attitudes toward seemingly dichotomous power relationships, we obtain more nuanced portraits of power. Furthermore, such an approach counters the tendency for female subjects to dissolve into a homogenous, Western concept of "woman" (Mohanty 1991). Instead of simply demonstrating isolated examples of resistance or accommodation, this chapter seeks to show how power relationships exist in interwoven, multiple forms.

Residential Schooling in the Soviet Era

In what ways did the Soviet boarding schools for indigenous Siberians initially invoke resistance? Assuming not all indigenous Siberians resisted, who did and did not resist and why? Given Foucault's assertion that all members of society, even those who are marginalized, are participants in the exercise of power (1980: 78–133), resistance itself becomes a problematic category. Are there reasons people might not resist forms of state power?

In taking a historical perspective on the Evenk situation, it is difficult to state definitively that the Soviet system was more of an "oppressive" system than the emerging market system. From a Eurocentric, feminist perspective, the collectivized childrearing of the Soviet system "freed up" women to take advantage of a whole new set of opportunities and to excel in academic and professional settings (Kollantai 1977; Goldman 1993). The market economy emerging in the 1990s and into the twenty-first century threatens to drive the cost of childcare and professional training out of range for many people (Moghadam 1993), including many Evenk women. From another perspective, however, this collectivized childrearing established in the Soviet period was an attack on indigenous Siberian systems of knowledge, and it imposed a set of idealized, Western gender roles rooted in the idea that women need to be "liberated." Drawing on an evolutionary vision formulated by Engels in *The*

Origin of the Family, Private Property, and the State (1972), laborforce participation and success in mastering European systems of knowledge were yardsticks used to measure degrees of women's "liberation." In the Soviet Union the residential school was meant to be the first step toward increasing indigenous Siberian women's labor force participation and thereby incorporating them into Soviet society.

In widely different locations around the world, residential schooling has served as a key aspect of nation-state attempts to control and assimilate indigenous populations. This has been accomplished in part by instilling historical and cultural amnesia that disrupted the transmission of knowledge between generations. In examining the anthropological literature on residential schooling, one finds widespread themes of indigenous peoples resisting, retaliating against, and rejecting schools that sought to radically transform them (Child 1998; Lomawaima 1993; Haig-Brown 1991). In general, the literature has underscored how residential schooling has become emblematic of a painful loss of language, traditional subsistence knowledge, and even self-respect (Ing 1991). Where residential schooling has been curtailed, as in North America and Australia, few are nostalgic about the past system.

Despite many parallels in the form that residential schooling took in these locations and among the Evenki, a range of factors has coalesced so that the Evenk women elders riding the town bus in 1994 proudly referred to themselves as "part of the collective" formed in Soviet residential schools. While one might expect these women to lament the Soviet state attempts to erase and transform a traditional past, many of the older Evenk women I met were instead affirming the way the state inscribed them with a collective sense of belonging. Moreover, as I demonstrate later in this chapter, this affirmation suggests the complex and unique way that socialism accomplished its task of solidifying a nation-state. As an inclusive model that posited indigenous peoples as the downtrodden heroes to be assisted and promoted at all costs, with indigenous Siberian women receiving special attention, this affirmative action approach to solidifying the nation-state anchored the allegiance of many. Still, this case raises questions about the processes of power and identity formation in a socialist context.

"Culture Bases," Gender Roles, and the Collective

Nearly four generations of Evenki have experienced the collective upbringing in the residential school. The *internatskie*, or Evenki raised in residential schools, like the women mentioned at the outset of this chapter, have a sharp sense of this experience as a shared, formative one. Since the late 1930s, a majority of school-age indigenous Siberians has attended residential schools. In many cases this has distanced them from a traditional way of life and caused severe hardship and loneliness. For many, however, the residential school also came to be instrumental in incorporating them into Soviet society. The schools provided a route to social mobility and simultaneously imprinted a collective identity.

The schools originated as part of a system of fifteen so-called "culture bases" (*kul'turnye bazy*)—outposts of Soviet political administration—established by the Committee of the North in what it called the "darkest corners" of Siberia.[15] Each outpost was meant to have a medical unit, a "House of the Native" (*Dom tuzemtsa*), later to become the "House of Culture" (*Dom kul'tury*), a veterinary unit, and a residential school. Prior to the establishment of the Tura culture base, teachers were already traversing the taiga (see Anderson and Orekhova 2002: 92). In the early 1920s Soviet teachers in the North worked in mobile "red tents" (*krasnye chumy*), promoting literacy and political instruction among herders and hunters in the region, and encouraging Evenki to become active in the new structures of self-government, the native councils. By the fall of 1926 the Tura culture base was firmly established and the red tents increasingly gave way to the fixed structures of administration in Tura.

Figure 5. Russian man conducting 1926 *Household Census of the Arctic North.* Evenk District Regional History Museum, Suslov Collection.

As a key element in the Soviet project's massive effort to incorporate and assimilate indigenous peoples, the culture bases established across Siberia were in many ways similar to the Russian Orthodox Church missions in an earlier era. Like the missions, culture bases offered indigenous Siberians temporary food and shelter and access to trading partners. However, unlike the missions, culture bases also initially sought to provide services that were much in demand, especially the veterinary care of reindeer. The services provided at the culture bases drew indigenous Siberians into the networks of Soviet administration, including the residential schooling.

As discussed in Chapter 1, the expansion of the Soviet administrative and educational infrastructure corresponds to the growing domination of the Soviet state. The first systematic household census in the North conducted in 1926, the *Household Census of the Arctic North* (Tsentral'noe statisticheskoe upravlenie 1927), was central to the state's later efforts to collectivize farming and herding throughout Russia. Beginning in 1932 in the Evenk District, herds of reindeer were converted into regulated *kolkhozy*, or state collective enterprises (GA EAO 1932: 68). Efforts to collectivize herds and agricultural land were followed by the period of violent purges carried out throughout the Soviet Union and most often associated with the period 1937–38.[16] On the local level of the Evenk District, the years of organized repression began with the government efforts to collectivize reindeer herds and the corresponding native efforts to resist collectivization in the early 1930s.

The Volochanka Rebellion, carried out by Evenk, Dolgan, and Sakha herders in an area north of the Evenk District in 1932, was the most violent example of resistance in the history of the immediate region. Four of those protesting collectivization and twenty Communist Party members were killed in the altercation (Anderson 2000: 49). Throughout Siberia large numbers of reindeer herds were also slaughtered by herders who chose this option over surrendering their herds to the state; other herders traveled far to avoid the collectivization (Anderson and Orekhova 2002: 95).[17] In this same period, in the Evenk District, Soviet authorities imprisoned about twenty people, identified in documents as Evenk and Iakut *shamany* and *kulaki*, shamans and kulaks. Both terms were applied to people considered to be in opposition to state policy, but the term *kulak* was also applied to reindeer herders in this region who either had hired laborers or had more than the regionally proscribed number of privately held reindeer, 30 or so. From the 1930s to early 1950s, the term *kulak*, the Russian word for "fist," came to be used as a catch-all label for anyone who was not abiding by local government efforts, in this case to collectivize herds and administer this area of central Siberia.

Beginning in the early 1930s and extending into the 1950s, the Soviet state consolidated most indigenous Siberian men in state cooperatives, where they continued to herd reindeer, hunt, or fish and turn over the end products to the state. Women, however, were increasingly segregated from these subsistence practices. In the case of the Evenki, women tended to be excluded from these spheres of production and instead concentrated in villages, where they were employed in offices, processing sites for furs, and social services such as medicine and education. During World War II, however, while men were at the front, women dominated the herding and hunting operations for nearly five years. Children, adult women, and the elderly often spent summers with their male herding relatives, but most of the year male reindeer herders lived without these family members. The Soviet organization of state collectives among reindeer herders allowed for just one woman, a "woman tent worker," or *chum-rabotnitsa*, to be employed to carry out what were viewed as the domestic tasks of cooking, sewing, and tending the camp for each reindeer herding brigade (Fondhal 1998: 70).[18] Any other women who chose to remain in the camps received no wages or pensions, and in effect they were encouraged to live sedentary lives in villages and towns. This pattern continued up to 1993, when the state-organized reindeer herding was dismantled as financing from the central government disappeared.

The disruptive role of the Soviet state in the lives of indigenous Siberians clearly influenced the degree to which Evenki felt incorporated into the Soviet project in general. Aside from pure repression, however, aspects of state infrastructures—veterinary services, housing, medical care, literacy, and opportunities for social mobility—played an important role in influencing Evenki to participate in the Soviet project. Education was one incentive that apparently appealed to the majority, who lacked the large herds associated with status according to traditional Evenk systems of power. Beginning in the 1920s, those Evenki on the margins were drawn in and nurtured to become intellectuals within the new systems of power being introduced by the Soviet state. These government tactics enabled some Evenki to secure the footing to take part in the broader Soviet society in subsequent decades, and many Evenki found their new positions provided them with types of power to which they otherwise might not have had access. Women in particular were offered extensive opportunities for social mobility and means of making a living outside of herding groups. Most significantly, women became central to national discourses of "liberation" and the creation of a new Soviet society.

Scholars have widely indicated that nation-building discourses often situate women as symbolically central in embodying the idea of the nation (Parker et al. 1992; Chatterjee 1989; Yuval-Davis and Anthias 1989; Mani 1987). As Schein has noted for China (2000: 100–131), and

Abu-Lughod in regard to the Middle East (1998), "woman" has been a key trope in periods when the pursuit of modernity seizes imaginations across the world. Women have been widely seen as reproducing the nation, both biologically and socially as they raise the next generation, and also as the bearers of tradition. For instance, debates over women's "liberation" and corresponding control of women's sexuality and identity have been at the center of resistance movements against the perceived cultural hegemony of global capitalism. This has been especially the case in Islamic revivalism in Malaysia (Ong 1990), and in tensions over veiling in France in the 1990s (Bloul 1994).

Likewise, ideas about modernity in the early Soviet period were produced and reproduced through an opposition of "modern" to "traditional" spheres, with the status of women being one of the central indicators of modernity. One historian of the early Soviet period has described the Soviet state's efforts to transform society, writing that

> Women's liberation [was] based on women's full and equal participation in public life through the socialization of the domestic sphere. . . . *Its vision extended far beyond the establishment of one more laundry or daycare center to the complete reconfiguration of family life* on the most intimate and daily of scales. It aimed at no less than a structural transformation of women's roles, the family, and the larger society. (Goldman 1995: 8, emphasis added)

The Soviet state's vision of modernity from the 1920s through the 1980s closely linked the "liberation" of women to radical structural change. From the perspective of the Soviet project, civic participation was central to an ideology of "emancipation." Among indigenous Siberians, engaging indigenous women in public meetings was a first step. It was hoped that women would transform their social positions (and consciousness) and then bring about a Soviet consciousness in indigenous Siberian communities. At the core of this vision of new roles for indigenous women was the idea of Woman as critical in the socialization of children and the transformation of local communities, but also Woman as the bearer of tradition. Therefore radically altering the gender roles of indigenous Siberian women was tantamount to beginning to instill socialist visions of modernity and to displacing the "backwardness" of herders' lives.

Administrators of the culture base of Tura took careful note of the "cultural work" with women. For instance, one administrator wrote: "With each health discussion [he notes 27 in 1929], women became increasingly active. There were cases where women even began to argue with the doctor! . . . This activity on the part of women began to affect the general native meetings; women actively made speeches and made very concrete (*delovye*) suggestions."[19] Residential schooling was a critical component of the state's attempt to mold all indigenous Siberians, but especially women, into "active" (*aktivnye*), "productive" (*produktivnye*) participants in building a Soviet society.

Residential Schooling in the 1920s

According to the Committee of the North, eighteen residential schools were in place across Siberia by 1926.[20] Indigenous students were also attending local schools that were not organized as residential schools. For instance, in 1926 five schools in the Siberian region (from the Urals to Kamchatka) had a solely native student body, and another twenty-six schools held classes for first and second grades, with a total of 751 indigenous students attending as day students (Itygin 1927b: 124). While initially educators had difficulty attracting students to the schools throughout Siberia, by 1938 this changed dramatically. By World War II, eighty percent of school-age Evenki in the Evenk District were studying in the residential schools and living away from their families for six months at a time (Trofimov 1965: 140–42, cited in Dunn 1968: 7). After World War II, residential schooling became a defining feature of indigenous Siberian identities.

Soviet educators-cum-administrators designing residential school curricula were inspired by the teachings of the American philosopher and educator John Dewey, and in particular by his "action"-oriented curriculum (1900).[21] They saw this as a means of breaking away from the old, rote methods of tsarist education, and some adapted Dewey's methods to emphasize production-specific curricula.[22] The emphasis on production was meant as part of a broader educational goal—to inculcate in indigenous Siberian children a sense of the inherent value of their own sociocultural "stage." As one educator-cum-administrator wrote, "In the primitive conditions of native life, combining the study of the region with socially useful work is easier, more lively and more unavoidable than in the social conditions of a more complex society. In . . . the subsistence type of the northern zone knowledge and action are woven into a unified whole" (Leonov 1928: 120). Educators-cum-administrators considered the establishment of schools among indigenous Siberian populations as both an embodiment of Communist philosophy where a society with the most "unified whole" could be realized and as a necessary element for incorporating indigenous Siberians into the new Soviet society. Those in charge of implementing the residential schools also considered the "action"-oriented approach as important for preparing students to become valuable promoters of technological changes in subsistence methods.

Educators were keenly aware of the need to appeal to students and parents alike, and they successfully argued for the necessity of teaching classes in the given native Siberian language for at least the first two years of instruction. (One woman fondly recounted to me how she had studied in first and second grades with Evenk as the language of instruction; she described her teacher as a patient Russian with amazing ability in the language. This woman was one of those whose education was affected by the language debates of the mid-1920s and early 1930s in which at least one Evenk educator was involved.)[23] Educators also promoted focusing on teaching skills related to the given subsistence of a region, such as sewing fish nets, both to potentially improve this technology and to maintain student and parent interest. One educator emphasized that "This is the only way to make school make sense . . . for [subjects] to be dear to the student herself and to attract the interest of the parents" (Dobrova-Iadrintseva 1928: 81). (This same author's writings draw on her observations in residential schools, including the one in Tura, where she describes the fish nets, skis, and sleds that were created as part of a school lesson.)

In general, educators found that parents were hesitant to send children to school. For instance, one of the early directors of the Tura residential school complained of the difficulty in attracting and retaining students. The director wrote that in 1930 the Evenki only sent children who were considered useless in the household or in need of nutrition; the school had three "mentally deficient" students that year.[24] An elderly Evenk woman confirmed in an interview in 1994 that, in fact, her parents sent her off to study at the residential school in the mid-1930s because they already had ten mouths to feed, and they wanted one less girl to provide for. Other women of the same generation reported similar reasoning behind their parents' willingness to send children to study.

Schooling, Resistance, and Russification

Even though people in their sixties and seventies with whom I consulted did not elaborate extensively about resistance to schooling in their own lives, there were resistances across Siberia to residential schooling in the early years, when the first students were attending these schools. For instance, teachers working in the Tomsk District in western Siberia and at the other end of Siberia in Nikolaevsk-on-the-Amur, in the Far East, recounted in 1926 that native parents threatened to take students out of school because local Russian peasant children were taunting them.[25] In a more direct case of resistance, Balzer (1999:110–16) describes an episode in the early 1930s in western Siberia, as the Soviet state sought to collectivize herds. In this "Kazym uprising," the Khanty and Nentsy refused to send their children to the school or to participate in Soviet efforts to establish local councils and then demanded that the school be closed. In the end the uprising, which involved about one hundred people, resulted in fifty indigenous Siberians being found guilty of rebellion; fourteen were sentenced to death for treason.

In a 1936 incident, this time in the Evenk District, a group of Evenki set the Baikit residential school on fire. Tragically, six children died in the fire. I found no detailed documentation of the event, although a few passing comments were made to me about the perpetrators being shamans, or alternatively government provocateurs, seeking to ensnare any Evenki who might be planning an uprising at the time. The Evenk District Museum's photographic collection includes several pictures of the children's coffins and some penciled notes suggesting that an "enemy of the people" (*vrag naroda*) was responsible.[26] Following events such as the Kazym uprising, the Baikit fire, and the Volochanka rebellion against reindeer collectivization discussed earlier, the pace of collectivization in the North and efforts to gather students in residential schools were both slowed. After World War II, however, these aspects of Soviet state consolidation were reinitiated with new vigor.

Given the instances of unequivocal resistance to residential schooling noted above, at least on the part of some indigenous Siberians, it is particularly striking that there was relatively little discussion about resistance among the women with whom I consulted in the 1990s. After World War II, however, when financial support for outlying regions was more forthcoming and collectivization was more extensive, schooling took firm hold among the Evenki and these women, like other school-age Evenki, were required to attend. As schooling became a normative experience for increasing numbers of Evenki, it significantly defined Evenki as being members of a Soviet society. For instance, in 1931 only one kindergarten was in place in the Evenk District (in Tura), and fifteen Evenk children from the ages of four to six years old attended it. By 1965, however, children were distanced from familial settings at increasingly early ages and twenty-three kindergartens serving 1,067 children from the ages of one to six existed in villages throughout the Evenk District (Boitseva 1971).

After World War II, attendance at residential school became mandatory and Russification was a generally acknowledged aim; educators were no longer worried about appealing to parents and students as they had in the 1920s. Even before World War II, teaching was no longer done in native languages but solely in Russian, and the curriculum no longer emphasized local patterns of subsistence. There was increasing emphasis on a sexual division of labor according to then current patterns in Soviet society, including gender-segregated vocational classes.[27] By the end of World War II, the residential school emphasized training young Evenki to be productive workers with distinctively gendered skills. In addition to the standard Soviet academic subjects such as Russian language and literature, physics, history, and math, boys took classes in carpentry, while girls were encouraged to bake and sew.[28]

Residential schools prevailed, in part, because of the coercive success of collectivization but also because of material inducements such as food, clothing, and opportunity for travel and education, and immaterial inducements such as imagery of indigenous Siberians as subjects of Soviet state-building ideals. By the post World War II period, a shift in consciousness was already emerging, and the second generation of students to attend the schools became inculcated with ideals of modernity linked to European systems of knowledge. These government efforts in the Evenk District were carefully documented in photographs taken by local administrators from the 1930s to 1960s as they took note of the government's proclaimed successes in transforming gender roles and creating a new, modern woman who was "liberated" from "traditional" ways. As one photograph donated to the Evenk District Museum in the early 1960s reflects, Evenk women were valorized as building socialism by "being capable of anything." Evenk women were also depicted as "fighters for the seven year plan," the state-defined plan for production extending to all spheres, including industry and agriculture as well as hunting and herding.

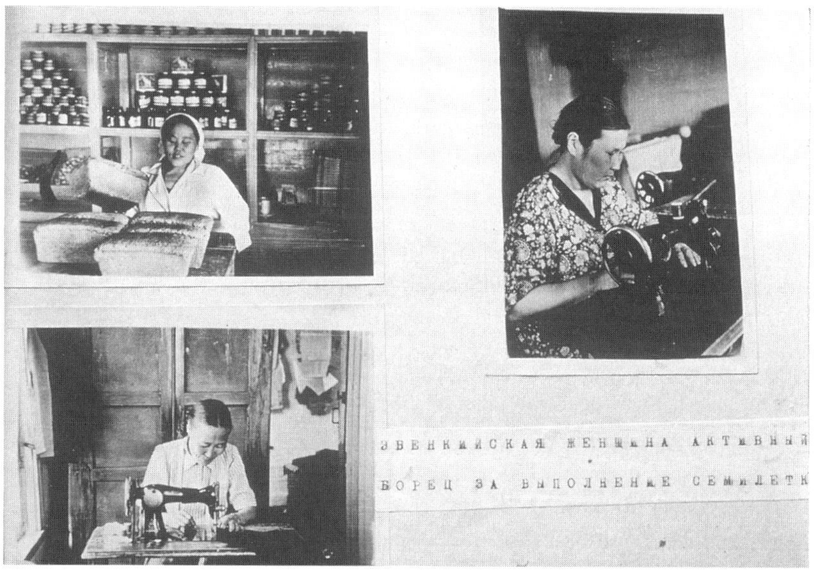

Figure 6. "The Evenk woman actively fights to fulfill the seven-year plan," circa 1955. Evenk District Regional History Museum.

The visual discourse imparted in these photographs was one in which assimilation of indigenous Siberian women would require them to adopt the "superior" European, and specifically Soviet, value systems of formal education, wage labor, and rigid sexual division of labor. The residential school was part of an effort not only to educate indigenous children, but also to free women for becoming involved in Soviet administrative and cultural praxis. Particularly during World War II, when women's labor was critical to the war effort, children were sometimes placed in residential schooling even when kin resided in Tura. Thus the discourses around women's liberation and residential schooling are closely intertwined with discourses around nation-building in a time of crisis in the Soviet Union.

The rhetoric of inclusion in this historical social experiment was all-pervasive. As Evenk women's narratives in the next section demonstrate, contrary to a binary model of power, Evenk women did not automatically resist the Soviet hierarchies of power. Some resisted, but many also accommodated or negotiated with the system. Many were proud to be part of the Soviet society, and by extension reflected fondly on the residential school in our conversations in the 1990s.

Women's Narratives on Residential School and Belonging

Given the radical transformation of gender relations for indigenous Siberians in the twentieth century, examining Evenk women's narratives provides a powerful means for learning what this experience meant for people. These narratives, drawn from the dozens of life histories I conducted with Evenk women in the 1990s, resonate with experiences of Soviet power structures and the negotiation of power in contexts such as the residential school. The narratives were gathered among three generations of Evenk women from various social backgrounds ranging from educated to unlettered reindeer herder to nouveau riche. This section focuses on five Evenk women elders and their life histories reflecting a plurality of perspectives on the residential school. In my initial research, I expected to find ample reflections on resistance to the residential school, but in fact the relationship to this instrument of the nation-state was more complex. Women's narratives emphasize the critical role the residential school plays in an ongoing negotiation of power. At times Evenk women recounted how the system was openly resisted, but more often women described their relationship to the system in instrumentalist and even nostalgic terms. The residential school served their needs and gave them a sense of belonging.

From the early days of the residential schooling, Evenki were often trained to act as administrators, teachers, and caregivers in the system, for, as Caroline Humphrey has described in her work on Mongolia, "the rhetoric of socialism required the plucking of people from obscurity to participate in the drama of power" (1994a: 24). People were not always "plucked from obscurity," but unlettered and semiliterate indigenous Siberians were drawn into this system. This multifaceted nature of the residential school experience was elucidated in the fond memories often recounted by a generation of Evenk women who received higher education in the Northern Faculty at Leningrad State University; many graduates returned to the North in the late 1920s and 1930s to work in the residential school system.

The following section explores the case of one woman who, like many in her generation, felt a deep sense of loss with the fall of the Soviet Union. I argue that in taking Praskov'ia Nikolaevna's account seriously, assumptions about "false consciousness" are challenged, and instead, we must consider the ways that a range of discourses, or what Bakhtin calls "heteroglossia" (1981), operate in relations of power.

Figure 7. Northern students and their teacher at Leningrad State University, circa 1931. Evenk District Regional History Museum, Suslov Collection.

"Plucking" Pedagogues for Residential Schools

Praskov'ia Nikolaevna, an eighty-five-year-old woman who studied in Leningrad in her youth, explained to me: "Those were wonderful years. . . . We lived well. When I look back at those years I am proud to have lived in the Soviet era." My acquaintance with Praskov'ia Nikolaevna began through younger women's accounts of their time in the residential school; these former students often mentioned Praskov'ia Nikolaevna as one of their favorite teachers.[29] Praskov'ia Nikolaevna spent her life working in the residential school system as a teacher and caregiver in the dormitories. Her family moved from the Katanga region in 1929 when her father completed training in a Communist Party school in Leningrad and was assigned to Tura to work in the Party administration for the Evenk District. In Tura, Praskov'ia Nikolaevna's mother was in charge of the house and gave birth to twelve children, although only three of them survived to adulthood. As a Katanga Evenk, Praskov'ia Nikolaevna had learned to read and write at a young age and was one of the first Evenki to attend the Northern Faculty at Leningrad University. She studied elementary education there from 1931 to 1935 and subsequently returned to Evenkiia to work. From 1935 to 1946, Praskov'ia Nikolaevna worked in five different villages in and around the Evenk District, traveling via reindeer each time she was reassigned. In 1946, after her husband died, she moved to Tura to live with her mother and teach in the residential school until her retirement in 1965.

Praskov'ia Nikolaevna's first teaching assignment in 1935 was in Sulomai, a village to the west of Tura, near the Enisei River, in a region that was primarily populated by the Kety, an indigenous Siberian group that also relied on reindeer herding for subsistence (Aleeksenko 1967). I had read about the residential school in this region when examining photographs in the Evenk District Museum. In a fine, penciled script on a picture depicting a crowd of Kety, the director of an ethnographic expedition had written in 1929 that not all the guests present at the October Revolution celebration were in the picture. The note explained that "ten men refused to be photographed . . . since Babkin [the culture base director] accused them of being *kulaki* . . .[for] carrying off children from the school." These efforts to collect children from the school were a precursor to the more adamant demands made in the early 1930s by Khanty in the same region of Kazym, as discussed earlier in this chapter.[30]

When I asked Praskov'ia Nikolaevna about children running away during her tenure in Sulomai she was dismissive:

PN Where could they have run away to? There was nowhere to run to. . . . You wouldn't run away into the taiga. At that time it was really bad. Parents were really poor there. . . . The Kety, they drank.

AB Did they bring their children voluntarily?

PN Yeah, well how else would they have fed their children? They didn't have a house, nothing, and it was cold.

Later in 1939, Praskov'ia Nikolaevna was sent to teach in Chirinda, an Evenk village located to the north of Tura. Again, in discussing her work as a caregiver during that time, I asked how the children felt about being in the residential school.

AB They didn't want to return to their parents?

PN No, they didn't want to. What would they do in the taiga in the winter? It's cold there.

AB How did you convince them to stay in the residential school ?

PN Well, all the kids were there. No one wanted to stay behind [with their parents]. There it was good and warm and besides that they were fed. Why not stay?

Praskov'ia Nikolaevna's depiction of the benefits of the residential school reflects one version of reality for indigenous Siberians at the time. From her social position, located above the Evenk children among whom she worked, she left out a sense of the students' hardship of living without family. Her perspective was certainly influenced by her life-long career in the school system and her role as one of the new "cultural workers" in the 1930s.

As a child Praskov'ia Nikolaevna lived at home and attended nearby schools and only came into contact with the residential system when she became employed in it. Although she identified as Evenk, she had a distinct background; the Katanga Evenki came into intensive contact with Russians and had access to education at least two generations earlier than Evenki in the area around Tura (Sirina 1995: 79). As discussed in Chapter 1, many Katanga Evenki played an integral role in establishing the Soviet infrastructure, and consequently they tended to be strongly allied with the Soviet ruling elite. Like many Evenki of her social background, Praskov'ia Nikolaevna was unapologetic about her role in the Soviet project. From her perspective there was little need to resist a modernization process with which she was allied; her own concept of self was closely tied to the part she played in molding a Soviet version of modernity among generations of Evenki.

Praskov'ia Nikolaevna's uncritical perspective on the residential school reflects how she viewed herself as a product of the Soviet project. The success of the residential school among indigenous Siberians was a critical indication of how well the Soviet project as a whole was progressing.[31] Like Praskov'ia Nikolaevna, many Evenki who actively took part in the excitement of creating Soviet infrastructures and inculcating Soviet ideals in Evenk youth view their lives retrospectively as part of a generally successful Soviet modernization project in the North. To be critical of schooling as a process that detached Evenki from distinct cultural practices would also involve questioning the Soviet project in general. Like many older Evenki in the 1990s, Praskov'ia Nikolaevna actively played a role in the "drama" of Soviet power in which she herself promoted the Soviet legacy and in this process gained a sense of belonging to it.

The First Generation of Students

Given the nature of alternative histories—especially under state socialism in which information was tightly controlled—they are rarely reflected in officially documented history. As discussed further in this section, the promise of modernization heavily counteracted initial attempts to actively resist the Soviet project. Like other modernization projects in the twentieth century, the Soviet state narrative was framed by an evolutionary perspective featuring "backward" peoples who "progressed" to become modern. In the Soviet case, reindeer herders were envisioned as progressing through stages of "development" to the pinnacle of socialism. While this depiction of the ideology so central to socialist economic development appears utopian and perhaps difficult to imagine as appealing to indigenous Siberians, in the following accounts I seek to demonstrate how an ideology of progress could be embraced by some who were featured at its center. Drawing on life history narratives provides fresh perspectives on nuances of state-periphery relationships and can foster discussion on the nature of post-colonial relationships to state power without homogenizing experience. As the following four narratives demonstrate, the sense of belonging felt by Praskov'ia Nikolaevna was not limited to those who played active roles in the drama of Soviet power but also often included those who were more marginal and had a place on the sidelines.

Vera Anatol'evna

I met Vera Anatol'evna in 1992 during a helicopter trip into the taiga where she was herding reindeer with her husband, daughter, three grandchildren, and two nephews. Vera Anatol'evna exchanged opinions with the helicopter pilot regarding the latest news on Moscow politics and the impending Clinton/Bush election. She then turned to me and invited me to join her and her family for a meal consisting of tea and sugar, *lepeshki*—an Evenk raised-bread dish cooked in a skillet over a small steel stove positioned in the center of the tent—and fresh reindeer meat lightly seared over the fire (*chukin*). I joined them, and tossed a few drops of vodka into the fire for an offering. As we reclined on the larch boughs spread around the tent for matting, Vera Anatol'evna recounted something of her life.

When Vera Anatol'evna was a child in the 1930s, her family had very few reindeer, and they primarily depended on hunting and fishing for subsistence. Her parents and grandmother died when she was young, so her grandfather raised her until she was eleven. In 1939 her grandfather tried to enroll her in the residential school in Baikit, but she was refused. (During the war children were not always admitted because the school had limited resources to care for the students.) In 1940 she was admitted. She finished the eighth grade at the school in 1948. Just before her grandfather died, Vera Anatol'evna recalled him saying: "I won't be here and you will be alone so decide what your fate will be." Vera Anatol'evna added, "I thought and thought and in a year I had decided everything, 'When I graduate I will go somewhere. Who will feed me? Who needs a poorly educated girl? I'm not fit for the taiga. Maybe I will be capable of something there, in Tura.'"

Vera Anatol'evna returned to Tura to enroll in the medical training college. Although she had enthusiastically sought to study in Tura, the first year at the medical training college was so difficult materially that Vera Anatol'evna considered at least temporarily reentering the residential school where she thought she would be better provided for.

According to Vera Anatol'evna's account, she (and her grandfather) actively sought out the residential school and medical training college. Vera Anatol'evna's retelling of her life placed her as an active, conscious decision maker, but she was also a product of her social circumstances, which dictated that she "be capable of something," as she explained. With no close kin left alive and no resources of her own (she had no reindeer or ability to provide for herself in the taiga), the academic training she received in the residential school and medical training college offered her the possibility to become self-supporting in a predominantly cash economy. In the case of Vera Anatol'evna it is clear why she ultimately felt fortunate to have attended the residential school; it served concrete material needs at a time in her life when she had few options. While for others, less practical and more emotional concerns are central to their accounts and to how they viewed the residential school, the narratives all reflect a pattern of radical state intervention in reindeer herders' lives. As the following narrative illustrates, Evenk reactions to state power were by no means homogenous. When the Soviet state imposed certain rules, some Evenki sought to evade them.

Zoia Viktorovna

In contrast to many accounts like Vera Anatol'evna's, which emphasize an instrumental perspective on the educational system, the accounts of other women in her generation tended to focus more on a pattern of radical state intervention in reindeer herders' lives and less on individual choice. Relative wealth, in terms of reindeer, as well as generation and gender, played a role in defining the variable appeal that a Soviet system of social mobility had for different Evenki. Many older women's accounts such as the following suggest that within families parents and children also had different views about the educational system.

I met with Zoia Viktorovna at the Tura tuberculosis dispensary, where she was completing one of her many hospital stays.[32] As we approached I could see that Zoia Viktorovna was sewing "*kamus*"—reindeer skin—for *unty*, the warm Evenki traditional skin boots that today are worn by many Evenki and other locals in the cold months of the year. Zoia Viktorovna planned to sell these to supplement her small monthly pension checks of 113,000 rubles (about $25 U.S. per month).[33] I noticed that her life of herding reindeer under harsh conditions in the taiga and tuberculosis had taken a toll on her health; at sixty-three she appeared as old as her favorite former teacher Praskov'ia Nikolaevna did at eighty-five.

We sat on a pile of lumber outside the hospital and between puffs on her unfiltered cigarette (*papirosa*) Zoia Viktorovna recounted that she had spent her childhood in the 1930s in Ekonda. Both her mother and father had come from relatively poor families with only a few reindeer of their own. Zoia Viktorovna's father was killed by "bandits" in a village skirmish when she was a child. The "bandits" may have been herders who refused to surrender reindeer in the collectivization campaign, or they may have been Russians who were avoiding state control or were exiled to the area. Zoia Viktorovna was not sure. Significantly, this was a period of unrest in reaction to the initial Soviet attempts to collectivize reindeer herds; the Volochanka Rebellion took place in 1932, just three years after Zoia Viktorovna's birth.

Zoia Viktorovna spent her childhood accompanying her mother at her post where she provided rested reindeer for travelers to continue their month-long trek to or from Tura. In the pre-Soviet period, Evenki and other indigenous Siberians in the region traveled long distances transporting goods for trade. In the Soviet period, prior to the late 1960s and the expansion of aviation to the North, reindeer caravans were the primary means of supplying state collectives, transporting goods for scientific expeditions, and moving people between population centers.[34]

Although there was pressure for Zoia Viktorovna to go to school, she only began studying in 1945 when she was thirteen. After finishing eight grades at the residential school, she was accepted to study in the Tura medical training college, but her aging mother convinced her to return instead to Ekonda. There she initially worked in the day-care center. When her mother encouraged her to marry a young reindeer herder because "things were tough and it would help out" with their situation, Zoia Viktorovna acquiesced and began reindeer herding. She spent the rest of her life working with reindeer, first transporting geologists and other specialists involved in oil exploration and later working with *sovkhoz* reindeer herds.

In contrast to Vera Anatol'evna's account of her success in the education system, Zoia Viktorovna emphasized her mother's role in the course of her life: "My mother . . . did not want to give me up. *She tried all kinds of methods to dissuade them from taking me. . . . She always took me with her.* I did not want to leave my mother alone. . . . We had to leave. . . . Everyone was required to study in Tura" (emphasis added). As an unlettered reindeer herder and subsistence hunter and fisher, Zoia Viktorovna's mother was able to avoid giving up her daughter for three or four years. She avoided contact with officials who might attempt to take her child off to school. The post from where she supplied travelers with rested reindeer was over a months' journey to Tura and thus was not frequented by Soviet officials in charge of gathering up children for the residential school.[35]

In contrast to Vera Anatol'evna's account of gaining social standing through the education system, Zoia Viktorovna's account emphasizes more resistance to it. Her account also suggests, however, how the education system simultaneously created possibilities for new career trajectories and potential for generational conflicts over responsibilities to parents.

Galina Petrovna

In addition to forms of instrumentality or, conversely, resistance to Soviet educational structures, ambivalence toward the Soviet system was also frequently expressed. Many older Evenki were reluctant to discuss a history of repression and forced assimilation, and instead their accounts reflected the multiple ways in which they felt a sense of belonging to Soviet society. These sentiments were sometimes expressed in terms of nostalgia, but sometimes with more ambivalence. As the following account reflects, Evenk lives were tightly enmeshed with instruments of the Soviet state. At different points in history, members of one family could experience state coercion or instead choose to accommodate or resist state programs of social transformation imposed in the North.

Galina Petrovna's daughter Nadia, who worked as a bookkeeper for the Association of Peoples of the North in the early 1990s, invited me home for lunch occasionally and this was an ideal time to converse with her mother (see Chapter 2). While Galina Petrovna's grandson sat nearby and played with his hand-held Tetris, Galina Petrovna and I prepared lunch, peeling potatoes and talking about her life.

Like Zoia Viktorovna, Galina Petrovna also arrived by reindeer from Ekonda to attend the Tura residential school in the 1940s. Her background was very different, however, from that of Zoia Viktorovna. Her mother's and father's families were relatively wealthy, and her husband's family had deep ties to shamanism. Although Galina Petrovna's father-in-law was the son of an influential shaman, as a young man he came to be a "*stakhanovets*"; he was decorated for his hard work and for being a committed Communist, which necessarily entailed taking a stand against any type of shamanism.[36] Galina Petrovna's own father was a reindeer herder with over 600 head. When Soviet organizers began collectivizing herds in the early 1930s, he resisted giving up his herd, but eventually he was forced to relinquish all his reindeer. In the course of one of our discussions, Galina Petrovna told me these reindeer had just gotten sick and died, but when Nadia contradicted her, she said the herd had been collectivized. This exchange reminded me of how Galina Petrovna's and others' accounts were very much tailored to the audience.[37] It is possible that had Nadia been absent, Galina Petrovna might have chosen to keep to the story of the reindeer dying from disease. My identity as an American researcher was often weighed carefully by those I met as they considered what they wanted to become part of a story about their lives and their ties to local structures of power.

When we spoke about the residential school and her time there, Galina Petrovna recalled that her parents sent her because "then you had to send children to school. There was no choice." Galina Petrovna described how the residential school used to send out a special group of people to gather up children from the reindeer herding brigades. Although at first she was scared, she recalled, "I got used to the school, but I cried when my father came (to visit and left)." This was part of the experience left untold by teachers like Praskov'ia Nikolaevna.

After finishing school, Galina Petrovna went to Krasnoiarsk, where she trained to become a film projectionist. After graduating, she returned to the Evenk District and married. She spent most of her professional life traveling around to villages and reindeer brigades in the Evenk District showing films. Her husband died very young. In 1998, at the age of 73, Galina Petrovna was living by herself in an apartment in Tura, although she cooked meals at her daughter's house, and she continued to work part-time in the town's fur-processing organization.

From the perspective of Galina Petrovna and many other women in her generation, after the initial trauma of losing herds, the Soviet project offered reindeer herders a chance to become "modern," to take part in the new Soviet society. These contradictory aspects of the Soviet state's role in Siberian lives were sometimes reflected in an ambivalence about speaking of the past. Perhaps Galina Petrovna was hesitant to reflect on the collectivization of her clan's reindeer precisely because she was speaking to an American. Galina Petrovna was aware of how Soviet power was wielded against her family, but it is possible that she also did not want to provide fodder against a society in which she had spent decades as an active participant.

Polina Mikhailovna

In many cases older Evenki not only expressed a deep sense of belonging to Soviet society, but they were also nostalgic about what was lost with the fall of the Soviet Union. This was the case for Polina Mikhailovna, who, despite personal tragedy, spoke of a sense of belonging to and nostalgia for the Soviet era. Polina Mikhailovna's narrative reflects, however, the great personal cost the state imposed on those whom it perceived to be resisting the redistribution of wealth, in this case reindeer. Polina Mikhailovna's account especially highlights the need for a careful discussion of the indigenous Siberian experience in Soviet society as distinct from, but in some ways intersecting with, that of other indigenous peoples faced with power imbalances imposed by nation-states. When I met Polina Mikhailovna in 1995, at sixty-three, she was a retired nurse working part-time as a doorwoman for the district administration building, or the "white house" as Turintsy called it.

One evening while we sat at her post, Polina Mikhailovna recounted something of her life, beginning with reflections on her father. He was from what is today the Sakha Republic and had been exiled to Essei, a village north of Tura about two hours by small plane. In Essei he met Polina Mikhailovna's mother and they had six children, one of whom died in infancy. For Polina Mikhailovna the most difficult aspect of her childhood began in 1938 when her father was accused of being a *kulak*, or of owning too many deer.

Materials in the Evenk District archive indicate how the government's mechanisms for marginalizing those who were thought to be resisting attempts to collectivize herds were gradually implemented in the early 1930s. Those labeled *kulaki* were sanctioned in certain ways. For instance, 19 *kulaki* in the Evenk District lost their voting rights in native council meetings in 1932. Those labeled *shamany* were also harassed; 13 Evenk men who were accused of being shamans lost their right to vote in the native council meetings (GA EAO 1932: 68).[38] Archival records do not indicate when exactly those labeled *shamany* and those labeled *kulaki* were being sent to prison in Krasnoiarsk. Oral accounts confirm, however, that those who were accused then stood trial and were sent via barge to Krasnoiarsk to serve time in prison.

In the late 1990s one woman, whose primary profession was as a caregiver in the Tura residential school, told me about her role as an interpreter (from Yakut into Russian) in the interrogations that were held in several northern villages in the Evenk District. Several people recounted to me how the "wealth"—mostly furs—was sent from these villages to Tura when these *kulaki* were put on trial. A former barge captain who transported some of the accused recalled that most of them were Evenki or Sakha who were locally considered to have prestige, often in the form of a connection to shamanic powers. However, a few *sibiriaki*, or longtime non-indigenous residents, were also among those the captain transported south to serve prison sentences.

In Polina Mikhailovna's case the local collective herding operation appropriated the twenty reindeer the household owned and Polina's father was imprisoned. Polina Mikhailovna remembered: "They did not leave us even one reindeer. My mother said that they took everything. . . . He was in prison for four years in Krasnoiarsk I think. . . . They wanted to shoot him and then that was rescinded. . . . They imprisoned a lot of people. Lots did not return. . . . A few did time and then returned." The imprisonment of Polina Mikhailovna 's father was extremely hard on the household. Polina Mikhailovna's mother was forced to support five young children on her own, and the surrounding community was relatively hostile toward the family. Only the exiled Latvians and Volga Germans helped out with firewood and some food.

The ostracism on the part of the community continued even after Polina Mikhailovna's father returned home when she was in the second grade at the residential school. At this age in Soviet society, children usually joined the children's division of the Communist Party, the Young Pioneers.[39] Polina Mikhailovna was not permitted to join, and later she was also denied membership in the youth division of the Communist Party, the Komsomol. Nearly sixty years later she recalled: "They called us 'Kulak Children' (*deti kulaka*). . . . The Komsomol would not accept us and the Pioneer camp would not take us. *We wanted to wear those red ties. . . . We hankered after those.* Everyone wore them, but we couldn't. They didn't give them to us" (emphasis added).

In Polina Mikhailovna's narrative the import of the red ties—which Pioneer and Komsomol members wore around their necks to indicate belonging to Soviet society—was unshaken by her personal experience.[40] Given Polina Mikhailovna's personal history, one might expect her to have a very different attitude toward the Soviet state and its instruments of power. Instead, like many in her generation, Polina Mikhailovna was nostalgic for a bygone era; perhaps as she witnessed how material conditions significantly improved in the North between the 1930s and 1950s, this outweighed her knowledge of the brutality of collectivization. Many Evenki continue to wish for the red ties of socialism to return and the concomitant stability they associate with it. Polina Mikhailovna particularly equated Stalin's era with ideals she viewed as lacking in Russian society of the 1990s. She whimsically reflected, "*I respect Stalin all the same.* . . . He jailed my father, but I don't feel malice [*zlo*] toward him. Because of Stalin we are honest. We grew up honest. We were never late for work, we didn't smoke, and we didn't drink. So there's the result of the 'Cult of Stalin'" (emphasis added).

This forthright statement raises interesting questions about a range of issues, including how to think about a subjected people's relationship to power. A certain type of "internal colonialism" appears to be at work, but, one must remember again the context in which this statement was made. Polina Mikhailovna's sentiments of nostalgia for the Stalin era were widely held by this generation of Evenki, not because these Evenki necessarily felt sympathetic toward the repressive measures of the state, but because they saw their material conditions and official stature within socialist society radically transform in the period under Stalin (see Verdery 1983; Grant 1995a for a similar point). The childhood trauma suffered by people like Polina Mikhailovna was "forgotten" as they became openly nostalgic about Stalin's era because the "red ties" of socialism that they sought were later extended to them. They were able to become nurses, teachers, and film technicians and thereby esteemed members of their communities.

Contemplating Red Ties of Belonging

In thinking about the historical and cultural context that has resulted in such a wide range of perspectives on the residential school, I was first drawn to the lives lived in close contact with this institution. Evenk women's life histories reflect widely held attitudes toward the Soviet era and the residential school as an instrument of the state. As Vera Anatol'evna's and Polina Mikhailovna's accounts in particular indicate, a variety of social circumstances illuminate how these women and others their age tend to view the residential school today. The residential school is a site associated both with a Soviet era and with a certain incorporation into Soviet society. But this is not a homogenous perspective.

How can one explain this generation's range of perspectives—nostalgia, resistance, accommodation, and ambivalence—on the residential school system? Given the power of the Soviet state refracted through this institution, why was a theme of resistance so nominal in these women's accounts? Is it possible that the psychology of colonialism was so successful that Evenki became integrated into and even sometimes embraced the system? Is it also possible that for many Evenki the benefits of the Soviet system outweighed the negative or "oppressive" aspects?

In reflecting on India's post-colonial legacy, Ashis Nandy claims that those who attempt to think in terms of the "benefits" of the colonial power structure are "collaborators" in oppression (1993: 3). But in fact, what if some Evenki have internalized this quintessentially Soviet institution as an important aspect of their identity? What if within the nested hierarchies of Soviet society elements of equality and belonging were extended to older Evenk women and cherished by some?

I would not claim that women spoke with me without their own reasons for sharing the types of narratives that they did. This is inevitable, but it does not change the fact that there was a wide range of positions expressed; these women's accounts do not fit into a rigid model of binary power relations. As discussed in the first part of this chapter, models of power and resistance too often assume a binary perspective. Instead of lumping people into "oppressed" and "oppressor" categories or looking for those in power vs. those victimized by power, the women's accounts presented here encourage us to consider the ways in which people are positioned through a wide range of factors. Perhaps one can better understand Praskov'ia Nikolaevna's comment that "When I look back at those years, I am proud to have lived in the Soviet era" and Polina Mikhailovna's "We wanted to wear those red ties" by thinking about the ways in which these women were evaluating their lives as members of Soviet society, as Evenki, as women, as students, as *Evenkiitsy*, and as members of their households. Their assessments of their lives involved multiple positionings, and for many the centrality of the state and the institution of the residential school was very much ensconced in nostalgia for bygone days of youth and opportunity.

Rofel's work (1994) is particularly compelling for thinking about the Evenk women's perspectives on the residential school as reflecting hierarchies of power. Rofel contrasts the "subject position" of an older generation of Chinese women whom she interviewed in the late 1980s and early 1990s with that of a younger generation that came of age in the midst of economic reform in the 1980s. She explains that with the 1949 revolution in China a new set of oppositions came to be central for evaluating Chinese womanhood; proper women came to be defined as those who worked (1994: 237). The older generation of Chinese women who worked went from being transgressors of pre-1949 gender sensibilities to becoming revolutionary, "liberated" women. The older generation framed the present (1990s) as an experience of "loss of frames of reference that had featured them at the center" (1994: 239), while the younger generation "yearned for modernity" that included denouncing the "liberation" tenets of the Cultural Revolution. Like the elderly Chinese women Rofel writes about, the Evenk women were often nostalgic about a time when they were "at the center" of a rapidly transforming society.

An older generation of Evenki very much identifies with Soviet idioms of modernity. For them, personal dedication in establishing an urban utopian society and dispelling with a "traditional" one was prevalent; in their youth they also "yearned for modernity," a Soviet version. As Geoffrey Hosking notes for the Soviet populace at large:

> Both in the macrocosm and the microcosm this dedication was achieved at the cost, not only of turning one's back on a rural childhood, but also of denigrating it, devaluing it, as something to flee from at all costs. . . . In a sense their years of individual dedication to the urban ideal replicated the total historical experience of the Soviet state, with its dedication to industry, technology, education, culture and mass media. (1987: 122)

Hosking's comments have an explanatory force, especially in conjunction with ideas about how people remember in former socialist societies. The way in which state socialism enforced "amnesia" and sought to deprive citizens of unapproved or unofficial memories provides a mirror image for understanding contemporary Evenki's remembrances of residential schooling. People recover and preserve memories in a very different light when confronted with totalizing accounts that act to erase individual experiences (see Watson 1994: 68). State-created "amnesia" certainly existed in the former Soviet Union. In the Evenk case, however, there is a new "totalizing" account of history to which people are reacting. For Evenk women the Soviet project, as embodied in the residential school, represented the enfranchisement of Evenki within the broader "modern" society. It makes sense that as harsh, new market conditions spread in Russia today, accompanied by widespread refutations of Soviet official histories, people are drawing on memories to secure themselves to the red or socialist ties of the past.

Given that these Evenk women elders chose to place me in the role of chronicler, documenting a slice of their past, they also sought to direct the way in which the past was recorded by someone from outside the community. Keith Basso has written, "Building and sharing place-worlds . . . is not only a means of reviving former times but also of *revising* them, a means of exploring not merely how things might have been but also how, just possibly, they might have been different from what others have supposed" (1996: 6). It makes sense to consider Evenk women's reflections as active efforts to influence and augment late 1990s public discourse on the continuing legacy of Soviet cultural and political practice in the lives of indigenous Siberians. As the women at the onset of this chapter emphasized, a sense of the socialist collective has permeated and in many ways defined their identities as Evenki; in the late twentieth century being part of the Soviet collective was interwoven with being Evenki and having a sense of place in the social order. These perspectives are not a matter of false consciousness preventing women from seeing true structures of power; instead these narratives reflect a historical consciousness of taking part in history.

As the next chapter demonstrates, historical consciousness is very much contingent upon how subjects are positioned in structures of power, including in generational terms.

Chapter 4
Young Women Between the Market and the Collective

> [The fact that] American Indians attended government boarding schools in increasing numbers during the 1930s . . . is not necessarily a sign that after decades Indian people had finally warmed to the idea of residential schools for their children. . . . When the deprivation of Indian families became acute during the 1930s, the boarding schools filled with children.
>
> —Brenda Child, *Boarding School Seasons*

> Dear Evenk women! . . . the former . . . government in this country consisted of a mere fifteen percent women. Can a society be considered democratic if, even when they are in the majority, women are excluded from participation in the political process, including at the highest levels? Maybe this is why it is so difficult to solve the country's social problems and why women's position in society has worsened. Like never before our country is in need of a united women's initiative. We should become that force that will assist in change . . . and extinguish the flames of interethnic conflict.
>
> —Handbill for candidates campaigning with the political party "Women of Russia" in the first elections held in the Evenk District in the post-Soviet Russian Federation, December 12, 1993

A post-colonial analysis of indigenous Siberians' position in a post-Soviet era might focus on liberation from decades of oppression, but, as indicated in the last chapter, this would not accurately reflect how a wide range of Evenki interpret their experience of Soviet power. At the start of the twenty-first century, people in formerly socialist countries, especially those on the margins, are widely lamenting the loss of the benefits the former systems provided (Hivon 1995; Berdahl 1999; Bridger 2000). The case of the Evenki suggests that it is important to consider post-colonial relationships in their specific contexts of interwoven power dynamics, particularly in post-socialist societies. As one author writes in regard to Poland, "the flaws of the centralized system, its extensive and highly visible levels of corruption . . . and Russian imperialism, all served to mask the ways in which actually lived socialism did in fact succeed in making daily life better in some ways for many people" (Pine 1996: 133).

For women especially, contemporary market conditions are a stiff reminder of the benefits of the past system. In terms of civic participation, under late socialism gender equity was officially promoted and for extended periods, popular representations portrayed both women and men as strong and able workers. Since the mid-1990s, imaginations have been awash with other imagery as a flood of Western-style glossy magazines locates women as subordinate to men, most often in kitchens, nurseries, or bedrooms and rarely at work in fields, offices, or factories (Einhorn 1993; Pine 1996). The multiple social roles in which women engaged during late socialism were facilitated by generous maternity benefits and job security; now the demands of neoliberal economics encourage formerly socialist governments to slash budgets for these "inefficiencies." In short, the late socialist paradigm of providing basic necessities for all prevented a widespread division between those with access to material possibilities and those without.

The younger generation of women who are the subjects of this chapter grew up in an era when Evenk social life had already been collectivized and molded through the residential school experience for over three generations. In contrast to the older women featured in Chapter 3, these women, aged twenty-five to thirty-five, had less intimate links to the traditional economy. In fact, while as children some had visited relatives in the taiga, as adults none of these women had ever lived in the taiga or herded reindeer. Their reflections on the residential school had less to do with taking up a "modern" way of life and more to do with the residential school as either a resource or, conversely, an unwelcome confinement. The perspectives the women expressed depended equally on their place within the emerging social stratification and on the new public discourse stigmatizing collectivism and social programs meant to provide for those in need. In conversation about the residential school, women in this generation often reflected on the new categories of "need" becoming associated with the institution. Young womens' attitudes toward residential schooling ranged from a sense of entitlement to government resources and educational opportunities for all indigenous peoples to a view of the institution as emblematic of the social stigma of being identified as one in need.

As indicated in the previous chapter, in the 1990s the residential school continued to be an important force in Evenk lives. Here I explore how various social circumstances (age, economic clout, profession, and personal history) influenced the ways in which young Evenk women evaluated the role of the residential school in their lives. Unlike the sentiments of nostalgia or ambivalence expressed by Evenk women elders for the Soviet era as embodied in the residential school, younger Evenk women tended to reflect on the institution in more instrumentalist terms. Many young Evenk women drew on the resources of the residential school in raising their own children; the school was very much part of an attempt to ensure household material well-being. Association with the residential school was increasingly defined by class rather than ethnic identity, and some young women like the head of the Kislov household described in Chapter 2, were opposed to being affiliated with the residential school. Young women's reflections on the residential school indicate ways in which emerging class categories are sometimes resisted or reconfigured by women as they react to new conceptions of "need" that stigmatize affiliation with the residential school in class terms. In examining young women's narratives in this chapter I also explore how the ways young women think about the institution are integrally tied to the ways they themselves are socially constituted in the shifting power relations of central Siberia in the 1990s.

Residential Schooling as Resource

Zhenia

For many young Evenki, sending their children to the residential school in the 1990s primarily served a material function. As tenets of individualism came to predominate in the emerging market economy, some young people still looked to the residential school as a mechanism for providing material well-being for them and a large portion of the indigenous community. Some young women explained that in sending their children there, they expected their children to excel. They viewed the institution as an important resource that would promote their children's interests specifically because they were indigenous. These accounts reflect the women's idea of "need" as a naturalized category allowing indigenous Siberians to look to the state for support without particular stigma. In accounts of their own lives growing up in the residential school, these young women reflected on the stability it provided.

This was the case with Zhenia, a twenty-nine-year-old woman I met in the pediatric division of the regional hospital in 1993. Zhenia was making a living doing odd jobs, including washing floors, but she was finding it difficult as a single mother of two children, aged ten and five at that time. Zhenia spent her early childhood traveling with her father, who worked as a musician in the Houses of Culture located in the various villages in the Evenk District. During one of our discussions, she quietly recounted, "My dad gave me up for a bit to relatives in Chirinda when mom died, but he was lonely so I soon joined him." Zhenia's father had a drinking problem, and she noted how happy she was to go off to the residential school at age six. She confided, "I only felt safe in the residential school, where we even had clean sheets."

After graduating from school at age sixteen, Zhenia studied art for five years in an institute in Krasnoiarsk. However, as much of the employment formerly available in the arts was drastically cut back with the collapse of the former Soviet Union, in subsequent years Zhenia primarily earned a living washing floors in the residential school. At the time I met her in 1993, Zhenia was selling stacking dolls (*matreshki*) for extra money, but by 1995 she was working as a laborer on a newly established pig farm.[1] As discussed in Chapter 2, in 1995 Zhenia and another single mother had decided to avoid what Zhenia called the chaos of the town. They moved into small houses allocated by the town administration that were located away from the center of the town. Unlike her friend, Zhenia was sending her older child—then twelve—to a residential school. It was located in the Sakha Republic, and because his father was Sakha, Zhenia's son received a full scholarship to study in a specialized music program.

Zhenia's case demonstrates the active choice some Evenki were making to retain ties to the residential school system in order to bolster an alternative identity and to obtain material support. In contrast to the single-mother household described in Chapter 2, Zhenia considered sending her son to the local residential school. Ultimately, she chose to send him to a residential school that she thought would best serve his musical talents and simultaneously ally him more closely with the more plentiful Sakha resources. This choice also alleviated some of the financial burdens of raising an additional child.

Lena

Lena's narrative also demonstrates how allying oneself with the residential school could provide a sense of stability and serve as a resource for young Evenki. I met with Lena, a thirty-year-old woman, during a quiet spell at the job she held in the early 1990s at the local meteorological station. As I accompanied her in checking rain levels and wind speeds, Lena recounted how she had spent all her childhood attending state institutions. Lena's parents had been reindeer herders in a brigade outside Tutanchan, a village west of Tura along the Nizhniaia Tunguska River. Her mother died when Lena was born, and her father was killed soon afterward in a hunting accident. Lena's relatives chose not to raise her and instead sent her to the district crêche in Tura. Once she entered the residential school, Lena had barely any contact with these relatives; as she explained, they only actively recognized her as one of their relatives when she returned to Tura with higher education. Lena reflected that in many ways the residential school came to play the role of the stable community that she lacked as a child in the taiga: "*The parents constantly drank* . . . and there were always a lot of people, at least until the end of summer when they [the officials] came and took away the kids, at least that's how it was for those who had parents. The rest of us constantly lived in the crêche or the residential school. *It was quieter there* and our class of twenty-eight or so got along well" (emphasis added).

When I met with Lena in 1995 she and her husband had recently begun raising her sister's twelve-year-old daughter. Lena's sister had died from gunshot wounds inflicted by her drunken husband. Although Lena's niece could have attended the town school, Lena made arrangements for her to attend the residential school as a day student. Lena explained that the child had grown up at home and would have a rough time living in the dormitory at the residential school. Lena avoided sending her niece and her daughter to the town school, however. As discussed in the following chapter, in contrast to the town school, the residential school was often viewed as more welcoming for Evenki. It had more Evenk teachers, a student body consisting of predominantly native students (most of whom were Evenki), a curriculum with an emphasis on Evenk traditional culture (including Evenk folk music, language, and ethnography), and a student body that was much less economically stratified than in the town school. Not surprisingly, in the 1990s many Evenk parents living in the town of Tura, like Lena, sent children to study in the residential school as day students. According to parents, the reasons for this choice were wide-ranging, including the additional material support—meals and some clothing—provided by the residential school; the additional academic support provided in cases in which children were viewed as developmentally slower than their cohort at the town school; and the less rigorous teaching styles, which demanded less from students who had personality conflicts with teachers at the town school. Lena also insisted that Evenk children were often taunted at the town school where most of the nearly 900 students in 1995 were Russian.

Lena's support for the residential school was tempered by the sense of community she found there during her childhood. She viewed the residential school as a refuge and a resource. This was particularly apparent as she dealt with providing care for another child who was growing up without her parents. Lena lived with her husband and two children in a one-room apartment; supporting a third child was difficult. The arrangement with the residential school, which provided three meals a day, even for the day students, allowed Lena to stretch her household's resources somewhat further.

For Zhenia and Lena, and many other women in similar circumstances, the residential school system served clear instrumentalist purposes that were dictated by their material situations. Zhenia's and Lena's decisions to send their children to residential schools were also motivated by a concern with ethnic allegiances. Like the Labinko household discussed in Chapter 2, they valued the educational opportunities that continued to be linked to residential schooling and they also wanted their children to be proud of their ethnic heritage. Zhenia's and Lena's decisions reflected an active resistance to a broader racially charged environment that they sensed existed in the town school. As discussed in the following chapter, students and parents reported that they were often made to feel inferior in the town school and Evenk cultural traditions were belittled or ignored. In contrast, the residential school's predominantly Evenk student population and numerous Evenk teachers provided a basis for a more supportive atmosphere.

New Hierarchies of Power?

In contrast to the experience of the older generation who were compelled to attend the residential school in the early decades of Soviet society, Lena's and Zhenia's accounts reflect attitudes shared by a segment of the younger generation. They actively chose to send children to the residential school in the 1990s. The range of attitudes toward the residential school, from one of nostalgia among older women to one of an instrumentalist and even political nature among younger women, could be viewed as a shift in the "hierarchy of power" (Abu-Lughod 1990). In these new hierarchies, where poverty among town Evenki was sharply emerging, the residential school was a resource.

The perpetuation of residential schooling among indigenous communities in Russia could be explained in terms of simple material need. In spite of the residential school's legacy of distancing children from their families and heritage in Siberia, many Evenk parents continued to look to the residential school for support in the 1990s at a time when government subsidies for food, housing, and transportation, as well as employment, were all radically diminishing. The Evenk situation also highlights, however, the shifting conceptualizations of state entitlements in post-socialist societies more broadly. While in the past, attending the residential school was not marked in any pronounced way, by the mid-1990s attending the residential school over the town school was widely viewed as either politically marked or marked by poverty.

For those Evenki flourishing in their newfound professions as entrepreneurs, like the younger Polgogirs discussed in Chapter 2, the allegiance to an Evenk identity was not appealing and the residential school was not considered a resource. Among the small segment of the population that embraced the market economy in the late 1990s, success was viewed as closely tied to independent accomplishment. The striking internalization of the basic market tenet of individualism clashed directly with the socialist tenet of the collective. The few "successful" Evenki viewed the collective Evenk identity that resonated in the institution of the residential school to be threatening and too interwoven with a socialist ethic they openly opposed. The following narrative particularly highlights these attitudes allied with a shift in social status that occurred along with success in the market economy.

Tamara Polgogir

I met Tamara through her mother, Nadezhda Sergeevna, whom I had known since 1992. As discussed in Chapter 2, from the time Tamara was young, Nadezhda Sergeevna actively engaged in "cultural work," primarily writing songs in Evenk, sewing *solnyshki*—"traditional" souvenirs symbolizing the sun in the form of circular fur items decorated with small, bright beads—and teaching decorative arts in the special education division of the Tura residential school. Until 1993, Tamara had also worked for nearly ten years as a teacher; at that point she gave up her profession and emerged as one of the new entrepreneurs. She began regularly traveling between Tura, Krasnoiarsk, China, and Saudi Arabia for her business as an importer of foodstuffs and clothes.

In the course of an interview in 1992, Tamara recalled her childhood and discussed what she considered to be happy years spent largely in the residential school. Although Tamara and her two brothers lived at home with their mother, they attended the residential school as day students. Nadezhda Sergeevna worked intensively, often seven days a week, and it was easier for her children to attend school where they could be looked after and fed. Tamara recalled: "I only saw my mother at school and there she would check to make sure I was dressed warmly enough and had eaten. . . . But I'm not sorry [that I attended the residential school]." Tamara's attendance at the residential school was not just convenient; it was a critical arrangement for Nadezhda Sergeevna, who was attempting to meet the consuming demands of her job while raising three children as a single mother.

In contrast to her comments in 1992, Tamara expressed a quite negative perspective toward the residential school in 1995:

> It seems to me that the whole residential school system should just be shut down! They are no longer needed at all. Children should study at home and live with their parents. First of all, it [the residential school] harms the role of parents. They get used to the idea that their children are somewhere "there." They only spend summers with parents, and the parents don't have to do anything. The school feeds and clothes the children and looks after them. [Second], it spoils the children. Someone cleans up after them, feeds them, takes care of them. . . . When children live at home they have their own chores, but after the residential school they . . . become so lazy!

Tamara's shift in attitude toward the residential school corresponded closely with her new career in business, and her attitude reflected her allegiance to the growing public discourse around individualism. In our discussions in 1995, Tamara emphasized what she considered the negative aspects of a communal culture in the residential school:

> If you live in your own home, you know that when you go out and close the door no one will come and touch your things. But in the residential school, when they go to class anyone can come and take something. They don't even really know if this is 'mine' or 'yours'; everything is common. So, if I have some sort of pretty toy, well it is really everyone's. . . . You see it doesn't matter if it is yours or his. Someone can just come and take it. It's not pleasant.

Tamara's account of the residential school demonstrates her years of work as a teacher in the residential school system, but it also reflects her perspective as someone distressed by collective tenets. The lack of private, personal property disturbed her more than the idea of women attempting to run a household without the support of the institution, and she did not view the school as a nexus for Evenk cultural revitalization. Tamara's success in the market represented her ability to absorb new cultural values, as well as her access to capital. For Tamara, as for the few others in positions to gain in the newly emerging market economy, the symbolic capital of the residential school as a nexus for Evenk community had little relevance. Possibly because she was embracing individualist values of the emerging market economy, she was no longer concerned with the collective needs for which the residential school could provide.

Oksana

There were only a handful of successful Evenk entrepreneurs in Tura, but some other young women who were not directly involved in business were also critical of the residential school. In some cases a critical stance seemed to be a direct result of negative experiences in the residential school. In most cases, however, this critical stance was closely tied to a social position of difference that set these young women apart from the local Evenki. For instance, Katanga Evenk women, like the woman heading the Kislov household discussed within the section on marginal households in Chapter 2, were often the most vociferous critics of the residential school. Instead of viewing themselves collectively as Evenki, the Katanga Evenk women I came to know first defined themselves as belonging to a class of people distinct from other Evenki. In fact, as detailed in Chapter 1, the Katanga Evenki do belong to a segment of Evenki that has been closely involved in Soviet politics, human services, and education since the early 1920s, and this continues into the present. In the 1990s those Katanga Evenk women whose families had been successful in the power structures of Soviet society for decades also tended to intermarry with Russians, which meant that they had more access to resources and opportunities that were largely controlled by newcomers in the community. As with the Kislov household discussed in Chapter 2, while this position of relatively advantageous social capital did not always result in prosperity or even stability, Katanga Evenk women tended to be well positioned to make use of social capital. The example of Oksana discussed below is typical of Katanga Evenki in that, like many, Oksana was able to build on her social capital and create a stable life.

Oksana was on leave from her job as a medical technician in the tuberculosis dispensary when we met in 1993. Oksana described how she had grown up in the town orphanage and she focused on her feelings of being controlled and catalogued as if she was not an individual. She explained that because she was orphaned, she did not even know the date of her birth when she was a child. She was given March 8 (International Women's Day) as her birthday, and only in the ninth grade did she learn that her actual birthday was August 1. Aside from resenting bureaucratic oversights, Oksana asserted that she and other orphans were angered by the way they were singled out in the residential school. Students particularly resisted being separated out as orphans during mealtimes, and they regularly tore down the list indicating that the orphaned children eat at certain times. Oksana noted, "I didn't like how people related to us. . . . They pitied us. . . . Why did they need to separate us out? . . . I remember how the older kids tore the list down. They were always tearing it down."

Oksana viewed herself as distinct from other Evenki, and not just because she was an orphan. In 1993 she commented: "My life is working out. I wouldn't want to live like some. . . . They give birth, and without education, then they suffer with these kids. They don't know what to do. I know what to do. I am a qualified midwife. *I won't have to wash floors for my whole life. I know I can make it*" (emphasis added).

Oksana's allegiances were more bound up with class than with an affiliation with a broadly defined Evenk identity. When we met again in 1995, Oksana was going through a messy divorce from her Russian husband, who had begun to drink heavily. Oksana recently had found a well-paying position in the regional Department of Public Health. Although she was now a single parent, she was not eager to rely on the residential school for material support. She emphasized a number of times that she did not plan to send her daughter to the residential school; she would manage without inflicting that stigma on her child.

Perhaps Oksana was more resistant to the residential school precisely because of its symbolic capital. She viewed the school as a place marked by its role in the socialist welfare state, and she strongly contended that the school created a dependent psychology. In her own life she claimed to be successful as a result of her hard work, and only in spite of the residential school. In a way Oksana was the product of two systems. Although she grew up in the collective setting of the residential school, she also grew up aware of her background as a Katanga Evenk; she was aware of her status within the hierarchy of local groups. The pride she drew from this awareness compelled her to "make it" on her own. This self-made aspect of her experience was elevated in the context of an emerging market economy.

Reconstituting "Need"

In central Siberia in the 1990s, the residential school was not simply a holdover from a colonized Soviet past. As reflected in these portraits of young Evenk women, the residential school was perceived in a wide range of ways, including as an emblem of a time when the state provided resources, albeit centrally defined, for people on the margins. Among the wider Evenk community, as among these young women, the benefits of residential schooling became part of a discussion about the degree to which the state should support those in need.

Prior to the early 1990s, the definition of those "in need" was most closely linked to ethnicity, and the category of "small peoples of the North" was invoked as a means of "helping" these indigenous people. By implication, the "big" ethnic groups were assisting the "small" ones; often the paternalism was palpable. Similarly, in another formerly socialist context, Haney (1999) demonstrates how categorizations of vulnerability and paternalism operated. She argues that in Hungary by the late 1970s former socialist state policies created paradigms in which women were conceptualized only in terms of motherhood, and social welfare allocations were viewed as linked primarily to motherhood. These conceptualizations created resistance to social welfare.

The residential schooling system, like social welfare, is now contested in part because of what it represents. For some it is a reminder of condescending state policies, and for others it is an institution in which the state sought to promote affirmative action measures and social mobility for indigenous Siberians. Haney's (1999) work set in Hungary helps sort out the shifting attitudes toward socialist institutions and social welfare practices. Haney makes a compelling case for how a new type of "need" has emerged in the market economy, in which in the 1990s social welfare has come to be linked to class instead of to motherhood or ethnicity. Haney writes that with welfare reform in Hungary in the 1990s, "the [new] focus on individual need gave rise to a preoccupation with individual defect; the materialization of need led to the pathologizing of the welfare client" (1999: 172). As in Hungary earlier, where women were eligible for social benefits on the basis of assumed inherent maternal responsibilities, in the Soviet era indigenous Siberians as a group were eligible for social benefits on the basis of their assumed inherent characteristics. The Evenki, for instance, were considered to be handicapped by a heritage of reindeer herding that had defined them as seminomadic and rooted in a system of knowledge that was closely allied with subsistence practices and land, rather than book knowledge. For both categories of people—mothers and indigenous peoples—the state benefits had been widely naturalized; in the late socialist systems there was a widespread sense of entitlement to the benefits that were designated for each group. With the rise of neoliberal economics in Russia in the 1990s, however, a stigma became attached to those receiving benefits or attending the residential schooling. "Need" came to be defined as a sign of weakness or an indication of an inability to adapt to the new social conditions in which class schisms were emerging.

While the difference in the tenor of accounts from elderly Evenk women and younger women may merely reflect the nature of shifting perspectives as people age (see Kan 1989), I argue that younger women's positionality is distinctly different because the implications of being in "need" are changing.[2] While in the late Soviet period and into the early 1990s, Evenki could make claims to resources based on minority entitlements as indigenous peoples, much in the same way Hungarian women could make claims based on motherhood, by the mid-1990s this had changed. The pressures of the market economy—including austerity measures demanded by the International Monetary Fund and the World Bank—and the growing discourse of individualism as superior to collectivism were influencing regional priorities as well as popular opinion among young people. Instead of being viewed as promoting ethnic affirmative action ideals, in the 1990s the residential school was increasingly viewed as a place serving marginalized, or struggling families, those who could not "make it" on their own.

Haney's point, that the conceptualization of "need" shifted in post-socialist contexts from one based in a group category (motherhood or ethnic identity) to one based on marginality, is a useful way to think about the relationship of a younger generation of Evenk women to the residential school. Young women's accounts reflect two general positions around association with the residential school. Generally, those like Zhenia and Lena who found it necessary to draw on the residential school as a resource spoke of the institution in instrumentalist terms of how it satisfied their needs. Those who were more financially stable with extensive social networks, like Oksana and Tamara, invoked a discourse of individualism to vilify the residential school. From the second perspective, to be in need is not to be successful. This binary framework for understanding young women's perspectives is also intersected, however, by a range of factors that complicate such a clean division. For instance, close affiliation with a sense of indigenous identity was a factor for some of the women choosing to send children to study at the residential school.

In general, the complex historical relations between the Soviet state and indigenous peoples belie a simple analysis of unidirectional oppression. I suggest it is more productive to consider the ways in which power was refracted in this community. In thinking about the residential school as a site where ideas about "need" were being negotiated, it is instructive to consider how differential positionings took shape. For instance, while Zhenia, Lena, Oksana, and Tamara share the experience of attending the residential school, their accounts reflect distinct subject positions of marginality, or conversely, relative privilege. Zhenia's and Lena's less critical perspectives on their time in the residential school were closely linked to their relative lack of material security. Typically women in their situation in the Evenk District were raising children without another adult or without the material and physical assistance of another person. Furthermore, like many women of similar material circumstances and with similar attitudes to the residential school, Zhenia and Lena lacked a broad social support network. They had family in distant villages but the cost of helicopter travel was prohibitive for frequent visits. These women were significantly more disempowered than some others who self-identified as Evenki, such as Oksana and Tamara. The more marginalized women tended to belong to the local, Illimpei (not Katanga) Evenki and marry classmates from the residential school. Their experience of the residential school was as a site of symbolic capital tying them to their Evenk identity but also providing them with material support. As women with little invested in the new market conditions, they found themselves especially threatened by change and the demands of a cash economy.

In contrast, Oksana's and Tamara's accounts reflect the sentiments of a group of young Evenk women who felt dissatisfied with the residential school system. These women viewed the school as having carefully groomed them and taught them few skills, while not preparing them for the "real" world. Both Oksana's and Tamara's accounts reflect a tension between the system that significantly molded them and cared for them and their resistance to this system as something oppressive. Positioning herself as successful, Oksana categorized herself as distinct from many other Evenki. Unlike them she was not "in need"; she could make it on her own.

Oksana's relative sense of resistance to and articulation of the power relations reproduced in the residential school can be clearly linked to her position in the community. As a person identifying as a Katanga Evenk, she maintained a certain amount of distance from the collective identity molded in the residential school. Evenki with roots in the Katanga region were keenly aware that many early Evenk intellectuals in Tura came from the Katanga region, and this internal stratification provided the basis for a worldview more allied with the prevailing power structure than necessarily with Evenki as a whole.

Those Evenk women who recognized themselves as Katanga Evenki often had familial links to the town and regional power structure and tended to intermarry with newcomers, especially Russians. Thus despite a residential school experience allying them solidly with an Evenk identity, they were also more likely than relatively marginal Evenk women to take an active part in the local power structures that were dominated by Russians. They were also likely to have a strong, varied network of family and friends built upon Evenk, Russian, local, and newcomer social ties.

Many new Evenk entrepreneurs like Tamara viewed the residential school as a holdover from Soviet times. They saw the new market reforms as a release from the confines of a system that marked them as a distinct group in need of special attention. As Tamara remarked to me in 1999 over a cup of coffee at a café in Krasnoiarsk, "It's just like that Abba song, 'Money, Money, Money' [at which point she rubbed her forefinger and thumb together]; with the market system, we are all the same and only making money matters." From this perspective, the market system seems to erase the ethnic lines reinforced by the residential school.

As examined in the following chapter, this erasure of ethnic difference is precisely the problem for Evenk intellectuals seeking to solidify Evenk interests. Class interests have made the creation of a consolidated Evenk identity politics difficult, and by the mid-1990s the market mentality focusing on self-realization emerged as a threat to realizing collective concerns.

Chapter 5

Inside the Residential School: Cultural Revitalization and the Leninist Program

> Earlier they were able to rely on references to building communism and the heroes thereof. . . . They just don't know what to teach without the Leninist program. . . . Today was Lenin's birthday, but teachers cannot use their familiar materials for marking this event. . . . People are just at a loss for the purpose of their teaching.
>
> —Educator in the Tura residential school, author's fieldnotes, April 22, 1994

> In education one is dealing with children in whom one has to inculcate certain habits of diligence, precision, poise (even physical poise), ability to concentrate on specific subjects, which cannot be acquired without the mechanical repetition of disciplined and methodical acts.
>
> —Antonio Gramsci, "Observations on the School: In Search of the Educational Principle"

When I first saw the Tura residential school in 1992, I thought it was some type of aging factory instead of a place where children lived and studied. Approaching the once robin-egg blue, L-shaped, wood and brick building, I wondered if it was about to be torn down. When I returned to Tura in 1993, the residential school building was in no better shape than it had been when I had first seen it a year earlier. On both floors of the building, many windows were cracked and a few were boarded up. Inside, the linoleum floors had heaved and left humps to stumble on in the dark hallways. The poor physical state of the building reflected the ambivalence of the regional administration toward the institution and the difficulty of financing repairs with the federal funding for education so reduced.

Despite the lagging federal support and despite the history of the school as a vehicle for assimilation, in the 1990s many Evenki continued to support this institution. They viewed it as a type of refuge, an ethnically based school (*natsional'naia shkola*) where they could expect some modicum of respect for indigenous Siberian cultural issues and space for establishing viable self-representation in a post-Soviet era. Furthermore, the residential school has remained central to a sense of Evenk identity for an older generation, partly because it has preserved elements of the familiar Soviet collective and the Soviet forms of order. For the older generation, these elements have anchored the Evenk community in a common experience.

My personal introduction to the school was part of this intimate tie that Evenk intellectuals felt to the institution. At the request of the Association of Peoples of the North, *Arun*, in 1993–94 I taught an English class in the residential school for several months. I became aware of how the younger generation of Evenki often felt alienated from the collective which the school embodied for the older generation. On the first day of class I began by calling out the names of students and asking them to introduce themselves. I taught two classes that met twice a week, grade seven and grade eleven. In the younger class we began with the alphabet, but in the upper-level class we quickly moved to conversational practice. The students especially wanted to discuss their favorite rock-and-roll bands, including Michael Jackson, Ace of Base, and Abba. No one mentioned a Russian or Soviet band as they practiced English adjectives to describe their favorite groups. Later that week many of my students were to take part in a talent show called *Star Tinaidzher* ("Star Teenager") in which they performed by lip-synching songs played by these same Western groups.

The students' fascination with Western rock-and-roll and lack of interest in Russian or post-Soviet contemporary music, let alone Evenk-language music, made sense considering what they knew of post-Soviet society; like the residential school itself, post-Soviet society was suffering from dilapidation. While the residential school, the very embodiment of the Soviet collective, crumbled around students, market imagery grew increasingly vibrant. For instance, in the classroom in which I taught, water dripped from the ceiling for nearly six weeks, leaving large, splashing puddles where it missed the bucket. In contrast to this disrepair, after classes students packed into the television area located in their dormitory common room, where they were miraculously transported into a glamorous world of the Hollywood soap opera *Santa Barbara* or the MTV videos broadcast nearly all day long.

The students in the residential school could be described in a multitude of ways, including in terms of ethnicity, favorite music, and economic status. One of the most prevalent ways in which they distinguished themselves was in terms of being either day students, literally "home" (*domashnie*), or boarding (*internatskie*) students. Those who came from villages where there was no school, or no school beyond the fourth grade, comprised the majority of boarders, but there were also orphans among them. The day students lived in Tura with their families but studied at the residential school.

Students could also be distinguished by ethnicity. There were Russian and indigenous Siberian students, predominantly Evenki, whose parents preferred to send their children to the residential school instead of to the town school attended by most students residing in Tura. While some of these students attended the residential school as day students because of scholastic or interpersonal conflicts at the town school, a sizable group of the Evenk day students attended the residential school because their parents openly thought it offered a more welcoming atmosphere for indigenous Siberian students. In 1994, of the 255 students, aged seven to eighteen who were attending the residential school, 65 were day students. Of the 255 students, 231 of them were identified as native (*korennye*) students by the Evenk District Department of Education. Most of the students were Evenki, but there were also a few Sakha and Kety students.

The Tura town school, located just a few minutes walk from the residential school, was primarily attended by Russians. While attendance

Figure 8. Residential school entrance with sign reading "Welcome," *Dobro pozhalovat'* (in Russian) and *ikeillu alatcheireiv* (in Evenk). Photo by Marliss Taylor, 1999.

was open to any resident of Tura, of the 882 pupils, only 62 were non-Russian in 1994. Generally, Russians and other non-native residents of Tura—Tadzhiks, Volga Germans, etc.—avoided sending children to the residential school and first enrolled students at the town school. It was generally believed, however, that the demands of course work there made it difficult for weaker students to succeed. As discussed later in this chapter, non-native students requiring remedial courses or extra attention were sometimes transferred to the residential school.

By 1998, the number of residential school students living at home with their parents or close relatives was increasing as Evenki like the Yoldogirs discussed in Chapter 2 moved into Tura from villages. In many cases families moved specifically because the municipal services like the village schools were being shut down because of a lack of government financing for staff and heating. In Tura many Evenk families and families with one Evenk parent, like the Labinkos and the Zubovs discussed in Chapter 2, sent their children to the residential school, even though they had the option of sending children to the town school. The parents of one student in my upper-level English class transferred her to the residential school for the last semester of her senior year; the student's Evenk mother explained to me that her daughter was being unfairly treated at the town school. Given that this student's father was not Russian, the parents very likely thought their daughter would have a better chance at being admitted to university when applying as a residential school graduate.

In discussion with Evenk parents, they often noted that their children just felt more comfortable in the residential school than in the town school. One woman explained: "Ours [village Evenki] try not to send kids to the town school. Turintsy are not so friendly toward us. I wouldn't send my kids to the town school. . . . The teachers, especially the ones who just arrived in Tura, even degrade kids sometimes." These types of responses perhaps reflect just as much about what went on in the residential school as what went on in the town school.

While in 1998 the curriculum at the residential school varied little from the town school curriculum, the general sensitivity to issues of Evenk identity was heightened. For instance, in addition to a range of standard high school classes, including Russian humanities courses and a class in computer skills, students at the residential school took classes in Evenk language and ethnography. They also had the option to take part in Evenk music and dance clubs. In addition to the curriculum, however, the composition of the staff at the residential school was also significant in drawing Evenki to study there. In 1998 nearly one-third of the personnel directly involved with the students were Evenk, while in the town school there were no Evenk teachers.

Social Stratification Inside-Out: Teachers and Staff

The composition of those employed by the residential school demonstrates some of the challenges to the school's role as a locus of contemporary Evenk identity politics. The overwhelming number of women employed in the institution was an indication of the ghetto status of the school from the perspective of the district administration controlling pay scales. The ghettoization of teaching as a "female" profession, noted for the Soviet Union as a whole (Lapidus 1978), was intensified in this post-Soviet setting that was stigmatized by the dominant Russian community. This situation was in marked contrast with the town school, where men taught history, geography, English, biology, computers, physics, and chemistry, in addition to the industrial arts and physical education classes.

In the 1990s teachers and staff of the residential school were predominantly women. In 1993–94 the staff was comprised of fifteen teachers, dormitory caregivers, a school director, bookkeeper, and support staff—including cafeteria, laundry, and cleaning personnel. There were only five men. The director and four male teachers—the industrial arts instructor, the physical education instructor, the itinerant history teacher who taught a few seminars for older students, and a music and dance teacher. The Evenk director only served from 1993–94, however, before his post was relinquished in 1995 to a long-time resident Ukrainian woman. (As discussed later in this chapter, she had strong ideas on how to shift the direction of the institution.)

In terms of ethnic composition, Evenki only taught at the residential school. Evenki and other indigenous Siberians comprised nearly 50 percent of the staff, including teachers, caregivers, and other personnel. In 1993–94 there were seven Evenk teachers, two of whom taught art, one history, one Evenk language, one industrial arts, and two general education for elementary classes (grades one to six). By 1998 there was an additional indigenous staff person, a woman with Sakha and Evenk heritage who was teaching cultural history. The doctor and dentist on the staff also identified themselves as Evenki. Furthermore, several indigenous women were employed in less skilled labor at the school—washing floors, cleaning and mending laundry, working as caregivers, and staffing the library. The teaching staff at the school also included, however, several Russian women who were often unfamiliar with or antagonistic toward Evenk cultural heritage. These women generally taught science, math, and Russian literature.

Among the teachers and staff, there were other schisms in addition to gender and ethnicity. A predominant schism was related to the degree to which teachers viewed themselves as a permanent part of the Tura community. This component of local identity was significant beyond the residential school as well. As discussed in Chapter 2, the categories of "newcomers" and "locals" had a salience in this town, as in others in the North in Russia. This division was reproduced in the residential school; newcomer teachers often pined for the urban centers of St. Petersburg and Moscow and made regular reference to the "backwardness" of Tura and its population. The newcomers maintained tight links with kin and friends living in urban centers in the south. These social ties resulted in significant material differences and opportunities for newcomer teachers, particularly in terms of education for their offspring. In the 1990s newcomer teachers could afford to send children for higher education to Moscow and St. Petersburg by arranging for them to live with relatives or friends. In contrast, local teachers were rarely able to afford to support their offspring as students in the large urban centers.

The local teachers, both Russians and Evenki, were more wedded to their locale than were the newcomer teachers. They rarely vacationed in the large urban centers and instead spent time camping in the surrounding taiga or visiting relatives in Evenk District villages. While the local teachers had been educated in the urban centers of Moscow, Leningrad (St. Petersburg), Krasnoiarsk and Irkutsk, they had grown up in the Evenk District. Their allegiances, network of social support, and familial ties were rooted in the surrounding area. Furthermore, unlike the newcomer teachers, the local teachers often had spent some years living or teaching in the Evenk District villages. For instance, the Evenk art teachers, history teacher, and language teacher all had grown up or taught for several years in villages from which many of their students came. In a very real sense, they were more closely allied with the residential school collective than were the newcomer teachers. It was common for the local teachers to invoke students' kin ties during lessons; in one case the Evenk language teacher reminded a student to pay more attention because the student's uncle had written the poem under discussion.

Labor Relations and the Collective

Throughout the 1990s, the sense of a "collective" was consciously inculcated in students even though the adjective "Soviet" was no longer used. Perhaps one of the most emblematic aspects of the disciplined collective in school culture was reflected in how labor was delegated. While minor repairs in the residential school were generally carried out by the industrial arts teacher and major repairs by the town department of sanitation and repairs (*kommunal'noe khoziaistvo—"komunkhoz"* for short), students were responsible for mopping the hallways of the classroom area and the dormitory. Each class was responsible for one week of mopping, and each month the class completing the best work was recognized. Until 1993, there were also weekly Saturday sessions called *subbotniki* in which the whole school community took part in general repairs around the school and in picking up garbage in the yard.[1] This type of volunteer communal work was incorporated into the obligation each person had as a student or employee, whether working at the town newspaper, the town hall, or the local oil exploration outfit.

From early 1993 the school no longer arranged collective work sessions, and instead students were sometimes hired by the school or by teachers to do specific tasks at the residential school. Two of the students I came to know were often busy mopping teachers' classrooms and wiping off blackboards after school was out at 4 P.M. They made a pittance, but they were happy for the rare source of pocket money. Unlike most other students, who came from outlying villages and returned there for winter and summer vacation, these students were orphans and could not depend on relatives to help them out; there were twenty-five orphans at the school in 1993. These two twelve-year-old girls spent most of their meager savings on candy, but they were also saving for shiny synthetic leggings (*losiny*), which adolescent girls in Tura often wore under skirts in the mid-1990s.

Discipline, Punishment, and the Collective in a New Era

For a younger generation, the sense of a collective valued by the older generation of Evenki, and the forms of discipline embodied in it, directly clashed with the growing emphasis on individual rights and individualism portrayed in the Russian media. Popular media and songs have constantly reflected this conflict between collective and individualistic identities; one song in particular, "It's My Life" by the Swedish band Ace of Base, was so popular that children of all ages were memorizing the English lyrics and double-checking the translation with me whenever they had a chance. The tune could be heard booming from dormitory rooms and being sung by groups of students between classes. The chorus includes the following words: "It's my life. I'll do what I want to do. Don't bother me. It's my life."

Until the early 1990s, the collective at the residential school was defined in a number of concrete ways. There were required courses in Communist philosophy and history, and attendance was required at Komsomol-organized events. There were also standard-issue uniforms consisting of blue pants and white shirt for boys and blue skirt and white blouse and pinafore for girls. By 1992, however, these outward manifestations of the collective had almost completely disappeared. In fact, the "lack of discipline" in the society that accompanied the shift from compulsory behavior and appearance had become a central concern of many community members reflecting on changes since Perestroika. By the mid-1990s, the residential school teachers often complained of the students' "lack of discipline," and they lamented the lack of regimen and the "proper" conduct of students.

Despite the widespread concurrence that discipline had waned since Perestroika, in significant ways subtle attempts persisted to maintain discipline and thereby maintain elements of the former collective in the residential school. These surfaced at several points during my tenure in the residential school, and one of the most vivid instances occurred during one of my English lessons. I was teaching a group of tenth graders when two school nurses attired in white with gloved hands and white-masked faces burst into the room and approached the five students. As the students resisted the nurses' efforts by leaning away in their seats, the nurses efficiently combed through each student's hair and sought out head lice. One student particularly protested the nurses' actions, explaining that she was a day student and so should not be subjected to the medical procedures standard for the boarders at the residential school. The nurses all but ignored the protests and forcefully completed their examination. When they were gone, students complained loudly among themselves about the residential school and the way it treated them like animals.

In addition to nurses "medicalizing" students (see Ehrenreich and Ehrenreich 1987) and thereby emphasizing their position as objects of state control to be disciplined, caregivers (*vospitateli*) often belittled students for having become objects of state control.[2] Thus in the residential school students were simultaneously subject to the remnants of compulsory, medicalizing practices of a socialist collective and to the antagonism of caregivers critical of collective upbringing. As caregivers, staff members were in charge of overseeing daily life in the dormitory. This involved everything from getting children up and dressed in the morning to preparing them for bed to coordinating the daily upkeep of the students' rooms to arranging for occasional excursions to the museum to gathering the children for their weekly visit to the town sauna. In short, they played a significant role in the daily life of the boarders at the residential school.

Some caregivers had empathy for the children. In spring 1994, when I visited the dormitory for children aged six to twelve, the caregiver there, Veronika, explained to me that of the eighteen children who were in her care, only ten were "officially orphans." Veronika was outraged that, of these "orphans," two children's parents had disowned them and the other six children had parents who only occasionally visited them.

Caregivers like Veronika related how sorry they felt for these children, and during my regular visits I witnessed the care Veronika and one or two others took to make the setting more appealing. The rooms occupied by four small beds were spartan but neatly maintained, with curtains hung on the window and children's drawings affixed to the wall. In the playroom where children also sometimes waited turns to be "quartzed," or stand before a sunlamp in the dark winter months, wallpaper displaying Disney figures of Goofy and Donald Duck vied for attention with children's watercolor depictions of tents and reindeer; the latter were inspired by a recent visit to the museum.

Frequently, however, children were the objects of the anger of employees' who felt overworked and underpaid. Some caregivers were antagonistic toward these children and viewed them as "pathetic wards of the state," irrespective of their ethnic background. As one caregiver told me in a voice wavering with resentment: "One girl's parents are Ukrainian, her mother is a drunk and left her father. The father lives here in Tura and lives well—with a *kottedzh*, a private sauna, and who knows what else, but he leaves his daughter here in the residential school while he works three jobs." On another occasion the same caregiver was merciless in chastising a young boy who had recently arrived in the residential school following the death of both of his parents. The caregiver yelled at him that his parents had died because they were drunks and then asked him why he was repeating a year in school.

When I questioned this caregiver about her mean attack on the boy, she blamed her angry feelings on the pressures of her job caused by cutbacks. She explained that the dormitories were chronically understaffed in 1994; for the six- to twelve-year-old age group there were "two-and-one-half" staff, while in 1993 there had been "four-and-one-half" staff. With fewer than three people, the caregivers were responsible for covering three shifts, seven days a week, except on Sundays when the caregiving was an all-day responsibility. According to the weekday schedule posted in the dormitory, the following routine was carried out:

Morning duty, 6–8 A.M.
Children to be awakened, washed, dressed, and sent off to breakfast.
Afternoon duty, 3:30–5 P.M.
Children to be prepared to go out to play, supervised while they complete homework or take part in after school clubs, and gathered to attend dinner.
Night duty, 7:30 P.M.–6 A.M.
Children to be prepared for bed; caregiver to rest in an adjoining room.

Besides being severely overworked, the caregivers were poorly and irregularly paid because of shortages of money in the local bank. The lack of accountability in the school administration complicated matters.

In 1992, for instance, the woman who had served as the director of the residential school for three years was terminated because she was suspected of embezzling funds.[3] Several caregivers explained that they resented caring for others' children when no one cared for theirs and they could not even count on their paychecks being paid regularly. Many caregivers expressed the opinion that the residential school was a special service illogically provided for irresponsible or, at the very least, undeserving parents. As among the young women discussed in the previous chapter, a frequent topic of debate among caregivers was the idea of "need" and the state's responsibility to provide for both Evenki and nonnative children.

Ethnicity was not necessarily a determination of how staff placed themselves within the power relations perpetuated within the system. I observed over the months both native and Russian staff members who were genuinely interested in the children's welfare. This was expressed most often in tones of voice, or an extra attempt to be tender with a child. Still, these individual efforts to support students had to compete with the alienating aspects of the institution that sometimes also permitted cruelty on the part of staff.

One dark April morning in 1995, I took up an invitation to join an Evenk caregiver employed in the special education division of the residential school. Maksim was one of the very few popular caregivers and students bestowed him with the nickname "Papa Maks." He was particularly patient with these students, who suffered from a wide range of mental disabilities, but predominantly from fetal alcohol syndrome.[4] Unlike other caregivers, Maksim loved to joke around with the children.

I met Maksim just before 7 A.M. for the morning wake-up call for young students aged eight to twelve. We made our way to the dormitory for the special education students located across the muddy path from the main residential school. From the outside it appeared to be a condemned building; the windows were boarded up and the main entrance was blocked off. The primary entrance had been temporarily tacked onto the back of the building for more than three years.

When we arrived at the room labeled "bedroom six," all twelve of the boys were still asleep. I followed Maksim into the room and peered around the criss-crossed clothesline laden with green-and-black-checked Chinese-manufactured shirts, rugged blue denim pants, and undershirts. I noticed that all but one of the sleeping boys looked indigenous, with dark features and dark hair; one boy was fair with blond hair. I stood by the door as Maksim walked from bed to bed, cheerily calling out, "Time to get up!" (*Pora vstavat'!*). A few boys opened their eyes on the first call. By the second call, most of them rolled out of bed; one of them pulled a cardboard box from under his bed and stroked two tiny

Figure 9. "Papa Maks" graffiti and students. Photo by the author, 1998.

kittens. Maksim gently reminded the boy that the kittens needed water. The next few minutes were occupied by anxious scrambles for stray socks and hurried splashes of water poured into cupped hands from a bucket, the only source of water in the room.

Then the students hurried out into the institutional green hallway to join others emerging for the morning exercises. The students lined up in rigid single-file lines, as if in a military formation, to undergo five minutes of morning calisthenics. The military atmosphere, paralleled in the historical accounts about regimen in schooling that some older Evenk women shared with me (see Chapter 6), was compounded by a booming woman caregiver's voice scolding students to hurry to breakfast. Downstairs at breakfast, which consisted of noodles served in warm milk and a cup of tea, a Russian caregiver leaned over to me and angrily confided, "You can't expect much from these slant-eyed ones. They don't have much upstairs to begin with." While some caregivers truly sought to nurture children and in turn were viewed as surrogate parent figures, a tone of racist interaction between caregivers and children was all too common in the daily life of the residential school in the 1990s.

Soviet Promises, Russifying Reality, and Language Revitalization

In the 1990s the residential school came to embody a contested legacy of extensive state support for the indigenous community. In 1998 I witnessed a controversy in the residential school that particularly underscores this situation and points to how some in the Evenk community were invested in the school. As the local education budget shrank, the Ukrainian school principal targeted the very defining features of the school as those to be discontinued. She sought to cut the Evenk music and dance program and to reduce the Evenk ethnography and language programs from five course hours per week to just three. This and other attacks on what many viewed as crucial elements of an ethnically based, or *natsional'naia* school incensed the president of the Association of Peoples of the North, *Arun*. In an article published in the town newspaper, she spoke out against the trend toward de-emphasizing the original mandate of the residential school as an institution specifically designed for educating indigenous Siberians:

> Ideal conditions should be created both at home and at school for spiritual revitalization, ethnic consciousness and self-worth, and the preservation of our native language. For these aims to be satisfied, the residential school *must* be an ethnically based school. We used to have such a school in the district—the Tura residential school (*Turinskaia sredniaia shkola-internat*). In 1971 an amazing, unique experiment was initiated and as a result of these efforts Evenkiia became

the first autonomous district where a native language was taught as a regular subject. But we do not value what we already have. (Pikunova 1998: 9)

In that same year, Evenk language and culture teachers met to consider revising the Evenk language program. In the course of discussion they also expressed their dissatisfaction with the shifting direction the school seemed to be taking. The Evenk District Department of Education was supporting the principal in her decision to cut back in Evenk language and cultural programming. The teachers argued, however, that they needed a massive infusion of resources and rethinking of the curriculum. Students continued to sign up for classes, but they were having difficulty with texts written for children with some knowledge of the Evenk language. Only a few students had enough familiarity with the Evenk language to excel in the program of study; most students were fluent in Russian and viewed Evenk as a "foreign" language, even if their grandparents still conversed in Evenk.

The teachers were frustrated because the curriculum needed updating, and had needed it for years now, to reflect the predominant new type of student that identified as Evenk but lacked even conversational ability in the Evenk language. As one teacher explained: "It is hard to teach the children who don't know the language. You end up teaching Russian grammar in order to teach Evenk. . . . Also, there are a range of students now. . . . Some, especially Russian students, are virtually imbeciles." Another chimed in, "Yes, and Evenk parents don't even speak in the native language at home any more."

The nature of the school began changing as the resources tightened throughout the 1990s and local administration was no longer bound by federal commitments to support programs for indigenous populations. While earlier the official mission of the school had been to educate indigenous students, by the early 1990s it increasingly took on remedial Russian students as well. The Evenk language and culture teachers were disheartened that their efforts to teach were hampered by having to contend with Russian remedial students. Their increasing presence in the school shifted the classroom tone. As one teacher explained at the same gathering mentioned above, the school was filling up with students who had failed out of the town school; the residential school was gaining the reputation as "the school for failures and . . . the school for the children of Russian freeloaders." Another teacher described the attitudes among many of these Russian remedial students as "arrogant and cheeky." Yet another teacher explained that students from the town school came to the residential school with the attitude that seemed to say "We're entitled, we're better [than Evenk students]." One of the senior teachers summarized the general feeling among the teachers, saying, "A new type of Russification is going on here . . . and our school is no longer a school for native children."

Given the history of the residential school as a site for Sovietization and assimilation, it may seem curious that there was so much support among Evenk teachers for the institution as a place for encouraging Evenk cultural identity. The above discussion reflects, however, that in the late Soviet period and early years of the Russian Federation the residential school became a site for the revitalization of indigenous Siberian cultural practices. Instead of focusing on the early role of the residential school as a site for assimilation, Evenk staff were instead lamenting that in the late 1990s the school, and by extension indigenous demands for a pedagogy centered around native concerns, was being sidelined by predominantly Russian regional administrators. From the perspective of these teachers, in the late Soviet period and up to the mid-1990s there had been resources to specifically promote the interests of native peoples. While the residential school continued to be organized according to Russian systems of knowledge and discipline in the 1990s, there was official support for maintaining a setting in which Evenk cultural practices could be at least respected.

Evenk language classes began being taught as early as the 1970s, and in the late 1980s and early 1990s the local Institute for Teacher Development (*institut usovershenstvovaniia uchitelei*) created a wide range of materials for use in newly designed Evenk ethnography and culture courses. Furthermore, the school was facilitating educational opportunity for Evenk students who often went on from there to vocational training as veterinary assistants, day-care workers, and nurses' aides or to academic training to return to the area as teachers. In the early 1990s, as federal government control of education was relinquished to more local control, many Evenk intellectuals had hoped for increased Evenk presence in the administration of the residential school. In 1993–94, an Evenk director was appointed for the first time. Evenk reformers hoped that the residential school, which had officially promoted the interests of native peoples in the Soviet era, could continue in the 1990s to play a central role in creating educational opportunity and in sustaining Evenk traditional culture. Instead, by the late 1990s the Evenk District Department of Education was seeking to save money by reducing funding for the residential school, starting with programs related to Evenk language and culture.[5] As in the late 1920s, the residential school was again at the center of local debates about Evenk representation and community interests and about the role of government in protecting and furthering Evenk cultural and political rights.

Chapter 6
Taiga Kids, Incubator Kids, and Intellectuals

> "The October Revolution saved the small peoples [of the North] from physical extinction!"—these words resounded in the ears of our party workers. "It brought happiness and enlightenment! We lived in poverty and ignorance, in primitive ways and in darkness. We did not even have such words as club, school, and culture!" (with sarcasm).
>
> —Alitet Nemtushkin, Evenk author, "Severed Song"

> Evenki—a unique people who, because of following their reindeer, occupy land from the Enisei River to Sakhalin Island—have been divided by false borders, divided as subjects of the Russian Federation. . . . If we all unified, we would be able to preserve our uniqueness. Territorial unification is unrealistic, . . . but we can actually establish . . . an information network, . . . open our own cultural centers, exchange experience and set up ethnically based schools and organs of self-government. If we succeed in unifying, it will greatly raise the self-consciousness of the people.
>
> —Andrei Isakov, Evenk educator and activist, cited in Pikunova, "Not What Your People Can Do for You, But What You Can Do for Your People"

As I was entering the residential school in Tura one day in 1992 a young boy ran down the hallway after another boy and taunted him, yelling "taiga kid!" (*taiezhnyi*). On another occasion during a school picnic, the same term was invoked by teachers in praise of an Evenk student who was particularly adept at lighting a campfire. Students at the residential school also were sometimes derisively referred to as "incubator kids" (*inkubatorskie*) by those who were not studying there. The general term used by the Evenk community, however, was simply "residential schoolers" (*internatskie*). These various terms heard in reference to those attending the residential school turned my attention to the complex place the school occupied in the local imagination. The residential school encapsulated the experience of three generations of Evenki and their relationship to the nation-state, but it was also emblematic of a shifting collective identity. What was perhaps most striking was how over the 1990s the residential school became a central focus for Evenk intellectuals' attempts to safeguard both cultural practices and Soviet era benefits for the native community.

The previous chapter discussed the context of daily life in the residential school and how teachers and other Evenk intellectuals sought to resist the demise of the school as an ethnically based school providing opportunities for social mobility. This chapter turns to consider the ways in which Evenk intellectuals have themselves been constituted, and how this has influenced how they were reenvisioning curricula in the 1990s. The residential school in Tura was the site of an intricate remaking of Evenk identities in the 1990s and Evenk intellectuals were engaged in a range of divergent approaches to consolidating Evenk identities.

A critical aspect of the Soviet identity inculcated in generations of indigenous Siberians through residential schooling involved a specific version of the modernization myth propelling industrialization and acculturation of indigenous peoples throughout the world. While this imposition of control was intended to make subjects in the Soviet state's image, it was not a monolithic control; there were resistances to it during

Figure 10. After school by the Nizhniaia Tunguska River. Photo by the author, 1995.

the Soviet era and there have been reappropriations of former state instruments, such as the residential school, in post-Soviet Russia. Evenk intellectuals in the 1990s largely continued to represent the Soviet era as a time of opportunity for Evenki; even the Soviet era language of "liberation" (*osvobozhdenie*) and "enlightenment" (*prosveshchenie*) continued to be invoked. This chapter examines discourses about identity and power that were being invoked by Evenk intellectuals in the 1990s, often in the context of residential schooling.

The subject of intellectuals and their role in crafting and opposing structures of power has been widely written about (see, for example, Gramsci 1971; Arendt 1966; Warren 1998). Instead of a Gramscian model of intellectuals as set apart from the populace and instrumental in perpetuating a certain cultural hegemony, I see intellectuals in post-Soviet Russia as producers of authoritative knowledge in a wide range of forms. Like Warren (1998: 26), I consider intellectuals to include elders respected by a community—leaders, teachers, healers/health practitioners, and officials. Intellectuals (*intelligentsiia*) in the Evenk District were a group of people who often self-consciously carried out their roles as interlocutors with a larger populace through teaching, writing, speaking, performing, or public service. Trained within Soviet institutional settings, Evenk intellectuals were tentatively critical of the former society and government structures, but they frequently defended the system that had allowed reindeer herders to join the ranks of Soviet politicians, academics, and professionals.

In 1994 there were seventy Evenki and several non-Evenki in Tura who listed themselves as members of the Association of Peoples of the North, Arun.[1] The list was not equivalent to a complete list of native intellectuals because some people chose to remain unaffiliated with what they saw as a special interest political organization. Arun membership did reflect, however, the broad range of native intellectuals—performers, teachers, curators, musicians, administrators, nurses, and academics—both in Tura and in the other two district branches of Arun, in Baikit and Vanavara. While the organization was open to all, in fact, few people who were employed in manual labor or reindeer herding, like Zhenia discussed in Chapter 4 or the Yoldogirs discussed in Chapter 2, were members of the organization. Those Evenki who were struggling to make ends meet, however, did appeal to Arun when they needed a grant for food or emergency transportation, as indicated by the funeral arrangements that were described in Chapter 1. In this way Arun was a sort of mutual aid society, but its main goal was to represent the interests of the native population to district and local administrations.

How a group represents itself through so-called "markers of authenticity" becomes especially important when the group has little access to economic and political power (Conklin 1997; Fischer and Brown 1996). In the 1990s, *Arun* as an organization, and Evenk intellectuals more generally, were involved in debates over how best to represent Evenk interests. Some argued that these would be safeguarded through a Soviet collective identity and structures of the former Soviet system, while others focused more on revitalization of specifically Evenk cultural practices. Markers of identity were critical as Evenk intellectuals, like other indigenous Siberians, were seeking to mobilize communities in the context of shifting political and economic access following the fall of the Soviet Union. In the case of Siberia, the rapid industrialization of the North, including oil and gas industries and the intrusive Baikal-Amur Railway (BAM) that developed in the late 1960s and into the present, took a high toll on indigenous Siberian subsistence practices (see Sangi 1988; Rytkheu 1988; Aipin 1989; Anderson 1991).[2] Similarly, in the Evenk District in the late 1980s a proposed hydroelectric dam would have flooded vast regions being used for reindeer herding and subsistence hunting and fishing, but the plan was eventually retracted. Throughout the 1990s the threat to natural resources was emerging in a different form as the Russian government continued to consider plans for privatizing land. Access to land for subsistence practices was also under question as multinational oil conglomerates moved toward investment in developing oil drilling in the southern area of the Evenk District. In this context the residential school became a central site for discussing what shape the collective identity of Evenki should take and how Evenk children could receive an education that would be most practical for them and the community.[3]

In the 1990s, as competition for former government resources grew, Evenk intellectuals often appropriated essentialized concepts that were used by the state to define indigenous Siberians in a Soviet era. In particular, imagery drawn from former dominant Soviet ideas of "tradition" and "modernity" was often invoked in Evenk intellectuals' discourse. The first part of this chapter explores how concepts of "modern" and "traditional" framed how indigenous Siberian intellectuals were constituted in the nearly seventy years of the Soviet era. The second part of the chapter turns to consider contemporary efforts by Evenk intellectuals to mobilize constituents and shape Evenk identities.

Tradition, Modernity, and Education

During the 1990s the residential school played a key role as the stage for discussions of "authentic" Evenk identity. One important reason was that many Evenk intellectuals were invested in the socialist symbolic capital embodied in the school. As discussed in previous chapters, the residential school had enabled two generations of Evenki to experience radical social mobility within Soviet society; as a result, perhaps, among indigenous Siberians the Evenki had one of the highest levels of Communist Party membership in the late Soviet era.[4] Education leading to social mobility for indigenous Siberians acted as a critical aspect of establishing a sense of belonging to the larger, "modern" society. As Benedict Anderson has written about the influence of the Dutch school system on "Indonesians" (1983: 111):

> From all over the vast colony . . . the tender pilgrims made their inward, upward way, meeting fellow-pilgrims from different . . . villages in primary school; from different ethnolinguistic groups in middle-school; and from every part of the realm in the tertiary institutions of the capital. . . . They knew . . . that all these journeyings derived their "sense" from the capital, in effect explaining why "we" are "here" "together." . . . Their common experience . . . gave the maps of the colony which they studied . . . a territorially-specific imagined reality. (1983: 111)

In the Soviet era (and in the 1990s to some extent) students could ascend from primary school to high school and finally on to universities in the widely esteemed metropole cities of Moscow and Leningrad. This trajectory was that of most indigenous Siberian intellectuals, including Evenki, and this "pilgrimage" forged a common sense of imbibing power from a central cache. Not all would go on to higher education, but this scenario of the path to the European centers was firmly part of a collective Soviet and Evenk consciousness about what it was to be modern.[5]

It would be inaccurate to label the Soviet project simply a "colonial" one parallel to the Dutch presence in Indonesia; but similar ideas of displacing "tradition" with "modernity" did propel extensive social change among indigenous Siberians in the aftermath of the 1917 Russian Revolution (see Grant 1995a: 68–89; Toer 1982 and 1996). Although some scholars (see Giddens 1990: 175–77) claim that "modernity" is distinctively "Western," in fact, many of the characteristics named as unique to the West also apply to the Soviet version of modernity established in the early twentieth century in central Siberia. The same "institutionalization of doubt" and "globalizing tendencies . . . [connecting] individuals to large-scale systems" (Giddens 1990: 177) were key elements of Soviet socialist society. These same processes, I argue, gripped the imagination of some Evenki in the 1920s and later and drew them to take part in the Soviet project, not as passive participants but as active agents in the transformation of social life in the North.

In the daily functioning of the Tura residential school in the 1990s, there were countless examples of how the Soviet system had neatly envisioned the future for indigenous Siberians. This was a system in which many people took pride, in a manner similar to what scholars have found among other marginalized populations in formerly socialist societies undergoing radical transformation (Dunn 1990; Haney 1999; Berdahl 1999). Especially in retrospect, as market pressures atomized communities and state supports faltered, a significant portion of people spoke nostalgically of having belonged to a productive, forward-looking collective. This earnest, production-oriented patriotism shared by many was distilled in a mural decorating the walls of the main assembly room in the Tura residential school in the 1990s. The walls were painted with stylized figures with Asiatic features dressed in garb reminiscent of ideal professions of the early Soviet society—those of pilots, doctors, engineers, and teachers—those professions viewed as integral to building a new society. Reindeer herders were also included in the imagery, in line with other "ideal proletarians." Their task was depicted as being as crucial to building socialism as the tasks of these "ideal" professionals were. From this perspective herding was not just part of daily subsistence, it was part of contributing to Soviet society.

The decoration on the walls quintessentially represented the supposed enfranchisement of Evenki and other indigenous Siberians as participants in modern Soviet society, one that revolved around production

Figure 11. Residential school mural of happy proletarians. Photo by the author, 1993.

and productive labor. While such imagery was often mocked by children in the school in the 1990s, this mural painted in the 1980s and other similar socialist realist imagery found on walls around town were not painted over. Those with firm allegiances to socialist principles evidently believed that these images embodied principles of modernity that they continued to find meaningful.

This imagery posing Evenki as "ideal proletarians" gainfully employed in professions viewed as crucial to modern Soviet society was countered by another prevalent theme allied with the idea of "tradition" (see Grant 1995b). In the school setting and beyond, Evenki were still seen as "children of nature" and associated with a timeless past (compare with Fabian 1983). By framing Evenki as "children" untarnished by "culture," this discourse insinuated that Evenki differed from Russians by being somehow locked in time, impervious to historical transformations. In this way indigenous Siberian cultural practices were essentialized and placed at the bottom of an evolutionary continuum with ever-progressing European society at the pinnacle. This idea of Evenki as "children of nature" is reflected in a song that was an essential part of the repertoire for public festive occasions in the regional center of Tura in the 1990s; the chorus follows:

My father is a reindeer herder	*Moi otets—olenevod*
On a clear autumn day	*V iasnyi den' osennii*
Even from far away	*Dazhe izdaleka,*
He will find his way	*On naidet svoi put'*
	—Belianin (1990)

In fact, these days most Evenki are not directly involved in reindeer herding. The intensive government efforts to settle Evenki in towns and villages beginning after World War II meant that by 1986 there were only forty households consisting of 145 Evenki engaged in reindeer herding, hunting, and fishing as a primary means of subsistence in the Evenk District (Amosov 1998: 85). By the late 1990s, the number of people engaged in these subsistence practices as a means of making a living had fallen by half.[6] Nevertheless, reindeer herding carried a symbolic weight among town Evenki, and an image of herding was central to local intellectuals' discourses about what it was to be Evenki.

All across Russia today local intellectuals are becoming increasingly active in defining the discourses around belonging to communities. Some have postulated that given the lack of democratic traditions in Russia, intellectuals have often played a critical role in its history. Similarly, in the dispersed regions of Russia, intellectuals play a unique role today as new political possibilities create space for neo-traditional discourse (Drobizheva 1996: 3).[7] As Evenk intellectuals have become involved in remaking identities in this post-Soviet period, they have often invoked a dialectic of the "modern" and the "traditional." The dialectic of "traditional" and "modern," a common underlying theme in Soviet and post-Soviet social science (see Pika and Prokhorov 1996), that is readily recognized by the general public, has been a driving force justifying the Soviet state and the Soviet project in the North. As market forces permeated the Evenk community in Tura in the 1990s, however, this binary model represented through images of "ideal proletarians" and "children of nature" was increasingly challenged by images of Disney, MTV, and discotheque chic occupying the imaginations of younger people.

Evenk intellectuals often countered these images of globalizing forces by invoking the Soviet discourses, the ones that were meant to signify Evenk belonging to a Soviet collective. In this way their actions were similar to the Islamic fundamentalists that Aiwa Ong (1990) describes, who relied on impositions of conservative controls over women's sexuality in an attempt to resist the threatening forces of a global economy. Both the Evenki and the Islamic fundamentalists were drawing on "tradition" as a means of symbolically positioning themselves apart from global forces. Especially as state control over natural resources loosened and access to these resources became more contested, Evenk intellectuals grappled with new types of collective identity that could be used to inculcate youth and thereby solidify a power base. It is not coincidental that, given its deep roots as a site for the transformation of identities in the North, the residential school served as an important vehicle for this purpose. The following section further explores how a "Soviet" sense of belonging equated with a move from "traditional" to "modern" became firmly rooted in the consciousness of many Evenki through the disciplining of their bodies in the school setting.

"Skins," School, and Dressing for Modernity

The contemporary sense of the "collective" was molded over time and was at different points enforced by various Soviet government practices, but the tension between the "traditional" and the "modern" remained central. This was perpetuated in a number of ways, including through schooling practices. As Foucault (1978) and others following him have emphasized (see, for example, Constable 1997; Lomawaima 1993), a fundamental element of the molding and controlling of subjected peoples—be it in prisons, hospitals, household labor, or schools—is the disciplining of bodies.

For women in particular, clothing emerges as an important theme in narratives reflecting government efforts to "modernize" Evenki. As Carol Hendrickson also indicates in her work on the Maya practice of wearing huipil to mark Maya identity, clothing can play an instrumental role as a "socializing agent" that can be tracked throughout the life cycle (1995: 99). In the case of several Evenk women I came to know, they recalled their first encounters with authority figures seeking to re-dress them in the state's image of civilized students; these memories were associated with their early schooling.

Elderly Evenk women's narratives often reflect proscriptions on what could be worn and proscriptions on movement, not unlike those described by Tsianina Lomawaima in her work (1993) on the historical setting of a Native American residential school. Lomawaima explores the power relations of residential schooling by focusing on bloomers, or undergarments, as a theme in the undercurrent of resistance to the Euro-American morality embodied in school practices. Like the Native American women forced to wear bloomers, indigenous Siberians' bodies were also disciplined through a Eurocentric dress code. Especially in the early Soviet period, boys and girls in the residential school were required to crop their hair, march in military-like formation, and wear European-style clothing consisting of skirts and blouses, and felt boots in the winter.

Discussions of clothing in particular reflect the Soviet attempt to control Evenki through ideas about propriety that juxtaposed attitudes about "tradition" and "modernity." For instance, as Galina Petrovna [GP], an elderly Evenk woman, and her thirty-five-year-old daughter Nadia [N] explained to me [AB] in discussing schooling in the 1930s:

GP They re-dressed us. When you came they dressed you in residential school clothing [a blue uniform and white pinafore]. You couldn't wear your own anymore.

N Hah, they just had skins before.

AB You couldn't wear your own clothing in school?

GP How could we go around in *skins* in *school* [her emphasis]? They gave us coats. They gave us everything, dresses, pants, felts, boots, etc.

AB But now kids in the residential school often wear *unty* [the traditional Evenk reindeer skin boots that are usually embroidered and decorated with beadwork around the top].

N But they couldn't wear these then.

In re-dressing Evenki the state sought to signify the imposition of a "modern" way of life and control over students in the residential school. Simultaneously, the women's accounts indicate an internalization of the pervasive Soviet dichotomy between the modern and the traditional. Galina Petrovna's comment—"How could we go around in *skins* in *school*?"—particularly demonstrates the dynamic that was perpetuated, and sometimes internalized, through clothing. The "skins"—reindeer skin clothing—represented traditions of the past, and "school" represented the modern present and future.

Clothing was also contested as a symbol of the continuity of Evenk cultural practices. These practices coexisted with the Soviet attempts to transform the subsistence economy, but they were relegated to villages, away from the administrative centers and residential schools. As another elderly Evenk woman explained:

> When you came home then, in the summer, you wore all Evenk clothing—*unty*, etc. . . . There weren't any dresses. Only in school they gave us these, and shoes and boots. When we came home we always had our own Evenk clothing. . . . They [the teachers] didn't permit us to wear our own clothing; they didn't permit it. . . . [In Tura] we didn't go around in that. There was barely enough money for Russian clothing anyway. Earlier, people were embarrassed by Evenk clothing. I did have some *unty* for a while though. I took them with me [to Tura]. When I was leaving, an aunt gave me those very beautiful beaded (*bisernye*) *unty*. I looked forward to graduating when I would go home and wear them.

As this narrative indicates, clothing served as a symbol of belonging and as a touchstone for ties to an existence outside the setting of the Soviet residential school. While students were sometimes made to feel "embarrassed" by what the clothing symbolized, some also looked forward to being able to wear Evenk clothing freely.

As a further means of social control, the school also imposed a military-style of behavior on children. During World War II this was particularly pronounced. Galina Petrovna laughed as she recalled, "We went everywhere in [military-style] queues—to school, to eat, to work, to bathe, even to the movies. Even when we went for a hike we went in queues! Hah, hah, just like soldiers!" As Galina Petrovna indicated, this discipline extended to non-academic time as well. Students marched in formation as they set off to plant crops of potatoes and harvest them, feed cows, pigs, and chickens, and haul water for the school and dormitory.

Aside from regulating bodies through clothing and physical movement, social categories were also invoked to control residential school students and define them as being more or less "modern. At certain points in its history, the residential school served as a site where children were subjected to close observation and social analysis by teachers; as discussed in Chapter 4 in Polina Mikhailovna's account of being labeled a "kulak child," students also derided peers for deviating from a given norm deemed modern. As early as 1929, there were indications of the attitudes that were to become commonplace in the 1930s. One report to the executive committee (*ispolkom*) of the Krasnoiarsk regional government commented on conditions in a school in the Tazov region near Turukhansk, on the Enisei River. The author of the report chided the school director for not documenting the social origins of the students and suggested that the local council develop "exact indicators on students' social class in order to have a clear idea of the composition of the student body and also in order to make sure there are no shamans' children in the school."[8] By the early 1930s, teachers were keeping track of the "social origins" of students and recording them according to class labels, such as "hired labor" (*batrak*), "of average means" (*seredniak*), and *kulak*. In the 1920s, educators in the North had largely disregarded the social origins of students and had simply tried to persuade students to attend the school. Beginning in the 1930s, however, the social categories imposed by the Soviet government served as the primary basis upon which students were classified; this practice extended until well after World War II.

Evenk Intellectuals and Consolidating Constituencies

By the 1990s, Evenk students had been required to attend the residential school for nearly sixty years; in some families four generations had studied in this system. Given the history of students being categorized and regulated in the residential school, it is curious that community members continued to send students even after 1993 when they were no longer required to do so. As discussed in Chapters 2 and 4, a wide range of households were choosing this institution for their children's education, either out of a sense of solidifying a connection with Evenk cultural practices or out of more material considerations. Unlike the widespread, vociferous statements made by native peoples in North America against residential schooling and its role in undermining cultural continuity (see, for example, Child 1998; Ing 1991), in the 1990s these types of narratives were not widely voiced by Evenk intellectuals. A few people wrote of the negative impact of the institution on indigenous cultural continuity (Nemtushkin 1992; Popov 1993), but many also viewed the institution as a place for rejuvenation of Evenk cultural practices (Shchapeva 1994) and for political mobilization (Pikunova 1998). In their interaction with the institution, Evenk intellectuals generally sought to alter the residential school system for their needs rather than discard it.

A poignant example of the complexity of the relationship to this institution is reflected in the experience of one Evenk woman who taught for many years in the school. The teacher told me how her brother had greatly disliked being in school and in the fourth grade decided to run away. He set out on foot up the frozen river toward home. It should have taken him less than three hours to reach his destination, but he never reached home. Despite such tragic events related to the residential school, this teacher and other Evenk intellectuals were not seeking to close this institution. Instead, Evenk intellectuals were active in recommending changes in the curriculum and a rethinking of the overall purpose of the school.

In October 1993, I wrote the following passage in my fieldnotes: "'Nomadic herders never had to worry about anyone stealing anything. In those days Evenki did not do that,' pronounced the lecturer in the Evenk ethnography course. The multiethnic class of Evenk, Russian, Sakha, Ukrainian, and Tadzhik sixteen-year-olds snapped their bubble gum and stared blankly at the lecturer." By sitting in on these newly created ethnography classes, as well as attending community events such as political meetings and folk festivals, I observed a wide range of situations in which Evenk intellectuals were actively engaging and sometimes reimagining Evenk identities in the 1990s. The course in Evenk ethnography (*etnografiia*), which was introduced into elementary, high school, and post-secondary curriculums in Tura in fall 1993, represents the shifting influence of highly educated Evenki in the cultural landscape following the fall of state socialism in Russia.

The course was conceived of, and initially taught by, an Evenk woman who was a former Communist Party member with a degree in general pedagogy from the Herzen Pedagogical Institute in Leningrad. As the course became standardized in the curriculum by 1996, it began to be offered one hour a week for four consecutive years at the high school level. The course steered students through an impressive range of topics as detailed in the curriculum guide (Shchapeva 1994):

A.

1. Peoples of the North, with a focus on the lifeways of Tunguso-Manchurian tribes and their origins
2. Our district in the seventeenth to nineteenth centuries, with a focus on the lives of Evenki and the areas occupied by Evenk clans
3. The October Revolution and the establishment of Soviet power in the North
4. Natural history of the region
5. Traditional subsistence practices and lifeways
6. Settlements and housing
7. Traditional Evenk clothing, including headgear and decorations
8. Household objects
9. Evenk cooking

B.

1. Evenk worldviews: cosmology, origin myths, and the spiritual world

2. Religious beliefs among the Evenki, including shamanism
3. Traditional knowledge: ecology, medicinal practices, upbringing
4. Lifeways: traditions, customs, rituals
5. Family and kinship: traditional practices, contemporary practices, demography
6. Decorative arts: ornamentation, beadwork, carving
7. Evenk oral traditions: folklore, literature, and poetry
8. Musical traditions: instruments, contemporary composers, dance
9. Fine arts among the Evenki and artists depicting life in the Evenk District

As an amalgam of ethnographic, historical, and sociological topics, the course promised to consider Evenk culture from a far more dynamic perspective than would classic formulations of the concept of culture as fixed and unchanging. During my observations of this ambitious course, however, it tended to perpetuate a sense of Evenk identities as homogenous, essentialized, and trapped in time. While history was certainly addressed as critical to understanding Evenk cultural practices, the essence of Evenk "culture" was seen as unchanging, rather than shifting and malleable. Scholars have widely criticized such views of culture as something bounded and impermeable, somehow unaffected by change and historical processes. For instance, Abu-Lughod and Lutz argue that the very term "culture" too easily connotes what they call "timelessness in the meaning systems of a certain group" (1990: 9). They demonstrate that in identifying and essentializing "a culture" as being fundamentally different from others, the term is used very much like the earlier term "race" was used widely by social scientists in the first half of the twentieth century. In thinking about the Evenk ethnography lectures, the utility of a culture concept crystallizing and essentializing group identity becomes clear. In light of pressing political issues in the Evenk District, and across Siberia more generally in the 1990s, it was almost inevitable that Evenk culture would be depicted by an Evenk intellectual as idealized and timeless.

With the new intellectual freedoms and urgency for promoting Evenk collective interests following the fall of the Soviet Union in 1991, cultural revitalization efforts expanded. Like other indigenous groups facing political and economic marginalization around the world, in the mid- to late 1990s many Evenk intellectuals were actively seeking to differentiate their communities and even freeze their past in a tangible, recognizable moment. In firmly locating their history in a golden point in time, they were seeking to combat the dominant public perception of them as a people "without culture" (*nekul'turnye*) or "without history" (see E. Wolf 1982). In the late 1990s, many of the former Evenk Party members were involved in cultural revitalization efforts in the Evenk District that were funded by the Evenk District administration. Evenki in their fifties and sixties were employed by the Evenk District Institute for Teacher Development to create courses like the ethnography course described above and teaching aids focused on material culture such as traditional housing, subsistence hunting and reindeer herding technology, decorative arts, and oral traditions. By 1998 three full-time staff were researching and publishing on aspects of traditional Evenk culture.[9]

Such courses and teaching materials reflected growing concern among Evenk intellectuals about representations of Evenki in the context of an emerging market economy. The lectures were part of a broader effort sponsored by the Institute for Teacher Development. One of the four staff members at the institute in 1994 was also employed teaching Evenk language at the residential school. As part of her efforts to incorporate more ethnographic material into her course, she created a traditional Evenk calendar with the year divided into five sections, each one related to the types of fish and game traditionally caught in a given time of year. Another staff member traveled to several Evenk villages giving lectures on Evenk toponymy.

For the first time since the mid-1920s, Evenk cultural history was making its way into the classroom and beyond, not as an aside meant to illustrate how successful the Soviet modernization project had been but as a central subject. As the lecturer explained to the ethnography class I visited one morning in 1993: "Evenki have lived in this region for thousands of years, and yet most of us do not know about their history. . . . In this class we will learn what makes Evenki unique. . . . Evenki never lied or stole." The teacher made a conscious effort to emphasize how "in the past" Evenki had been pristine and honest, but she stopped short of discussing specific historical social policy (like collectivization or kulakization of shamans and others) as factors in local history.

In general, the teacher's essentializing perspective on Evenk cultural practice as limited to "traditional" and static elements was mirrored in public discourse. A vivid example of this emerged in public discussion in Tura following the showing of a Finnish documentary made in the Evenk District in 1992. The documentary, entitled *Taiga Nomads*, chronicles the lives of Evenki living in the taiga and in villages in the Baikit region of the Evenk District (Aaltonen and Lappalainen 1993). Many in the community, Evenki and Russians alike, were critical of parts of the film that had been made in a reindeer herding brigade. The ethnography teacher criticized the filmmakers most vehemently. As she explained, "Those Evenki didn't wear traditional clothing. They should have filmed people in traditional clothing!" Others were annoyed that the director had chosen to include scenes in which Evenk children were loudly swearing as they cleaned the cafeteria in the residential school. Significantly, the film was not used as a source of teaching material during the course of the school year, although copies were available to the public in video format.

In general, the ethnography course "othered" Evenki through a decontextualized emphasis on their past spiritual traditions and no reference to troublesome periods in local history or to contemporary lives and ritual practice. By preserving and promoting one view of Evenki as timeless "children of nature," this ethnography course relied on the Soviet binary markers of "traditional" and "modern" and thereby left unexplored questions about contemporary culture and its messy reality lacking boundaries of definition.

For indigenous groups threatened by increasingly less access to economic and electoral power, imagery associating indigenous peoples with the timeless, pristine past carries symbolic weight. As scholars have indicated in regard to the Maya in Guatemala, control over the representation of everyday life and history has practical implications (Fischer and Brown 1996: 3). Groups such as the Evenki, which lack significant economic resources, can at least draw on symbolic capital to mobilize their constituents. Indigenous intellectuals are not bound, however, to an unchanging set of "markers of authenticity" (see Conklin 1997). These markers can be reproduced without much transformation, or they can be actively remade and reappropriated. The following sections provide illustrations of several ways in which Evenk elite are invoking a range of markers of identity in their efforts to mobilize Evenki.

Contesting Imagery of School and Nation

From mid-1993 on, the Communist Party no longer officially controlled socioeconomic and political life, but many of the same forms of governance and practices of campaigning were perpetuated. The fact that indigenous Siberians never lived under reservation systems, unlike many indigenous peoples in the United States, Canada, or Australia (Armitage 1995; Fleras and Elliot 1992), is reflected in the configuration of their political power today. In the early 1930s, the Soviet government established a system of "autonomous regions" (Svensson 1978), one of which was the Evenk Autonomous District. Despite the names of the regions suggesting some type of autonomy based on ethnicity, the ethnic groups after which the areas were named did not have control over the political, economic, or cultural development of a given region. Even the native councils established by Soviet organizers in the 1920s were disbanded by the early 1930s in favor of a single, unified judicial and political system for indigenous Siberians and newcomers (Miller 1994; Tugolukov 1971). From 1931 to the present, the Evenk District has had its own representatives in the central government, but not until 1993 were they elected by the general populace.[10]

In late October 1993, campaigning for the first democratic elections to the Russian Federation Duma began to gather momentum. The Evenk District had two slots to fill for the Duma, and more than ten candidates emerged. Instead of door-to-door campaigning and public debates or discussions of candidates' platforms—a format familiar to me—the campaigning largely took place at different organizations. (In addition, candidates printed up handbills for broad dissemination with a description of their platforms and often a photograph.) Thus candidates would contact the administration of a given organization and arrange for the members of the work collective to gather for a meeting. This type of campaigning focused on place-of-work was familiar to Turintsy because it was exactly how the Communist Party had conducted meetings leading up to elections.

Attending one of these meetings in the residential school, I had a sensation of déjà vu, as if I were at a former Party gathering, only now several people actively challenged the candidates. The incumbent Duma representative was an Evenk man who had been in politics for many years and continued to identify himself as a Communist Party member. He spoke about his innocence in connection with the storming of the Parliament or Duma (*Belyi dom*) on October 4, 1993. (While most representatives exited the Parliament in protest of the military-backed attempt to oust Boris Yeltsin from power, this incumbent and about one hundred other representatives remained resolutely inside the Parliament building.)

The Evenki—teachers of fine arts, health, Evenk language, and ethnography—sat quietly to one side. Near the back of the room the Russians—teachers of physics, geography, and Russian literature and the head administrator—sat clustered. One of them bluntly asked the candidate, "If there was no change [in the social conditions] for all those years you were in office, what will change now?" This challenge appeared to be what the speaker was waiting for; he readily explained that his efforts to improve the socioeconomic conditions in Evenkiia had been hampered because the Parliament had been half bought out by the U.S. Central Intelligence Agency.[11] At this point he looked toward me before once again energetically entreating those gathered to vote for him in the upcoming elections. This Evenk politician rallied for his vision of a reestablished socialist collective by posing this in opposition to the CIA, a powerful symbol evoking a binary of Russia versus the West, socialist Russia versus the bourgeois, spying United States.

Arun, Natural Resources, and "Evenki"

The president of *Arun* followed an alternate route in envisioning and mobilizing Evenki.[12] During the 1994 New Year's celebration in the residential school, she gave a rousing speech to the gathering of students, parents, and residential school staff in which she discussed her recent United Nations sponsored tour of several urban centers in the United States. The 1993 UN symposia marking the International Year of Indigenous Peoples included several indigenous Siberian leaders who traveled to four U.S. cities on a speaking tour and met with Native Americans and Alaskan Natives. In the association president's presentation she turned to me, asking for affirmation of the fact that in the United States many indigenous groups were well organized and among other issues, arranged for the education of their children in their native languages. (She had been especially impressed with the Apache schools in this regard.) In this event and again in graduation ceremonies later that year, she chided the organizers for creating a school function in which the proceedings were completely carried out in Russian, with barely a word included in the Evenk language.

Arun's president stressed raising political consciousness (*samosoznanie*) as key to improving Evenk living standards. In contrast to the call by the candidate for Parliament for a return to Soviet markers of collective identity in the form of oppositional Cold War rhetoric, *Arun*'s president underscored the need to focus on local group markers of identity such as language in mobilizing the Evenk community. She also emphasized access to and control over natural resources as central issues for Evenki.

With the collapse of state agricultural cooperatives in 1992, issues of land use became increasingly acute throughout agricultural regions of Russia, as well as in the North and *Arun* became involved in organizing Evenki to claim their "clan lands." (Claiming these lands was not de facto privatization but implied that these clans had primary rights over the use of the land.) In this period the Tura archive attracted an unusually large number of visitors as many sought documentation dating from the 1920s and 1930s to firmly establish the areas in which their clans had herded reindeer prior to collectivization. Such documentation was considered essential for substantiating clans' claims to land as privatization began to be considered throughout Russia.

These land claims were complicated for several reasons. First, in many cases serious conflicts developed over Russian versus Evenk land use. In one case, an area in which the district game warden had personally hunted for nearly fifteen years was recognized in 1992 as the "clan land" of a powerful Evenk family.[13] The game warden was compelled, not by law but by local pressure, to give up use of the contested land.

A second cause for conflict was the definition of identity internal to the Evenk community. Those with mixed parentage who recognized themselves as Evenki usually had "Evenk" stamped in their passports at age sixteen; but as discussed in Chapter 1, the community did not always recognize them as "true" Evenki. Especially if they grew up in town away from reindeer herding and hunting activity, conflicts arose when these town Evenki sought to lay claim to "clan land." Also, if a clan—which was correlated by surname—was particularly large, there often arose disagreements about which branch of the family should have use of the land.

The new possibilities for families and clans to have control over land raised difficult questions of ownership and community. These issues directly involved the Association of Peoples of the North as it sought to represent the rights of "indigenous" (*korennye*) peoples. Many questions arose such as: Who is Evenk? Who is "indigenous" to the region? Can you become Evenk? And who "owns" land that has been collectively controlled for more than three generations? Such questions were motivating Evenk intellectuals to define markers of belonging to the Evenk community, in part through academic publications and ethnography courses, but also through the introduction of practices such as the "winter picnic" into the residential school curriculum.

Anchoring Evenk Identities: *Taiezhnye* and Cheerios

One characteristic of symbolic capital as described by Bourdieu (1977) is that it is not all-encompassing. In reappropriating Soviet markers of "traditional" Evenk cultural practices, there are inevitably other competing ones. Early in April 1994 one event clearly illustrated this dilemma faced by Evenk intellectuals in their attempts to mobilize a new sense of collective identity. Although it had warmed up to just below zero degrees Celsius, two feet of snow remained on the ground when the students and staff at the residential school began setting up a winter picnic. As the school children unpacked their lunches, they pulled cookies from bright yellow Cheerios cereal boxes in which the residential school kitchen staff had packed them. The students then insisted on holding the boxes in their arms as I took several group photographs.

While the popular Cheerios cereal boxes served as a vivid reminder of how local culture is integrally tied to a global economy and to markers of global belonging (Appadurai 1991), the picnic had been intended as a practical lesson in "traditional" culture. The knowledge of the forest and necessary life skills such as building a fire were invested with unusual import as quaint skills unfamiliar to most of the students. The few who knew how to arrange the fire pits and get a fire going for this winter picnic were quietly called *taiezhnye*, or taiga kids, an appellation that simultaneously denoted respect for their skill and derision for their otherness. This winter picnic was one of many recent attempts to incorporate "traditional" ways into the residential school curriculum.

The picnic was reminiscent of efforts documented in photographs taken in mid-winter in the early days of the school.[14] As described in the text penciled on the back of the images housed in the district museum's photographic collection, at the time the photographs were taken in the late 1920s, Soviet teachers were learning about tracking techniques and trapping in an outdoor lesson. As these images attest, the government sponsored training for Soviet teachers to become knowledgeable about Evenk subsistence practices; this was considered invaluable for facilitating the ongoing work begun by the "red tents"—to familiarize herders and hunters with Soviet modernity in the form of political education, literacy, and an introduction to biomedicine. Conversely, in the 1990s Evenk teachers were leading applied lessons about subsistence practices in an effort to reinscribe a vehicle of the Soviet collective, the residential school, with new symbolic power, and thereby kindle a renewed sense of Evenk identity.

While legacies of Soviet governance and educational practices established the conditions under which Evenk intellectuals formulated markers of belonging in the 1990s, the specific agency of individuals was key to how the Evenki were becoming mobilized as a group. It remains to be seen how markers of authentic belonging, which have been rooted in the Soviet dialectic of "traditional" and "modern," will be interpreted and remade by a younger generation whose imaginations are strongly influenced by new markers of belonging to a global community. These identities may be situational and invoked at opportune moments. The essentialist or "primordialist" markers of Soviet-defined Evenk identity—the "children of nature" and the "ideal proletarian"—are in the process of transformation. They are anything but timeless. As explored further in the next chapter, Evenki are actively engaging a wide range of frameworks for representing their identities.

Chapter 7
Representing Culture: Museums, Material Culture, and Doing the Lambada

> With humans we enter into the realm of history
> (*Vmeste s chelovekom my vstupaem v oblast' istorii*).
>
> —Friedrich Engels, epigraph over the entryway to the ethnography hall, Evenk District Regional History Museum, 1998

> Modernity is the long cultural moment in which the positive and negative and close/distant axes of Indian otherness become inverted.
>
> —Philip Deloria, *Playing Indian*

When I visited the House of Folk Art in Tura in the summer of 1998, I was immediately drawn to the stenciled, bright wooden paneling protruding from the ceiling and demarcating dim cubicles left over from the building's brief incarnation as a night club in the mid-1990s. Wooden frames covered in black felt had been leaned up against the wall in several cubicles, and these served as a backdrop for contemporary artisans' work. This included circular beaded pendants and the fur appliqué and beadwork referred to throughout the North as "suns" (*solnyshka*).

Throughout northern Siberia, indigenous peoples make versions of circular beadwork depicting the sun. Historically, Evenki decorated gloves and other clothing with similar beadwork designs. They exchanged sable or squirrel pelts for the beads that made their way via American whalers or traders from China. In the 1990s, beads tended to be obtained in Czechoslovakia. The most popular colors in the Evenk District were ones that appeared traditional to the artisans selecting the beads and directing the projects. Royal blue, sun yellow, bright red, and black beads were especially in demand, but only if they were glass (not plastic) and the appropriate size for a needle to thread through. In borrowing the "sun" technique, one artisan's work featured in the House of Folk Art was a beaded mosaic profile of Lenin with a sable fur border.

As I reflected on the beadwork, the director lamented that the French businessmen for whose reception the exhibit had been especially prepared had still not arrived even though they had been expected for more than two months. Suddenly we were interrupted by the shrill notes of Russian pop music projected through the sound system in an adjacent room. The director turned her attention to criticizing her young colleague for spending far too much of his work time rehearsing pop music pieces for a discotheque commemorating the upcoming Russian Independence Day. He was supposed to have begun preparation of an Evenk folk music program for the upcoming folk festival.

A series of similar encounters in the Evenk District Regional History Museum, House of Folk Art, and broader community compelled me to think about the ways material culture was being used to bridge deep ruptures of knowledge and political economy in the Evenk District in the 1990s. Material culture, including museum exhibits and dance performances, was historically employed in support of the Soviet grand narrative of progress that traced a trajectory of human development from hunting and gathering societies to a pinnacle of social and technological development. In the early 1990s material culture in Siberian museum settings and elsewhere was less frequently used to invoke a unilineal, orthodox vision of social progress. In some areas of Siberia, this meant that curators engaged with critical perspectives by creating exhibits on some of the dissonant aspects of Soviet history—the collectivizations, village relocations, and religious repression. The Evenk District Museum remained, however, a space marked as safeguarding the grand narrative of unmarred progress.

As Carol Breckenridge has argued, in the second half of the nineteenth century museums became central in an "object-centered mythology of rule" (1989: 211). In the context of Russia in the 1990s, where the "mythology of [Soviet] rule" was recently challenged and is now being redefined, museums are also potentially important political vehicles. As the Russian government considers privatizing property throughout the country, indigenous Siberians like the Evenki are faced with possibly losing access to the land and natural resources that have formed the basis of their subsistence economy (Murashko 1996). As discussed in previous chapters, historical and contemporary representations of Evenki have also been closely linked with the emerging issue of control over local resources. But more than just "natural resources" have been at stake. Evenk intellectuals have been struggling with how the Evenki as a group could represent their interests when the familiar grand narratives of

Figure 12. Beadwork image of Lenin. Photo by the author, 1998.

inclusive Soviet progress are widely contested. In the 1990s many intellectuals believed that the new emerging narratives of individualist, market cultural practices would not benefit the Evenki. For them material culture played a powerful role in representing Evenk interests within public discourse, especially as individual profit replaced collective interests as the foundation of the prevailing ideology.

While the last chapter considered the role of Evenk intellectuals in forging and promoting Evenk identities, in this chapter I consider how the mobilization of Evenk identities is refracted through museums and material culture. In the first part, I consider the place of museums in nation-building projects, and specifically the place of the Evenk District Museum in representing the Evenk experience in Soviet nation-building. The second part considers how the concepts of culture presented in the museum intersected with those being played out in public culture. In particular, this chapter examines some of the ways in which Evenk intellectuals and Evenk youth were thinking about "culture" and symbols of identity in the 1990s.

Museums and Shifting Political Economies

The recent literature on anthropology museums and museum displays often situates its critique in terms of the West and the Other. This literature has defined the acquisition of objects from the periphery and the portrayal of peoples under glass as both representing and affirming the hegemony of the metropole (Stocking 1985; Clifford 1990; Hinsley 1992). The anthropology of museums has flourished with analyses ranging from thick description of the community politics of specific museum exhibits (Clifford 1990) to discussions of the role of museums in societies overall (Handler 1993; Stocking 1985). Frequently scholars examine the tight connection between museums and nation-state legitimization projects (Bloch and Kendall 2004; Kaplan 1994; Handler 1988).

The Evenk District cultural institutions are, however, part of a worldwide phenomenon in which self-representation is viewed as increasingly critical from the perspective of indigenous communities (Gorbey 1992; Mahuika 1992; Shchapeva 1994; Warren 1998). Scholars have taken note of the divergent aims and functions of museums and historico-ritual sites as they operate in diverse national and local contexts (Kaplan 1994; Schildkrout 1999; Cruikshank and Argounova 2000). Museums and similar sites where material culture is displayed can be viewed as locations where cultural hegemony is played out. They can also be viewed as sites where cultural representations are negotiated and contemporary, contested knowledge is constituted.

In less urban areas of Russia, museums continue to play a central role in how local knowledge and ideas about "tradition" are embodied; objects are presented for consumption not only for outsiders, but also for community members themselves. As the publics visiting these museums shifted in the 1990s and definitions of belonging were being contested, a new political economy was also taking form. For instance, like her colleagues around the world, the director of the Evenk House of Folk Art in Tura was faced with representing "traditional" culture under new circumstances in which material well-being was increasingly at stake. As multinational companies like the French one with interests in the Evenk District have sought out areas in which to establish business in lumber extraction, oil drilling, and mass production of mushroom and berry products, local Siberian museums have contributed to the wider attempts to court transnational capital investment.[1] Traditional culture was certainly appropriated in the Soviet period to serve the state's purposes (see Levin 1996; Doi 2001; Bloch and Kendall 2004), but with the market transformations in the 1990s there was an open competition between forms of expression for use in community representation.

In a context of decreased central government financing and control, regional history museums were often re-presenting their collections and simultaneously looking for sponsors. Officially, in the Soviet period regional administrations received funds from Moscow that were then parceled out to each subdivision, including the Departments of Health, Education, and Culture. For instance, the Evenk Department of Culture oversaw and theoretically financed the District Museum, the House of Folk Art, the House of Culture, and public celebrations and cultural events. In the early 1990s, however, the money funneled from Moscow to the various regions slowed to a trickle. In many regions while the administration of cultural organizations and events remained under the Department of Culture, institutions were increasingly forced to seek out private donors or raise money for operating costs through alternative means, such as tourism.

In the late 1990s some cultural institutions in the Russian Far East raised funds by organizing travel tours, as in the case of the Provideniia, Chukotka Regional History Museum, or by providing classes for school children, as in the case of the Magadan Regional History Museum (Bloch 2001). Members of indigenous communities were also taking initiative to create their own new community museums and open-air, historico-ritual sites (Cruikshank and Argounova 2000; Balzer 1999). Community museums, often called "apartment" (*kvartirnye*) museums because they typically began in someone's apartment, became common by the mid-1990s. These small private museums acted as alternatives to the state-run museums found throughout Siberia; they emerged in urban centers like Vladivostok[2] and in smaller settlements (Khelol 1997).[3] These museums often explicitly presented their mission in contrast to that of the government museums that were viewed as linked to a "continuous discrimination of [indigenous] culture, lifestyle and religion" (Donkan and Onodera 1998).

Unlike in the Russian Far East, in the Evenk District there were no cultural institutions using material culture to provide counter narratives to the grand narratives defining Soviet-era displays. One reason was that they lacked the financial backing to be independent of the local Department of Culture. Unlike the Provideniia Regional History museum, ideally located on the Bering Strait along the route of major pleasure cruises and accessible by tour companies operating in Alaska, the Evenk District cultural institutions were fairly isolated from tourism. Also unlike the situation in larger economic centers like Magadan, there were no local benefactors for cultural institutions in Tura, although an occasional exhibit reception was sponsored by local grocery store owners.[4] Evenk District institutions continued to rely exclusively for financial support on the local Department of Culture. As an indication of the dire financial situation that especially affected the arts, in June 1998 those people employed in Tura organizations under the aegis of the Department of Culture had not received paychecks for more than six months.

Also in contrast to the Russian Far East where apartment museums were emerging, there were no apparent efforts in the Evenk District to create physical spaces for alternative histories. The government-run Evenk District Museum and the related House of Folk Art remained the centers for community representations of local history. The beadwork image of Lenin on display in Tura underscores a very particular local history in which the Communist past continued to be an important part of how many Evenk intellectuals wanted to represent their community in the 1990s. As explored further in this chapter, however, while there were no alternative museum or exhibit spaces, there were alternative representations of Evenk public culture in other settings.

Nation-States, Museums, and Belonging

In the context of what Evenk elders tended to view as an onslaught of homogenizing market culture, in 1998 the Evenk District museum continued to serve the role of preserving "local culture" and claiming for the Evenki what Virginia Dominguez has called "legitimacy through history" (1986: 550). In other words, the museum was important because community leaders came to think of it as integrally tied to the recognition of their place in local history. While the Evenk District Museum played a modest role in the general structure of government institutions in the region in the 1990s, it was an important symbolic site for the community. In existence since 1928, the museum continued to serve as one of the important sites for a reiteration of nation-state power, despite a change in political power in the early 1990s and a virtual absence of financing since 1995. What was displayed as "traditional culture" fit into a narrative in which the culture of the majority indigenous population in the region, the Evenki, was effortlessly and almost enthusiastically incorporated into the nation-state. This version of history left out the painful elements of Evenk history discussed in Chapters 1 and 3, including collectivization in the 1930s, the demonization of shamans, and the loneliness of many in the residential school.

Despite widespread public outcry about conditions in the North beginning in the late 1980s and continuing into the 1990s (see Abriutina 1997; Vakhtin 1994; Rytkheu 1988; Sangi 1988), the museum continued to display the Soviet state's narrative that indigenous people prospered under socialism. The four permanent exhibition halls into which the museum was divided—natural history, human prehistory, ethnography, and Soviet history—reflected a classic evolutionary trajectory often found in anthropology and regional history museums internationally. The exhibits in these halls were intended to provide an overall picture of local history, including predictable images of the "progress" introduced in the Soviet era when industrialization in the North brought electricity, mining, and aviation. As in similar small government museums found throughout sparsely populated town centers in Siberia, material culture played a critical role in perpetuating social memory for the Evenk District community.

The museum exhibits not only acted to remind residents of the former way of life for indigenous Siberians, but also linked the region and its inhabitants into the larger nation-state through the logic of industrial and evolutionary social progress. The social infrastructures such as hospitals, schools, and collective farms established through the efforts of the Soviet state became validated through this logic. This same teleology of industrialization was reflected in museum exhibits that could only place Evenk reindeer herders and subsistence fishers in the distant past as subjects for nostalgia. Households like the Yoldogirs (see Chapter 2), which had maintained village and taiga residences since the early 1990s, were not included as part of the Evenk "culture" to be depicted. Like many regional history museums worldwide this museum was concerned with the past rather than the present lives of its subjects. In an era in which new representations were possible, it continued to depict the way in which indigenous populations "progressed" in the region as greater and greater numbers became literate, adopted sedentary lifeways, and became inculcated with Soviet patriotism.

The museum's centrally located Soviet history section reflected a continuous trajectory of Soviet nation-state consolidation. This was evident in label copy such as the following: "The Onset of Socialist Society in the North," "Collectivization of Agriculture in Evenkiia, 1930–1940," "[Communist] Party Organizing in Evenkiia," "The Establishment of Aviation," "Evenkiia Defending the Fatherland," and "The End of the War and the Return to Peacetime Activities." Black-and-white photographs and text taken from local newspaper accounts accompanied these labels. For instance, one featured a local Evenk man who became a national hero for his celebrated role in defending the Western front against the German incursion during World War II.

What was most compelling about these displays was how much was left uncritically examined. The official Soviet version of local history continued as the dominant theme in this museum. One particularly vivid example was a display of an early 1930s ledger from a regional council meeting held at a time when people were classified, like the students described in Chapter 6, as "poor," "hired," and "of average means." The minutes reported that 268 Evenk representatives were elected to the council in 1931–32; among them 186 were indicated as *bedniaki* ("poor"), 14 as *zaemnye* [sic] ("hired"), and 68 as *seredniaki* ("of average means"). There was no effort to contextualize this statement and explain that along with the Soviet efforts to classify the population for purposes of pitting groups against one another, there were also widespread repercussions for resisting state efforts to reorganize production patterns. In eliding these additional facts, as discussed in previous chapters, the exhibit was able to feature Soviet efforts to include Evenki in local political life as if this process was completely benign.

Overall, the museum exhibits lacked information on the variable success of local Soviet efforts to establish and maintain control over the Evenk population. This elision suggested the ongoing ambivalences of a contemporary indigenous elite that experienced a range of benefits in the Soviet era. As in some other museum contexts in which local history is contested, in this museum difference was "suffocated and dissolved in the all-encompassing embrace of national and revolutionary fraternity" (Alonso 1988).

While the museum continued to largely disregard the ruptures in favor of reproducing a seamless history from a Soviet past, there were segments of the local population that were quietly exploring the ruptures in recent history. In 1998, I met a local Sakha woman who was eager to share with me documents regarding her family's 1938 kulakization when her father was accused of harboring "anti-Soviet" attitudes; he was subsequently "rehabilitated" in 1996.[5] None of this legacy of the 1930s government collectivization policies was reflected in the museum's narrative.

A shamanism exhibit created in 1994 did reflect the new freedoms of exhibition that came with the fall of the Soviet Union. The lack of reflection on the Soviet government relationship to shamanism over time was a notable ellipsis, however, that could easily mislead viewers to think of the absence of shamanic practice in everyday Evenk life as a "natural" outcome of modernization. The exhibit's dearth of signage further emphasized the indecision of the local intelligentsia. If celebrating traditional culture as it fits into a Soviet narrative of progress was part of the effort to resist the influence of market forces, including the erosion of social benefits for indigenous groups, then critical commentary on how the indigenous population fared during Soviet rule seems to suffer. The museum director explained that there had been "no time" since the creation of the hall in 1994 to write text for the shamanism exhibit. It seemed more likely that there was no consensus about appropriate label copy at the level of the local Department of Culture. Whatever paths would be chosen for narrating the exhibit would certainly be contested by factions that would rather not deconstruct the Soviet seamless narrative of uncontested successes in building a socialist society in the North.

Public Culture, Cultural Revitalization, and a Golden Past

Museums and cultural institutions are a critical part of establishing the social production of memory for communities.[6] By linking the Evenk museums as sites for producing social memory with what Appadurai and Breckenridge (1992) have called "public culture," we can gain insight into the role of material culture in the shifting dynamics of cultural identity in post-Soviet Russia. Movements for cultural revitalization rely on a common social memory, but this is not simply constituted and is more often a matter of contest. Among Evenk intellectuals the museum served as one place where traditional culture was drawn upon to build community and promote group rights, but this coexisted with a broader public culture with which youths tended to more readily identify. The way in which the district museum's concept of culture articulated with public culture suggests that the idea of "cultural revitalization" needs to be critically considered. Cultural revitalization has tended to be treated as a homogeneous, unified process (compare with Warren 1991: 103–4), but in fact, in closely examining the dynamics of social position, generation, and social memory, the multiple factors competing to define a sense of belonging are revealed.

As for indigenous revitalization movements around the world (Conklin 1997; Brysk 1996; Meyers 1994), markers of authentic indigenous belonging are central in indigenous Siberian efforts for cultural revitalization.

Evenk intellectuals in the 1990s tended to invoke a concept of indigenous Siberian cultural practices as confined to "traditional," static elements as a means of challenging new types of conquest and assimilation, those brought on with global market influences.[7] It was not a mistake that the concept of "traditional culture" was reminiscent of how the concept of "culture" was viewed in classic Soviet formulations. Many Evenk intellectuals were firmly rooted in ideational frameworks that viewed the socialist era as a time when "traditional" culture, and by extension Evenk collective interests, had been safeguarded. The image of Lenin in beadwork was a visual embodiment of these ideas. While the concept of "traditional" culture elevated a golden past, it failed to appeal broadly to younger generations that were drawing upon globally connected, multilayered public culture for their sense of belonging (Appadurai 1991).[8]

"Baroness," Reindeer Herders, and Revitalization

While Evenk intellectuals sought to consolidate a collective identity by relying on homogenizing paradigms, young Evenki tended to be drawn to more hybrid expressions of identity such as the showy, individualistic behaviors that they associated with cultural practices of the West. One of the many examples of this generational tension was demonstrated in an event held in the Tura residential school at the conclusion of the school year in June 1998. The residential school held an event to commemorate the accomplishments of high school graduates, and a full program was planned. Parents and other community members were invited to attend and be entertained by students who sang, danced, and read poetry.

The highlight of the evening occurred when a fifteen-year-old girl of Evenk and Russian background gave a twirling, hip-swinging performance of the Russian pop song "Baroness." This song featured the tale of a rich girl's romantic encounter and her pining for her suitor. In the course of her performance, the young woman swayed her body to the beat, attempting a coy demeanor, and shyly baring a bit of leg under her miniskirt. While some of the crowd, including the mostly Russian teachers, heartily cheered, many of the parents in attendance, who were predominantly Evenk, looked on in tentative silence. (A similar disjuncture of reactions was evoked in 1999 when the graduation ceremonies I attended at the school featured student performances, including a rendition of the Lambada performed by two Evenk youth clad in midriff-exposing, bright yellow outfits.)

Two elements were striking about the graduation event in 1998. First, the popularity of the song "Baroness" among youth in this region of

Figure 13. Doing the Lambada. Photo by the author, 1999.

Russia was related to the recent reversal of folk concepts about wealth. Under state socialism extreme social stratification—exemplified by the terms "baron," "baroness," and other such terms of social position—was considered backward and contrary to the ideals of an egalitarian society. In the 1990s, however, young people in Russia tended to be openly enamored by images of wealth.

Furthermore, the residential school event differed from the many commemorative gatherings I attended between 1992 and 1995 in the Evenk District; there was a complete lack of any "traditional" Evenk songs or choreography. In other gatherings I attended, students performed dances and songs accompanied by the rhythm created with a skin drum; the students dressed in outfits made from cotton, with stylized fringe and fur edging, and they wore reindeer skin boots or moccasins. As Levin (1996) and Doi (2001) discuss in the context of Uzbekistan, the Soviet state historically promoted what was called the "national" dance and music of minority populations. These expressive forms tended to be rigidly stylized and homogenized in terms of internal regional variation and became reified as "traditional"; nevertheless, these state-sanctioned dance and music forms came to signify the belonging of minority groups to a multiethnic Soviet society. The lack of Evenk traditional forms at this school graduation was significant as more than just a cosmetic change in the program; in this context of a school predominantly attended by indigenous Siberians, the lack of these dance and music genres was politically laden. By removing traditional Evenk forms from the program, the Evenk cultural and political markers were being edged out.

The president of the Association of Peoples of the North said with disgust following the 1998 graduation ceremonies, "Baroness, Baroness," accompanied by a derisive wiggle of her shoulders, "Who needs that Russian junk! It took us years just to get Evenk language and ethnography to be taught in the school, and now they want to take it away!" The sexualized, popular culture perceived as "Russian junk" was viewed as displacing authentic forms of Evenk cultural practices. The activist's comments reflect one way in which a sexualized global youth culture was clashing with the version of an asexual, traditional Evenk culture created in the Soviet period. In fact, this same activist, trained in linguistics, was steeped in the Soviet-era ideas about traditional culture, and she had taken part in the legacy of state-supported "cultural revitalization" in the form of language programs. She spearheaded the effort to reintroduce Evenk language classes into the residential school in this region in 1971.

The 1970s movement was just one of a series of such "cultural revitalization" and "cultural integration" efforts over the past eighty years. As discussed in previous chapters, in the 1920s there were significant Soviet efforts to create writing systems for a number of indigenous Siberian groups, including for the Evenki, and classes in the residential school were initially held in Evenk. But as Russification and new policies of assimilation were introduced in the mid-1930s, school classes in the Evenk District were less frequently taught in Evenk. The early Soviet cultural policies emphasizing local cultural traditions (*korenizatsiia*) lost out to the dominance of Russian language and Soviet bureaucracy. In the early Soviet period of political-economic transformation in the Evenk District, there was confusion over the official stance taken on Evenk/Russian bilingualism. For instance, one editorial noted: "Often the local secretary of the village council studies Evenk language in order to work with the local population, while the whole population studies Russian in order to communicate with representatives of the administration. . . . Also there has never been an effort to get the local Russian workers to study Evenk language" (Ocherednaia zadacha, *Evenkiiskaia novaia zhizn'*, 1939).[9]

This situation led to the near complete lack of Evenk language use in local administrative and Party business in the 1930s (Boitsova 1971), and by the mid-1940s there was no longer discussion of Evenk language as one of the official local languages. By the late 1940s, Russification in schooling had accelerated significantly, and native language was only employed for preparatory classes; it was no longer the medium of instruction for even first and second grades (Boitsova 1971: 150). Native language instruction became just another subject (for indigenous Siberian students only) in the course of a week, while Russian language was used for instruction in all grades. By the 1960s, Evenk language was only taught sporadically in the residential school, and the textbooks were more than thirty years old. In this context, a native language movement throughout the North took shape in the early 1970s, just as indigenous Siberians began to establish themselves in greater numbers as intellectuals throughout the Soviet Union.[10] During the Soviet era, although the commitment to Evenk language use ebbed and flowed, there was constant government support for reified forms of traditional culture such as dance, music, and material culture in museums.

The audience disdain for the sexually suggestive dances like "Baronness," cherished by teens, can be traced to a disjuncture in value systems. The sexualized, global youth culture embodied in these dance performances was jarring for those thinking of Evenk culture as defined in terms of "tradition." An indication of a disjuncture existing in particular around young women's sexuality is revealed in reviewing the Evenk language publications and textbooks produced in the wake of this 1970s cultural rejuvenation in the North.

The text and illustrations of many Evenk language and literature books that continue to be used in classroom teaching situate young women as demure and either dedicated to the Leninist cause as young Komsomols or dedicated to practicing traditional crafts within the context of reindeer herding. Popular Evenk literature fitting within the realm of cultural revitalization tends to allocate young women a place viewed as "traditional"; it is an asexual, domestic space that young women occupy. For instance, in "Girl-seamstress" ("*Devushka-masteritsa*"), Evenk poet Nikolai Oegir equates the craft of a young seamstress to something akin to cultural tranquility and balance:

Like a scintillating glance at the stars,
And just as beautiful as the figure of a girl,
A seamstress's needle sews
Multicolored *solnyshki* of reindeer hide.
In their fur burrows,
Squirrels nestle and sweetly dream of
Larch cones bursting with sap in the spring.
At the end of the day beside the *chum*
My white reindeer takes rest.
The trees sleep in their white hats.
Only the *chum* isn't sleeping.
A slant-eyed girl sits in it,
Surrounded by pieces of fur,
With a delicate needle she sews and sews
A hide mosaic for her promised one. (1989: 34)

This poem and others with similar themes equating girls with domesticity, craft production, and maintenance of cultural balance were often studied in the music and ethnography programs of the residential school in the late 1990s. The coy "Baroness" performed by the student at the 1998 graduation could be viewed as resistance to such stylized depictions of young women's daily life. In the late 1990s, young people's interests often diverged from official depictions of Evenk belonging.

Beyond the confines of school, young people in this community were reinterpreting attempts to revitalize traditional Evenk culture and in so doing were remaking their own versions of social memory. This remaking of cultural forms built on and sometimes challenged attempts by elders to promote their own understanding of social memory. Given the elders' singular emphasis on "traditional" culture as marking authentic Evenk identity, it is perhaps not surprising that local youth were often disengaged from the official processes of cultural revitalization. In the mid-1990s they were more likely to be at the discotheque held nightly in town centers than at the local museum. For many Evenk youth, to be Evenki was not just to be knowledgeable about traditional culture. They appeared skeptical of a revitalization effort that discounted their daily experience of being Evenki and did not reflect the hybrid, ever-changing processes that were influencing their identities and interactions with the community.

The majority of Evenk youth I met were uncomfortable with their Evenk identity being simply allied with "tradition," especially in the school setting. Several girls in an eighth-grade Evenk language class told me: "We're ashamed to speak Evenk. . . .We don't like to study it because other kids laugh at us." Another fourteen-year-old girl quietly confided, "I guess I don't like to be different from the other [non-Evenk] kids." This devaluation of Evenk language was set in relief by what did interest many students. The most popular subject in school, "information science," held students' attention largely because the teacher allowed them to spend most of the class time crowded three and four to a computer to play PacMan.

Not surprisingly, in the 1990s some of the museum's toughest critics were the youth in town. According to the museum director, who self-identified as a member of the indigenous Siberian community, children were the most frequent visitors to the museum, and they were probably the most influenced by the radical changes in the public culture they encountered in the daily life in the town. The museum director explained that youth were faced with negotiating what were often posed as diametrically opposed worlds of "traditional" culture and "modern" lives.

This schism between an Evenk intellectual movement still largely celebrating socialist successes and predominant youth perceptions of the promise of market society was highlighted by the museum director's reflections. As she explained, young people often came to the museum and quietly derided the exhibited artifacts as she gave tours. She added: "You see, everywhere ethnographic exhibits are viewed as somehow not 'modern.' If you go to an ethnographic museum in the city you'll also see youth react in the same way, especially when exhibits show people who lived almost in the Stone Age." This evolutionary paradigm the director referred to and herself invoked is a familiar one; it is also firmly a part of the museum context rooted in a Soviet discourse that celebrated industrial progress and distance from traditional practices as the "modern" and desirable way to live.

The Evenk District Museum director emphasized what she viewed as a transformation in youth attitudes linked to the growing market culture. She noted how years ago younger children of seven or eight were exceptionally interested in the exhibits. They would often go to the museum on their own after school and would request to sit in the *chum*, the reindeer hide, tepee structure erected in the ethnography hall. In contrast, older children—who were often brought in school groups in the late 1990s—only expressed interest occasionally when the guided tours particularly illuminated parallels with contemporary life. The director concluded with some consternation: "Seven or eight years ago [1991] children came and even helped out. But now they have entirely different perspectives and goals. . . . They sometimes work [after school], and they also know now that anything can be bought. They don't really have patience for looking at exhibits now."[11]

A few youth, however, were bridging this gap and creating ways to use imagery of "traditional" culture to increase the visibility of the Evenki as a group. For instance, three enterprising young men collaborated in 1997 to create a small performance group that was invited to travel to Tunisia to an international folk festival. The performance group was accompanied by several elders who were known in the Evenk community for their beadwork, songwriting, and storytelling. One of the elders recounted to me how the success of the trip had spurred her to begin planning an "open-air" museum consisting of a birchbark *chum,* to be situated in the taiga in the south of the Evenk District where she grew up. Her daughter was also preparing to videotape the construction of the *chum* because they had heard that some museums in the West had already purchased such documentary materials from Sakha artisans.

In 1998 one of the performers who traveled to Tunisia was also developing what he viewed as more authentic depictions of contemporary life in the region than those often created by outsiders and local leaders. With the assistance of a local advertising company in Krasnoiarsk, this young man, Vladimir, was creating a webpage incorporating video footage of Evenk songs and dance interspersed with images of everyday life and contemporary pop music he had written. In his webpage, Vladimir particularly wanted to counteract information available over the Internet depicting his town in primarily static, statistical terms. He told me that he wanted to provide a visual sense of the strong ties he saw in the community to the everyday practices of hunting, fishing, and enjoying nature and to the artistic practices of dance, song, beadwork, and leatherwork. In one memorable clip, he and his colleague sit on a sled careening down a snowy slope toward the town center; they are outfitted in beaded headbands and reindeer skin boots crafted by their aunts. A rock-and-roll guitar tune composed by Vladimir plays in the background. In Homi Bhabha's terms, Vladimir was looking for ways to represent "an interstitial space, a space that was not fully governed by the recognizable traditions" from which he came (1994: 190). By using familiar symbols of belonging—beadwork and reindeer skin boots—in new amalgamations, this young man was seeking ways to tell his own story of contemporary life for young Evenki who were predominantly rooted in town rather than taiga settings.

Museums and the Shifting Use of "Authentic" Aboriginality

In the context of radical changes in Siberia, including shifting state-periphery balances of power, material culture continues to be critical for the articulation of new concepts of belonging being developed and contested in indigenous communities. While a slogan displayed in the Evenk language classroom in the Tura residential school in 1998 read, "When loud jazz deafens native melodies and a people forgets the music of its ancestors, it perishes as a people," this perspective was not shared by all in the Evenk District. Today jazz, rock, and pop music are openly an important part of Evenk youth culture. As elders age and youth come of age to take their turns at employing their own discourses to define what it is to be Evenki, competing concepts of identity will very likely be negotiated and played out in an array of contexts, including the museum and school. The social memory rooted in socialist practices and idioms that the older generation of Evenk intelligentsia continues to shape will surely take on new forms and directions as youth make further forays into video and webpage production, Internet contacts, and contemporary music production and as they move into positions of authority in the community.

Cultural forms exemplifying "tradition" among indigenous Siberians will surely continue to shift in the future. If international and even national (that is, Russian) investors begin to play more important roles in the economy of the Evenk District, including sponsoring cultural institutions such as museums, it is likely that the display of Evenk material and visual culture will be modeled according to new criteria. It would not be surprising if the next visit of a French investor to the region is greeted by yet another incarnation of "traditional" Evenk forms, perhaps with such media as video art incorporating images of local pop music performers and the construction of an Evenk *chum.* It is less certain what will become of Soviet cultural ideals of equality and collective good, as embodied for many older Evenki in the beadwork images of Lenin described at the outset of this chapter. These ideals may be deemed "inauthentic" or, conversely, "traditional" as a new political economy takes shape and new cultural practices define what it is to be modern in Russia.

Chapter 8
Revitalizing the Collective in a Market Era

> In the taiga and tundra regions of Siberia . . . the school not only did not give the students the vitally necessary habits and skills, but even nurtured in them a negative attitude toward the hunting-and-reindeer-breeding economy, which supposedly belonged completely in the realm of survivals of the past.
>
> —Iu. B. Strakach 1966, cited in Ethel Dunn, "Educating the Small Peoples of the Soviet North: The Limits of Culture Change"

> If place-making is a way of constructing the past, a venerable means of doing human history, it is also a way of constructing social traditions and, in the process, personal and social identities.
>
> —Keith H. Basso, *Wisdom Sits in Places*

The post-Soviet context, with its contests over new types of sovereignty and concomitant reevaluations of place, is one of the most dynamic contexts imaginable as a focus of study. The shifting representations of identity and unresolved questions over resources recently released from the monopoly of state control make the field of analysis akin to the unstable thawing ground in the taiga in early summer. The issues confronting indigenous Siberians are very much part of how indigenous peoples worldwide are reevaluating their relationships to nation-states in this era of "post-colonialism," or neo-colonialism (Biolosi and Zimmerman 1997). What makes the case of indigenous Siberians, and specifically the Evenki, unique is that they were inserted in many ways into the hierarchies of power that comprised Soviet society.

A time-tested tenet of ethnography turns our attention to the local and how lives are lived on a daily basis. Here I have focused on how men and women in one central Siberian Evenk community in the 1990s were making sense of the post-Soviet world and of the social and institutional legacies of residential schooling that shaped Evenk lives. In Keith Basso's words, the "place-making" of individuals within a community is critical to the way histories and identities become crystallized (1996). In the case of this community of central Siberian Evenki, "place-making" is not just about naming and retaining a link with traditional homelands, although this is critical as well (see Amel'kin 1996). In the 1990s Evenki were also struggling to renegotiate and identify the place of the "collective" in their daily lives. How this new collective is defined in the future will closely intertwine with questions of economic development, levels of sovereignty, and access to multiple systems of knowledge. As Basso eloquently states in regard to the Western Apache, "Knowledge of places is . . . closely linked to knowledge of the self, to grasping one's position in the larger scheme of things, including one's community" (1996: 34).

A sense of collectivist culture shaped a shared identity for many Evenk adults, but it is rarely viewed as a significant element by observers of indigenous Siberian community dynamics. Instead, tensions between "tradition" and "modernity" have been targeted by many indigenous Siberian intellectuals and social scientists as the crux of the challenge to guaranteeing an equitable future for indigenous Siberians. For instance, two Russian social scientists generally sympathetic to the plight of indigenous Siberians write: "Native people should neither whine nostalgically for the past, nor beg for subsidies for the future. Rather, native people need to use the increasingly severe economic conditions as a means of creating a genuine revival of native traditions in all spheres of life" (Pika and Prokhorov 1996: 269; Pika 1997). While the authors expressed this opinion within a broader set of recommendations that the Russian government must cede control of natural resources and social and political structures to indigenous organizations, the emphasis on "traditions" belies several fundamental stumbling blocks in imagining a sustainable future for indigenous Siberians. By overlooking the Soviet collectivist culture as a significant element of indigenous Siberian identity, social scientists run the danger of essentializing indigenous Siberians. They can be relegated to "traditional culture" and broadly conceived of in a contained, binary framework, but this is a thin representation of reality. Why should indigenous Siberians turn back to simply reviving "traditions" rather than demanding their fair economic proceeds for building their own transformed infrastructures, possibly growing out of former Soviet institutions?

Larisa Abriutina, an indigenous Siberian activist and doctor from Chukotka, questions ideas about tradition from a slightly different perspective. She argues that the occasional new Russian legislation about the "status" of native peoples and cultural revitalization efforts in the form of museum exhibits, folk dances, and native language classes will not make a difference for Northern peoples struggling to survive (1997: 19). What she says will make a difference are careful discussions with those people who continue to make a living in traditional subsistence practices, herding reindeer, fishing, and sea mammal hunting. Her comments reflect the anxiety felt by indigenous Siberians as federal legislation about the privatization of land was debated for years on end; a version of this legislation was finally passed in the spring of 1999, but in 2002 it was still pending implementation. As the entire country has undergone a massive transfer of government capital to private control (or long-term lease) since 1992, indigenous peoples relying on natural resources for subsistence have anxiously observed the course of federal legislation. Abriutina cautions that "casual land transfers to representatives of indigenous peoples of the North could lead to conflicts and the ultimate loss of parts of this subsistence land [to inappropriate people]" (1997: 19). As Abriutina's critical assessment makes clear, essentializing indigenous peoples as totally "traditional" is inaccurate and does not take into account the hierarchies of difference that exist among indigenous Siberian groups, even when they have a "collectivist" Soviet legacy in common.

Likewise, in considering the residential school as a vehicle for nation-state power in the Soviet era and as a site for Evenk identity politics in the post-Soviet era, I have sought to avoid a homogenizing perspective. The residential school was and continues to be a site for reproducing ideologies, but I do not argue for a simple dichotomous model of power relations in post-Soviet society. Instead, I have tried to demonstrate the wide range of ambivalences, resistances, and types of power that are imbricated in this institution. In the Evenk District power and resistance to power were intricately nested, often with no clear dichotomy between Evenki and Russians as oppressed and oppressor. There were, and continue to be, however, patterns in how these relations of power play out. In the former Soviet Union, given the history of scholarship privileging unidirectional power relationships, it is especially important to pay attention to the myriad ways that power in fact operates and to how people talk about it.

Through this analysis of multiple power relationships at different points in time vis-à-vis the residential school, I have sought to provide a sense of the shifting nature of power. For instance, Praskov'ia Nikolaevna (the Evenk teacher cited in the first part of Chapter 3) can be seen as wielding power over students as an educator while simultaneously herself being a product of the Soviet project. At another level, Katanga Evenki in general can be viewed as allied with a Soviet project in contrast to Illimpei Evenki, who were the primary subjects of the Soviet project in the Evenk District. A perspective focusing on Russians dominating the

Evenki also comes into question as Evenk intellectuals are actively engaged in transformative projects of their own that sometimes continue to be shaped by socialist ideals.

As many Evenk intellectuals emphasize the potential for the residential school to be a center for Evenk cultural revitalization, some Evenki contest this as well. Those who were invested in the former socialist system feel threatened by formulations of "cultural revival"; they view "cultural revitalization" as an attack on the Soviet state's educational programs, and in turn on their long years of work in the system. One older Evenk teacher and Communist Party member explained that she viewed the school as a place for Evenk students to become more "civilized." The same teacher angrily spoke against the growing trend to leave the Communist Party saying, "When people ask me how I can remain in the Party, I tell them, 'You entered the Party as a career move and so you can abandon it easily. I entered the Party because I believe in it, and I still believe in it.'" From the perspective of some Evenk intellectuals who were schooled in the social-evolutionary teachings of Marxist-Leninism, the concept "cultural revitalization" implies that Evenki were wronged during the socialist period and now must have their rights rehabilitated and their culture revived. It is both personally difficult for them to accept that they were part of a party that could be injurious to their community and politically unacceptable for them to believe that the Soviet period has not benefited Evenki as a group. From this perspective, Communist Party members ask what "culture" needs to be revived when the state has been actively involved in supporting folk dance, music, and native language programs for years. In contrast, those who resent that the Soviet government historically directed significant resources to indigenous peoples continue to ask why native peoples should receive any special benefits.

This question may be what led to a recent disaster in the Evenk District. In the winter of 2001, the residential school burned to the ground, leaving Evenki without a physical structure in which to pursue cultural revitalization or emphasize teachings tailored to native students. It remains unclear if the fire was set by an arsonist or was perhaps simply an accident. Given the passions surrounding this institution and the symbolic importance it holds for community members, this event was widely discussed, with news first reaching me via an e-mail from Moscow. For nearly a year the governor of Evenkiia refused to invest in rebuilding the structure, invoking cost-saving arguments. Following a huge public outcry by Evenki and some others, construction on the new school was initiated in summer 2002. It seems that at least for the immediate future Evenki will have a space of their own to continue the difficult process of establishing a sustainable means of safeguarding their community and their cultural distinctiveness.

As Evenki negotiate relationships with the post-Soviet state, the question of "culture" will continue to be debated. The residential school as a former central instrument of the Soviet project has emerged as a key site for the Evenk community to evaluate how "traditional" culture will fit into the lives of contemporary and future Evenki. Given the wide range of diverging perspectives in this community about what it is to be Evenki, the residential school will very likely be a site that remains contested for years to come.

Basso writes in regard to the Western Apache:

> Models of "the Whiteman" are consistently formulated in relation to corresponding models of the "the Indian." More precisely, it appears to be the case that in all Indian cultures "the Whiteman" serves as a conspicuous vehicle for conceptions that define and characterize what "the Indian" is not. . . . The "Whiteman" comes in different versions because "the Indian" does, and it is just for this reason—that conceptions of the former constitute negative expressions of conceptions of the latter (and vice versa)—that *in rendering Whitemen meaningful, "the Whiteman" renders Indians meaningful as well.* (1979: 5, emphasis added)

Basso's statement highlights why an "oppositional" identity, or a "boundary" identity in another formulation, is in fact problematic in considering the dynamics of group identity. If "Indian" (or Evenk or Western Apache) is a mere "oppositional" identity of "Whiteman," then how does one explain all the negotiation, nuance, and contest over identities described in the previous pages? Basso's formula for how identity operates reflects an essentialist approach. It glosses over the multiple contests that are always at play in the formation and transformation of identities and supposes a unified "Indian" identity, unperturbed by the political, regional, class, generational, and gender identities that compete for allegiances in any community.

A concept of "oppositional" identity does form a foil for reflecting on how competing notions of being "indigenous Siberian" are now emerging in the Russian Federation. In fact, this identity formation for Evenki is perhaps closer to what has been described as emerging among the Inuit of Greenland in the face of economic development schemes (Nuttall 1992: 179). As Evenki are faced with a political economy moving toward privatization of lands, reindeer herds, and areas for gathering, a uniform concept of an authentic Evenk person comes to serve a political purpose. Significantly, however, while the local herding, hunting, fishing, and gathering subsistence practices continue, those increasingly representing community interests both at a federal level and international level are often disengaged from these local communities. As social stratification increases in the region, the range of local interest groups also grows. Like the situation in Alaska after the Alaska Native Claims Settlement Act (ANCSA) of 1971 and the situation in

Greenland in the 1990s, the collective interests of this Evenk community are increasingly threatened by profit-driven, individualistic visions for community development. Thus, ironically, in this era that some view as "post-colonial," indigenous Siberians are often looking to Soviet cultural ideals and practices as a means for anchoring their communities with a sense of collective belonging in the post-Soviet era.

Notes

Abbreviations

Terms for Archives and Geographic Areas
EAO: Evenk Autonomous District (Evenkiiskii Avtonomnyi Okrug)

GA EAO: State Archive of the Evenk Autonomous District (Gosudarstvennyi Arkhiv Evenkiiskii Avtonomnyi Okrug)

TsGA RF: State Archive of the Russian Federation (Tsentral'nyi Gosudarstvennyi Arkhiv Rossiiskoi Federatsii)

GA KK: State Archive of the Krasnoiarsk Region (Gosudarstvennyi Arkhiv Krasnoiarskogo Kraia)

Preface

1. The Committee of the North (Komitet Severa), sometimes referred to as the Department of the North, was in existence until 1934, when it was disbanded. It was established again in 1993 but disbanded once more in 1999. At that point the Committee for Regional Politics was created; it was to subsume the former responsibilities of the Committee of the North. In the second major reorganization in the course of one year, the Committee of the North was reestablished in the spring of 1999 (personal communication with Tamara Semenova, 1999). For an overview of the original Committee of the North, its founding mandate, and its historical development, see Grant (1995a).

2. Unlike higher education, which is being increasingly privatized, secondary education continues to be officially government financed. Dash postulates this may be the result of central government fear of unrest over this issue in various regions of Russia (Dash 1998: 1232).

3. I use the term "intellectuals" following Kay Warren, who writes of intellectuals as "producers of authoritative knowledge and interpreters of social reality . . . elders, leaders, teachers, priests, healers, mediators, officials, and so forth" (1998: 26).

4. Several authors have written extensively about the broader Soviet and

post-Soviet education system. One recent ethnography conducted in St. Petersburg high schools found the structures of schooling and practices of socialization to have changed little since the late 1980s; however, students' narratives did re-flect the ideological shift. Students did not register a sense of Soviet historical consciousness; the majority interviewed did not consider the downfall of the Soviet state as significant in their lives (Markowitz 2000). An overview of the Soviet education system, especially focusing on collective culture promoted in preschool socialization, is provided in Bronfenbrenner (1970). Eklof (1990) has written on systems of education for the peasantry in nineteenth-century Russia, and Lempert (1995) has written on the system of higher education in post-Soviet Russia with a focus on St. Petersburg. Studies of school, society, and sexuality in Russia are growing as well (see Attwood 1996; Pilkington 1996).

5. All citizens of Russia continue to carry an internal passport in which they are required to indicate their "nationality" (Russian, Evenk, etc.), and until 1993 they were required to register (*propisat'sia*) with the town passport office in their place of residence. This regulation was variably enforced in urban centers by the late 1990s, but it continues to be important in rural regions of Russia. As a center for trade, politics, education, and health services, Tura on any given day has at least 400 temporary Evenk residents (primarily students and patients).

6. Those exiled from the Baltic regions and from southern Russia were considered potential collaborators during World War II. Germans in Tura tended to be farmers from near the Volga River; their ancestors had moved to Russia in the late eighteenth century during Catherine the Great's efforts to establish European settlements in southern Russia. When World War II broke out, they found themselves living adjacent to German occupied territory and the Soviet government suspected them of being collaborators, an accusation that was not always well founded. As of 1990, the German government was "repatriating" Volga Germans by offering them the opportunity to return to their German homeland, and those from the Baltics were able to return home in the 1950s. Only a few of these exiled families remained in the Evenk District in the late 1990s (personal communication with Joachim Habeck, 1998). Various indigenous populations on the borders of Russia were also accused of collaborating with the "enemy" during World War II; for instance, many Nivkhi on Sakhalin Island served time in prison because of "collaboration" with the Japanese (Im 1998).

7. Humphrey points out that demands for sovereignty and ethnic unification were quelled in the early 1990s with a presidential decree that equalized the status of autonomous districts and republics and created equal footing for them in their efforts to lobby for payments from Moscow (1999b: 50).

8. The Soviet Federative Socialist Republics (the Soviet Union or USSR) were comprised of a hierarchy of designations based loosely on population size, with the so-called "nations" (*natsii*) (e.g., Russia, Ukraine, and Uzbekistan) at the pinnacle. "Nationalities" (*natsional'nosti*) like the Sakha and Chechen were next in the hierarchy, and they continue to be organized into territorial units called republics (*respubliki*) within the contemporary Russian Federation. Ethnic groups such as the Evenki, which did not have the status of "nations" or "nationalities" in the Soviet period, continue to be officially represented by autonomous territories (*avtonomnye kraia*), or districts (*okruga*), depending on population size. Territories are also sometimes divided along administrative lines that are not ethnically based, with provinces (*oblasti*) designated. Districts are sometimes part of the provinces and sometimes independent entities, as in the case of the Koriak Autonomous District located to the north of the Kamchatka Province. Districts are divided into administrative regions (*raiony*), such as the three

in the Evenk District. "Autonomous districts" (*avtonomnye okruga*) only came into existence in 1977; from 1930 to 1977 they were called "national districts" (*natsional'nye okruga*) (Schindler 1997). For an overview of the local Soviet system of government and versions of "self-government" established among Evenki in the late 1920s, see Tugolukov (1971). For an extensive discussion of levels of Soviet administration, the contemporary reorganization of hierarchies, and the specific history of territory boundaries and local concepts of these in the area around the Evenk District, see Anderson (2000: 148–60).

9. See Balzer (1999) for a discussion of the context and individuals involved in the 1990 establishment of the umbrella organization, the Russian Association of Indigenous Peoples of the North (RAIPON).

10. The precursor of the Northern Faculty at the Herzen Pedagogical Institute was the Institute of Northern Peoples, or "Northern Faculty," founded in 1924 at Leningrad State University.

Introduction. Fieldwork, Socialism in Crisis, and Identities in the Making

1. See Slezkine (1994), Grant (1995a), and D. Anderson (2000) for a critical discussion of this classification of indigenous Siberians.

2. Catherine Verdery (1996: 4–6) makes a similar observation and notes that the Cold War had its own "cognitive organization of the world" that affected all, East and West.

3. This opposition to "bourgeois" cultural forms dates back to a 1934 pronouncement that socialist realism was to be the new genre for Soviet cultural production. For instance, the First All-Union Congress of Soviet Writers decreed in 1934, "Socialist realism . . . demands of the artist the truthful, historically concrete representation of reality in its revolutionary development. Moreover, the truthfulness and historical concreteness of the artistic representation of reality must be linked with the task of ideological translation and education of workers in the spirit of socialism" (cited in Tertz 1960: 148). Such was the proclamation of socialist realism as the new official genre for all Soviet cultural production. See *The Atomic Cafe* (Loader 1983) for the mirror image of the U.S. fear of socialism, with the Soviet Union as the epitome of this threat to ideals of "democracy" and "freedom."

4. In discussing the word *kul'tura*, David Anderson writes that when Russian newcomers, state authorities, and sometimes native intellectuals invoke this concept they collapse an assumption of basic social services with an expectation of some of the trappings of "high culture" (2000: 188). While it may be self-evident, it is important to note that this reference point of "high culture" is European without a doubt, with Russia's centers as one of the focal points but with western Europe, and specifically Paris, often placed at the pinnacle.

5. Vladimir Shlapentokh explores this issue in his work on public and private spheres in Soviet society (1989).

6. The drumsticks were called "Bush's legs" because they apparently appeared for sale following a trade agreement signed by George Bush in 1989 for surplus U.S. agricultural products—including chicken, butter, and cheese—to be sold to the Soviet Union.

7. Until 1991, the whole area of the Krasnoiarsk Territory (*krai*)—what is today the Republic of Khakassiia, the Taimyr Republic, and the Evenk Autonomous District—was considered a "closed region" for all foreigners, and even

for all Soviet citizens who did not have express permission to be there. This regulation of movement was in place supposedly to protect the then booming defense industry and strategic military installations in the region.

8. The situation in Siberian cities was mirrored in Moscow, where, according to one source, women formed 80 percent of the unemployed in the early 1990s (see Posadskaia 1993).

9. See Linnekin (1998) for an extensive discussion of the drawbacks of being a young woman in the field. She also emphasizes the ways taking family to the field shifts one's frame of reference from an identity defined by the classic lone fieldworker to an identity as a person rooted in social relationships. See Turner (1996) for an evocative example of how generational positioning shifts over a researcher's lifespan and how aging can create ideal subjectivities for conducting certain fieldwork. See Back (1993) for a discussion of masculinity and fieldwork with adolescents in South London.

10. As discussed in Chapter 2, prior to the Soviet period there were Russian Orthodox missions within several hundred kilometers of present-day Tura, but these missions were abandoned in the early part of the twentieth century. See Anderson and Orekhova (2002) for a discussion of missionary activity in the region in the nineteenth century.

11. The terms "tradition" and "traditional" have been widely discussed and problematized (Linnekin 1991; Handler 1988), including specifically in Siberian contexts (Rethmann 2001: 155–74; Krupnik and Vakhtin 1997; Grant 1995a). Chapters 7 and 8 discuss negotiations around the concept of tradition in the Evenk District.

12. See Béteille (1998) for a discussion of the potential political volatility of the term "indigenous," and Wilmer (1993) for the UN definition of indigenous peoples. In Siberia, contemporary indigenous groups have special status because their group histories, or "priority of settlement," as Béteille calls it (1998: 188), predate European "discovery" and colonization. Throughout this book the phrase "indigenous Siberians" serves as a shorthand referring to those populations inhabiting Siberia prior to the arrival of Russian and Soviet settlers. See Maybury-Lewis (1997) for a discussion of how the term "indigenous" contrasts with terms such as "ethnic."

13. Recent portrayals of socialist cultural practices are particularly poignant in literary form. For instance, Thu Huong Duong depicts the world of socialist Vietnam and emphasizes the ways a socialist society could break down capitalist relations while leaving untouched some ancient patterns of familial hierarchy (1993, 1995). Prior to the fall of the Soviet Union, Salman Rushdie also crafted a journalistic portrait of the challenges facing Nicaragua as it neared the tenth anniversary of its socialist revolution (1987). In his work, Ha Jin evokes images of social interactions and shattered dreams that imply a sharp critique of the culture of Chinese socialism (1997, 1999), while an array of Cuban women authors weave reflections on gender ideologies in post-1959 Cuba into their work (see Davis 1997). I am grateful to Madhav Badami for this last source.

14. Feminist anthropologists have criticized the anthropological canon for glossing over gender as a significant aspect of how the world is structured and experienced. See Reiter (1975) for an early critique of male bias in the discipline and Moore (1988) for a historical overview of feminism and anthropology.

15. Popov's (1993) rather iconoclastic consideration of Japanese childrearing practices and their implications for indigenous Siberians, reflects the spirit of new possibilities for envisioning childrearing at this time. See D. Anderson (2000: 33) for a discussion of Evenk pedagogy in regard to reindeer herding.

16. For a powerful literary treatment of education as a facet of state-building,

see Pramoedya Ananta Toer's novels on colonial Indonesia, and especially *This Earth of Mankind* (1982) and *Child of All Nations* (1996).

17. Ogbu (1991) argues that immigrants and non-Western peoples attending Western-style schools experience types of cultural discontinuity in systems of education that are distinct from the discontinuity experienced by native minority populations.

18. See Nemtushkin (1998) for his most recent collection. Nemtushkin usually writes in Russian, but he has some works written in the Evenk language as well. Unfortunately, his more than twenty-one books of poetry and prose are not currently available in English.

Chapter 1. Central Peripheries and Peripheral Centers: Evenki Crafting Identities over Time

1. Tura serves as the administrative, political, and economic hub for three regions: the Illimpei, for which Tura is also the capital; the Tunguso-chunsk, for which Vanavara acts as the capital; and the Baikit region, for which Baikit is the capital.

2. In the introduction to their provocative volume incorporating Maya and "foreign" intellectuals' essays, Fischer and McKenna Brown note, "Ironically, as they seek to proffer the elixir of empowerment, postmodernists are actually eroding the epistemological basis for the authoritative voice central to Maya scholarly activism through their rhetoric of multivocality and relational values, which denies authority to individual representations" (1996: 4).

3. See O'Hanlon (1988, cited in Reed Danahay 1996) for a discussion of the lack of agency addressed in these studies.

4. The Sakha in the Evenk District predominantly live in the northern village of Essei and maintain close ties with the neighboring Sakha Republic to the east (Okruzhnoi otdel statistiki EAO 1994). The Sakha in Essei prefer, however, the self-referent "Iakuty," the Russian language ethnonym by which they have been called since tsarist times. About half (1,000,000) of the population of the Sakha Republic identifies as Sakha, an indigenous Siberian group with Turkic linguistic roots. The Sakha were officially known by the ethnonym Iakuty until 1990, when they chose to reestablish their self-appellation as Sakha. In the late 1990s, the rest of the population in the Sakha Republic was predominantly Russian and Ukrainian, although there were also about 14,000 Evenki living there. For examples of ethnographic work on the Sakha see Balzer (1993, 1996), Tokarev (1988), Ivanova-Unarova (1998), and Cruikshank and Argounova (2002). This book makes use of the contemporary ethnic appellation of Sakha, except in historical references where Iakuty was the current term.

5. The 1989 Soviet census counted less than 1,000 Kety in the Soviet Union. The Kety have historically lived in close proximity to the Evenki in central Siberia; today they are concentrated near the Enisei River in central Siberia. The Keto origins differ from the Evenk origins, however, and they speak a language unrelated to the Evenk language. Keto is the only remaining language belonging to the Enisei family of languages (Alekseenko 1988: 211–12). In the early 1990s, there were 179 Kety recorded as living in the Evenk District (Okruzhnoi otdel statistiki EAO 1992).

6. In the early Soviet period, the Committee for the New Alphabet aimed to create alphabets for sixteen indigenous Siberian groups. At first it was thought that latinized scripts for Siberian languages would be the most accessible to

students and so be ideal in the gradual introduction of Soviet power. By 1936, however, there was growing pressure to Russify Soviet populations, and the Committee for the New Alphabet put aside the new latinized Siberian scripts, turning to writing Siberian alphabets with Cyrillic script (see Grant 1995a: 97). Contrary to the plan to create sixteen alphabets, by 1938 linguists had created only seven—for the Nenets, Mansi, Nanai, Eveny, Chukchi, (Yup'ik) Eskimo, and Evenki. Until after World War II, these groups commonly studied through the first grade in their native languages. Other groups, however, were forced to begin with Russian as a medium for learning.

7. See Kerttula (2000) for a thorough examination of the concept of "newcomers" as it is used in northeastern Siberia in Chukotka. In particular, she considers patterns of marriage between newcomers and Yup'ik and Chukchi (2000: 40–48). See Alaina Lemon (1995) for an important discussion on concepts of race in Russia, especially in regard to Roma.

8. Other terms such as "European" (*evropeets*) or "white" (*belyi*) could be used instead of Russian (*russkii*), but these are problematic in their own way. First, they are not how people generally referred collectively to "Russians." Second, the terms had separate primary semantic spheres; European was usually used in reference to west Europeans, not for people of European decent or phenotype, and white was most commonly used in commenting on race relations in the United States or Africa.

9. The term *rossiianin* (plural *rossiiane*) has been in circulation for a number of years, but was actively reintroduced into public discourse with Yeltsin's rise to power.

10. The 1989 People's Republic of China census indicated that 26,315 Evenki lived in China at the time; additionally, 1,000 to 2,000 Evenki live in Mongolia (Fondahl 1998; Ruofu and Yip 1993). In 1989 there were 29,901 Evenki in the Soviet Union (Gosudarstvennyi komitet RSFSR po statistike 1991: 9). For a discussion of Evenki in China, see China Nationality Photography and Art Press (1989).

11. The Buriat Mongols are concentrated in the present-day Buriat Republic in south-eastern Siberia on the border with China (see Humphrey 1983, 1999a).

12. The Eveny and Evenki are similar in that both groups occupy areas extending from central Siberia to the Russian Far East, and both are historically nomadic groups depending on a combination of hunting, fishing, and reindeer herding as a means of subsistence (Tugolukov 1988: 525–26). The Even language is also closely related to the Evenk language, with common roots in the Tunguso-Manchurian branch of the Ural-Altaic family of languages. At present the Eveny are concentrated in the Russian Far East, in areas of the Magadan and Kamchatka Provinces (*oblasti*), in the Okhotsk region (*raion*) of Khabarovsk Province, and in eastern regions of the Sakha Republic. The 1989 Soviet census counted 17,200 Eveny. Like the Kety, the Eveny have been historically concentrated in close proximity to the Evenki, but recent census data does not indicate any Eveny currently living in the Evenk Autonomous District (Okruzhnoi otdel statistiki EAO 1992).

13. From the Soviet side a long tradition of ethnography and anthropology of Siberian peoples dates back to prerevolutionary times. For an overview of the literature, see Slezkine (1994), Shimkin (1990), Grant (1995a), and D. Anderson (2000).

14. The tent, or *chum*, the Evenki historically constructed and in the herding brigades continue to construct takes the form of a tepee. A bundle of poles is tied together at its vortex, with the opposite ends splayed out in order to form a circular

space underneath; a hearth area is cleared at the center of the *chum* for a small iron stove. Since the 1970s these structures are more often covered with canvas sheets, although they can be covered with reindeer hides. See Monakhova (1999: 12) for a description and diagram of the Evenk *chum* construction.

15. Some scholars hold that the term "shaman" in various Turkic languages did not derive from the Sanskrit but evolved independently in each language (Laufer 1917, cited in Mironov and Shirokogoroff 1924).

16. I am indebted to Irina Borisenkova for her assistance in deciphering the handwriting in these nineteenth-century documents housed in the Evenk District Archive.

17. GA EAO, Tura, f. 29, o. 1, d. 1, l. 3. Vedomosti Turukhanskoi pokhodnoi tserkvi, 1754–1859.

18. GA EAO, Tura, f. 7, o. 1, d. 1, l. 5. Troitskaia tserkov' Turukhanskogo Severa.

19. GA EAO, Tura, f. 29, o. 1, d. 1, l. 3. Perepiska Eniseiskogo dukhovnogo konsistorii c Turukhanskoi pokhodnoi tserkov'iu.

20. GA EAO, Tura, Fond 29, o. 1, d. 11, l. 83. Perepiska Eniseiskogo dukhovnogo konsistorii c Turukhanskoi pokhodnoi tserkov'iu, 1868.

21. GA EAO, Tura, Fond 29, o. 1, d. 3, l. 8. Esseiskii sviatoi Vasil'evskii tserkvi Turukhanskogo kraia, Illimpiiskogo raiona za 1913.

22. The 1926 Soviet *Household Census of the Arctic North* contains a plethora of data reflecting the social relationships between the Evenki, other indigenous Siberians, and the Soviet state at the time. For instance, census-takers were careful to record the numbers and types of domestic animals, the use of staples such as salt and tobacco, and the common types of ailments for animals and humans (Tsentral'noe statisticheskoe upravlenie 1927). Information such as this was used in subsequent strengthening of state control over nomadic populations. David Anderson (2000: 74–81) extensively examines similar state control mechanisms and their links to the bureaucratic and social scientific ranking of groups in the region in the nineteenth and early twentieth centuries, as well as in the Soviet period.

23. Only by the 1960s were reindeer herds fully collectivized and consolidated in the North (personal communication with Igor Krupnik, 1997).

24. Grant argues that the resettlements of population resulted in a second-class status for the Nivkhi, an indigenous Siberian group concentrated on Sakhalin Island (1995a: 129). In the reorganization of *kolkhozy*, Nivkhi often lost their skilled and administrative positions to Russians.

25. For instance, in 1932 the total population for the area that is today the Evenk Autonomous District was 4,932; 81.9 percent, or 4,071 people were considered Evenki (Kurilovich and Naumov 1934: 44, cited in Habeck 1997). By 1939 the population for the Evenk District was recorded as 9,118, but without ethnic groupings indicated (GA EAO 1939). By 1959 the population had grown to 9,910, with 35.4 percent (3,506) recorded as Evenki, Sakha, and Kety, and 64.4 percent as other—namely Russians (Okruzhnoi otdel statistiki EAO 1965). The population of the Evenk District in 1998 was recorded as 20,033 (V zerkale statistiki 1998), with 2,805 Evenki (EastWest Institute report 1999: 1).

26. As David Anderson (2000) has noted, in 1995 Evenk was widely spoken in small villages.

27. Much has been written on the Evenk language. See Boldyrev (1994) for an overview of the history of the language.

28. In the early 1990s one Russian in Tura was renowned for his fluency in Evenk; he was married to an Evenk woman and for many years had taught Evenk

language in a nearby village. In the mid-1990s this self-taught linguist began working in the Institute for Teacher Development (*institut usovershenstvovaniia uchitelei*) in Tura, where he took on various projects (see Amel'kin 1996).

29. In writing about his research conducted among the Kwakiutl on the northwest coast of North America in the 1960s, Wolcott adopts Ward Goodenough's term "prospiospect" (1989: 142). Wolcott explains that such a term is useful to encompass the subjective views of the world that "each of us acquires out of the totality of our personal experience" (1989: 142).

30. In 1996, in a time when the Russian Federation was appealing to sponsors and potential students no longer sympathetic to socialism, the university was renamed from "Patrice Lumumba University" to "the Peoples' Friendship University of the Russian Federation"; at the same point the university lowered its percentage of foreign students from one third to one quarter of the total student body (CNN, June 1997). Patrice Lumumba University was originally named in honor of the first prime minister of former Zaire (Democratic Republic of the Congo since 1997). Patrice Lumumba founded the National Congolese Movement in 1958 to oppose Belgian colonial power in the Congo, and he was elected prime minister in 1960. He was killed shortly thereafter in a coup supported by the United States.

31. Another aspect of this job as a *kochagar* was that one had easy access to the showers installed at each of the coal-fired generator sites. This highly gender-segregated sphere, where women did not seek employment, was an important place for some men to pass their leisure time. It was common for even those men in town who did not work in the coal generator sites to gather there socially and take the opportunity to shower during a friend's shift.

32. As of 2002, this project was yet to materialize.

33. This service involved a fusion of iconography; at one point during the prayer and calls of "Christ is risen" ("Khristos voskres!") and "Yes, he has truly risen" ("Voistinu voskres!"), a cloth that organizers had draped to transform the office space had slipped slightly; I looked up to see an image of Lenin affixed on the wall behind the makeshift altar.

34. The *pominka* (*pominki*, pl.), or memorial gathering and meal, is generally held seven days, as well as forty days, and one year following a death. These Russian Orthodox funerary practices were perpetuated into Soviet, and now post-Soviet times, albeit with significant changes. (For instance, in the post-Soviet period crosses have reappeared on many gravestones, and priests are often asked to preside over burial rituals.) A similar pattern is observed widely in Russia among both Russians and others not necessarily considering themselves Christian.

35. Evenki in this region historically "buried" the dead by suspending them in trees. Even though this custom is no longer generally practiced in towns, many people continue to believe that the soul of the dead will be reincarnated as a young Evenk person. See Balzer (1999: 178–82) for discussion of similar contemporary and historical death and soul beliefs among the Khanty of western Siberia.

36. In 1996 in Tuva in southern Siberia, at least 725 recognized shamans gathered in the capital of Kyzyl (Drobizheva 1996: 254).

37. Personal communication with Craig Campbell, Vancouver, B.C., May 2000.

38. Among Evenk herders it is common to give people nicknames that suggest a connection between the animal and human worlds; nicknames usually indicate something about a person that is reminiscent of an animal's traits, for instance, the gait of a reindeer. Among other indigenous Siberians, naming continues to be a widespread way of preserving a connection with ancestors. For instance, in

regional towns in Chukotka, Chukchi children are often given a Russian name and a Chukchi name (personal communication with Vera Ivanovna Popienko in Provideniia, Chukotka, August, 1998; Kerttula 2000). The Chukchi name would be borrowed from a recently deceased relative.

39. The novel is set in the early nineteenth century and tells of Russian traders encountering Evenki, most notably a shaman by the name of Sinilga, along the Enisei and Nizhniaia Tunguska Rivers (Shishkov 1987).

40. Balzer (1996) writes that in the Sakha Republic shamanism has played an important part in assisting Sakha to reembrace tradition that was denigrated for years under Soviet and pre-Soviet Russian Orthodox influence. Not just shamanic practice is being revived or reinvented, however; in the Buriat Republic, Buddhism and shamanism have reestablished themselves as strong rivals (Zhukovskaia 1995). Others have recently written about shamanic practice and ritual belief among taiga-dwelling indigenous Siberian groups such as the Even reindeer herders in central Siberia (Vitebsky 1991) and the Koriak living in northern Kamchatka in the Russian Far East (King 1998).

Chapter 2. A Siberian Town in the 1990s: Balancing Privatization and Collectivist Values

1. This tension between state and household responsibilities for ensuring the well-being of social reproduction, or social welfare, is certainly not limited to Europe. See Chhachhi (1998) for a historical discussion of maternity benefits in India and the 1929 debates in the Bombay assembly.

2. Keith Basso explores how place-names operate to connect people mentally and emotionally to landscapes, but also to associations of time and space, of history and events, of social interactions and people, and of stages in one's life (1996: 76).

3. Sviridova (1995) carefully details the preparation of a wide range of fish, reindeer, and other traditional Evenk dishes.

4. In 1993 a friend working in a factory in Krasnoiarsk received her pay in the form of cookware for more than six months. She was forced to barter this for daily needs such as foodstuffs, and she found this difficult given the glut in cookware in the area. See Humphrey (1999a: 467–577) for a detailed analysis of how this type of barter operated in the context of Buriatiia.

5. In 1995 people living in regions designated as the "North" or "on the level of the North" on the basis of difficult living conditions were granted fifty-four days of vacation per year; other Russian citizens could take only forty-five days per year. In Tura in August 1995, vacation pay of 1,000,000 rubles (about $222 U.S. in 1995) was the average amount allocated for professionals like teachers, medical specialists, and administrators. This was considered a radical drop in benefits because the sum was approximately the price of just a one-way ticket to the popular vacation sites on the Black Sea. This cut in paid vacations was sharply felt in contrast to the benefits that had been in place since the mid-1980s.

6. The population grew rapidly in the 1970s and 1980s and then plummeted from 1992 to 1994. For instance, in 1964 the population of the Evenk Autonomous District was 11,830 (with over 4,000 Evenki); in 1984 the population was 21,430 (with 3,503 Evenki); the number of Russians in the district nearly doubled in just 20 years, 1964–1984 (Okruzhnoi otdel statistiki EAO 1965, 1985, 1993c). The population statistics are cited in V zerkale statistiki (1998) and East-West Institute report (1999: 1).

7. The inmigration and outmigration statistics for Tura were, respectively: in 1990, 428 and 425; in 1991, 211 and 498; in 1992, 143 and 691; and in 1993, 102 and 459 (Okruzhnoi otdel statistiki EAO 1993a).

8. The sharp drop in Evenk population in the district could also be in part, the result of misrepresentation in the statistics on the native population (*korennoe naselenie*) as consisting of just Evenki, without taking into consideration the Sakha and Kety. In Evenk District Department of Statistics calculations for the district as a whole, often the native populations were indicated without necessarily distinguishing between groups. While the number of Kety remained around 170 in the 1990s, the Sakha population in fact fluctuated in the Evenk District as families in the northern town of Essei considered relocating to the more prosperous Sakha Republic.

9. For instance, in 1993 over a period of ten months (January–October), 788 apartments were privatized in all of the Evenk District. Only 16 of the 788 applications granted for privatization were charged a fee. From those 16 the Russian government collected 697,966 rubles (about $700 U.S.), and the local administration received 8,064 rubles (about $8 U.S.) (Okruzhnoi otdel statistiki EAO 1993b). In Tura in 1993–94, 1,000 rubles was equivalent to about $1 U.S.

10. See Kerttula (2000: 32–40) for a discussion of parallel social stratification in Chukotka, in the Russian Far East.

11. While by the late 1990s, most people in the Evenk District could rarely afford to fly to their native villages, make trips to Krasnoiarsk, or even attend funerals of close kin in outlying areas, the airport was sponsoring some personnel to make annual trips to international soccer tournaments in Italy and to attend language classes in England.

12. In the early 1990s, in the absence of federal laws, each district or town adopted its own bylaws on private property. In the case of the Evenk District, land and capital (lumbermills or farms) could be rented from the government but not owned. For instance, in Tura in 1994 any resident was eligible to pay a small fee, 5,000 rubles or about $5 U.S., to rent a plot of land for personal use for a five-year period. Physical dwellings could be owned.

13. In Russian patronymics are frequently used to indicate respect, and particularly when a younger person is addressing an older person. While pseudonyms are used throughout, except in the case of public figures, I have retained the sense of varying formality between myself and consultants. I have retained the formal (with patronymic) or informal (without) depending on how consultants chose to interact with me. In conversation with me many older consultants preferred to be called by their patronymics, for instance Nadezhda Sergeevna.

14. *Masteritsa*, or seamstress, was a term specifically related to a craftswoman specializing in traditional Evenk material culture, such as reindeer hide and beadwork; the term was generally invoked in regard to older Evenk women who were respected for their craft.

15. In the late 1990s, those hunters and reindeer herders who had avoided being officially documented in the Soviet period were increasingly seeking internal passports (personal communication with Craig Campbell, May 2000). The dire material circumstances, with ammunition, gasoline, and basic foodstuffs like flour difficult to obtain, drove these older Evenki to seek out social assistance; this was only granted when they possessed an internal passport.

16. Tamara Polgogir recalled that in 1985 she had hoped to travel to Turkey as a reward for her excellence as a teacher. Because she was also the Komsomol secretary in the residential school, she had expected to be permitted to take

advantage of this vacation package (*putevka*). At the last moment, however, the vacation package was awarded to someone senior to her in the Party. The new freedom of international travel that emerged in the 1990s was an important aspect of the widespread youth resistance to a renewed Communist Party. Although many youth may never have the capital to travel internationally, overwhelmingly they support what they view as achieved status, for example, potential access to money, over the ascribed status of Party affiliation as a yardstick for access to resources.

17. In addition to mobile medical units, which dated from the early 1950s, there were also mobile "agitation-propaganda" (*agitprop*) groups, divisions of the Party Agitation and Propaganda Department. These traveled around the taiga to the reindeer herding brigades seeking to entertain and educate. They continued right up until the breakup of the Soviet Union in the winter of 1991. In addition to their intended purpose of disseminating information on hygiene, contemporary politics, and education, the agitprop groups also showed films and organized artistic performances.

18. A "family with many children" (*mnogodetnaia sem'ia*) is a classification used by social welfare services in Russia to distinguish those families who have priority in housing and other government benefits. Those families with two or more children were classified in this manner in the Evenk District in the 1990s.

19. In Tura in early 1993, this was roughly equivalent to $500 U.S. This was slightly higher than the standard rate at the time for a one-bedroom apartment in Tura because the apartment was in the *portovskii* block of housing maintained for employees at the airport.

20. *Arun* maintained a list of those households that had laid claim to land. By 1998 only a small percentage of those who had laid claim were actually herding reindeer. Some could not establish the necessary capital, and others were seeking the necessary expertise because many young people who had grown up in residential schools had never learned the skills required for life in the taiga. See Hivon (1995) for an interesting parallel discussion of the establishment of private farming in central Russia.

21. With the onset of a market economy across the North, reindeer herders began selling dried antlers to importers in neighboring Asian countries where there is a demand for antler because of the belief in its medicinal properties, including as an aphrodisiac. In the Evenk District in the early 1990s South Korean companies were the primary customers; initially they offered a wide range of appliances such as televisions, telephones, and microwave ovens in exchange for the antlers. In 1993 dried reindeer horn was being bought by Koreans (in Alaska auction houses) for $40 U.S. a pound (Bernton 1993, cited in Kerttula 2000: 91).

22. The name of the organization, the "Farmers' Association," was indicative of new legislation in the 1990s that applied across the country and permitted individuals to apply for the right to use land for personal (as opposed to government) ventures. The language reflects the agricultural reference point for this legislation. See Hivon (1995) for a discussion of how the "Farmers' Association" was implemented in central Russia.

23. While Evenki were seldom employed in quartz crystal mining and processing in the Soviet period, quartz crystal has long been valued by Evenki, as reflected in oral tradition. In his poem "*Aldun*" (quartz crystal in Evenk), the Evenk poet Nikolai Oegir (1989: 13) describes how the "flicker" (*kolykhanie*) of taiga campfires is reflected in the quartz.

24. The town administration actively sought to house women with "many children" ahead of others on its housing list. For instance, in 1995, out of the forty-two apartments it allocated, eighteen of those were for women with more than two children (S bol'noi golovy na zdorovuiu 1996).

25. This relationship to socialist, collectivist culture was sometimes quite extensive and personal. Through naming, socialist practices and political culture merged with personal lives. In 1993 one young woman told me that she was named Anzhela, a name rarely encountered in Russia, because her mother saw a picture of the prominent former Communist and American intellectual Angela Davis in the newspaper. In the 1990s it was not uncommon to meet women in their sixties and seventies named Oktiabrina, after the October Revolution, or Stalina after Josef Stalin.

26. Kay Warren (1988: 177–210) describes a similar situation for Maya intellectuals in Guatemala, where generational, religious, socioeconomic and geographic distinctions also influence how allegiances play out.

Chapter 3. Red Ties and Residential School: Evenk Women's Narratives and Reconsidering Resistance

1. *Internatskaia/internatskii* is a colloquial term derived from *internat*, the Russian word borrowed from the German word meaning boarding school. Given the elite connotation of the phrase "boarding school," in this book I have chosen to refer to these institutions as "residential schools." *Internaty*, or residential schools, are institutions existing throughout the former Soviet Union that care for children whose parents are unable to look after them. These are distinct from orphanages, *doma rebenka*, where children who are up for adoption generally live. In 1992, 77,200 children reportedly lived in orphanages and residential schools in the Soviet Union (cited in Creutziger 1997: 357). See the report by Human Rights Watch (1999) for an overview of contemporary abuse in such institutions located in urban settings. In the North residential schooling was established separately from the country-wide system; residential schools in the North were originally set up under the aegis of the Committee of the North, instead of under the Ministry of Education. I have not seen any official reports or heard of any abuse in these residential schools.

2. Verdery (1996: 7) also discusses the impact of the Cold War on social science research focused on Eastern Europe and the Soviet Union. She notes that anthropologists conducting research in this region have had to work at moving beyond the questions and paradigms of interest to political science—particularly questions about citizenship and nation-state consolidation—in order to engage more with the local cultural practices that are at the core of anthropological inquiry.

3. In the 1990s one of the most prominent changes in the landscape surrounding major cities such as Moscow, St. Petersburg, Krasnoiarsk, and Vladivostok, was the boom in residential construction. By most standards, and certainly by Russian standards, these houses were not modest; they were predominantly two-story brick structures with four and more bedrooms and garages. Because of economic uncertainty, and then the crisis of 1998 when the ruble was devalued severely, construction efforts often were abandoned, however, and the buildings stood in semiconstructed states waiting for water and electricity lines.

4. See Thompson (1966), Le Roy Ladurie (1978), and Wolf (1982) for early examples of work focused on oppressive power relations.

5. In their work on north Indian women's expressive traditions, Raheja and Gold (1994: 17) note that studies focused on mass movements or large-scale resistance have tended to exclude women because they are rarely involved in these types of resistance. Such studies tend to imply that women are apolitical. Raheja and Gold demonstrate, however, how expressive genres can voice discontent in wider political arenas (1994: 187). Thus taking informal and ritual resistance as a valid and critical part of analyses of power may reveal previously overlooked agency of many groups.

6. Scott describes "everyday forms of resistance" as those forms "deployed by a weaker party in thwarting the claims of an institutional or class opponent who dominates the public exercise of power" (1989: 21–24). He emphasizes that resistance does not have to be organized and collective to be recognized as an important element in class relations. Most importantly, for Scott resistance serves as an indicator of oppressive power relations and tensions.

7. Scott points out that resistance of the "foot-dragging" sort could easily be the basis for later mass revolution (1985: 23)

8. In defining resistance Scott's work makes little room for accommodation; he focuses on the intentions of actors rather than on the effects. Scott also emphasizes that his concept of resistance encompasses all those actions whose object is to either repudiate or make more palatable the demands of superiors or to promote one's own claims (1985: xvi). This broad definition of resistance subsumes any concept of accommodation in power relationships and suggests that subordinates are always in positions of agency. Scott's work thus rejects ideas of false consciousness; in direct opposition to a Gramscian world of cultural hegemony Scott embraces the idea that poor peasants can have radically independent thought.

9. These analyses are important in that they forcefully demonstrate the interconnected nature of modes of resistance, gender, and contemporary capitalist processes. Ong (1987) and Sharp (1990) in particular examine ways that resistance can be somatized when women's social experience is transformed in contexts of urbanization and market expansion.

10. Abu-Lughod writes about pitfalls in regard to analyzing aspects of consciousness: the problem of recognizing resistances without misattributing forms of consciousness to them, the problem of explaining why women both resist and support a system of which they are a part, and the problem of acknowledging that forms of resistance can be "culturally provided" without assuming that this means they are "safety valves" on some type of mechanistic cultural system.

11. Behar (1993: 295) also writes of the overly celebratory approach of many studies of resistance, while Ortner (1995) provides a cogent examination of the pitfalls created with simplistic studies of resistance.

12. Foucault does not use the term "accommodation" but identifies two types of resistance: "reverse resistance," which involves continued support of a power/knowledge discourse, and "resistance as freedom," which would require breaking away from and denying a power/knowledge discourse (Foucault 1990, cited in Guthrie and Castelnuovo 1992). This chapter uses the terms "accommodation" and "resistance" to refer to Foucault's ideas.

13. In Lamphere's work (1987) among New England factory women she examines how ethnicity and gender intersect to influence political action. She links the term "accommodation" with "strategies" to consider women's actions on the shop floor (1987: 29–30). In distinguishing between "resistance" strategies and "coping or accommodation" in her emphasis on women as active strategists, Lamphere shows how they employ types of informal strategies to have some

control over their work culture. Ultimately, the line between resistance and accommodation appears unclear.

14. Rofel considers the dilemmas of these terms in her work on women silk workers' negotiations of power in the context of ideologies of production speed-ups in China. When women take breaks supposedly to breastfeed children but instead spend time visiting relatives, Rofel argues that they are resisting pressures for higher productivity (1992: 94). If one interprets these actions as pursuing personal aims over the aims of capital, then the actions could be considered as resistance. Rofel also notes, however, that what she initially calls resistance could also be viewed as accommodation because it contributes to the social reproduction of prevailing beliefs in Chinese society that women are less productive than men.

15. The Committee of the North sought to assert Soviet administrative and economic power in areas of Siberia populated by indigenous Siberians (TsGA RF f.1397, o.1, d.1, l.1). See Slezkine (1994) for a critical overview of the establishment of culture bases in the North.

16. Alec Nove cites figures indicating the number of people executed for counterrevolutionary offenses in the USSR as a whole in this period varied radically from year to year. They ranged from 2,056 in 1934 to 1,229 in 1935 to 353,074 in 1937 (1993, cited in Grant 1995a: 183).

17. One scholar estimates that the reindeer population throughout Siberia dropped by one-third in just a three-year period, 1934–37 (Pika 1989: 320).

18. See also Kwon (1993) on women "tent workers."

19. TsGA RF, f. 3977, o. 1, d. 1110, l. 14. "Otchet po obsledovaniiu raboty Turinskoi kul'tbazy za 1929–1930." "Rabota po okhmatilau."

20. There were eighteen schools planned, but fifteen in fact in place by 1926 (TsGA RF, f. 1877, o. 1, d. 1, l. 1).

21. Educators working with urban Russian populations in the 1920s were also drawn to Dewey's emphasis on action-oriented learning. In particular, Anton Makarenko (1973) became well known for his reform schools for youth that were organized around principles of collective manual labor.

22. Dewey's "action"-oriented curriculum was intended to engage students with activities whereby they would learn reading, arithmetic, or geography (1900). Instead of merely reading a book, he would have students use reading to solve a puzzle. Instead of merely solving sums, he envisioned students building something, like a shed or a wagon, thereby gaining competence in arithmetic.

23. Egor Itygin, an Evenk educator who directed the Division for the Enlightenment of National Minorities in the Irkutsk Department of Education (Kraevoi otdel narodnogo obrazovaniia) from 1927 to 1928, wrote: "The delicate mind of a child (should) train in its native language from the beginning. . . . These conditions allow the child to develop in a proper, balanced, harmonious way. That's the physical and psychological way of humans. . . . Only when a child has an understanding of his familiar, native knowledge will he move gradually from the familiar to the unfamiliar. . . . Then he'll begin to study the language of the majority of the population [of the USSR]" (Itygin 1927a: 85).

24. TsGA RF, f. 3977, o. 1, d. 1110, l. 16. A. Ivanenko, "Otchet po obsledovaniiu raboty Turinskoi kul'tbazy za 1929–1930 gg."

25. TsGA RF, f. 3977, o.1, d. 134, ll. 5–7, Doklady uchitelei o rabote tuzemnykh shkol (Na kursakh po povysheniiu kvalifitsirovaniia letom 1926): Doklad na tsentral'nykh ekskursii-kursakh uchitelei narodov Severa po "uchetu mestnogo opyta"—kursanta-uchitelia Samoedskoi shkoly I.A. Dimova, and TsGA RF, f. 3977, o.1, d. 134, ll. 8, 11, Doklady uchitelei o rabote tuzemnykh shkol (Na kursakh po

povysheniiu kvalifitsirovaniia letom 1926): Doklad o rabote Ukhtinskoi tuzemnoi shkoly Nikolaevskogo na Amure okruga za 1925–26 uchebyi god.

26. Okruzhnoi muzei EAO, Tura, d. Narodnoe obrazovanie, Baikitskogo raiona, photograph 164, "Zhertvy pozhara, poselok Baikita, 1936." The Evenk District Regional History Museum (hereafter Evenk District Museum) houses the Suslov Collection, which consists of photographs taken by the ethnographer-cum-administrator Innokentii Mikhailovich Suslov from 1925 to 1927 during his three expeditions to the Evenk District. Most of the photographs are accompanied by Suslov's brief commentary written in pencil; in this case no further context or information was included. See Anderson and Orekhova (2002) for a discussion of the three generations of Suslovs engaged in social activism in central Siberia.

27. On Soviet, and particularly Russian concepts of sexuality and gender relations in the post-World War II period, see Attwood (1990, 1996).

28. Bell (1995) describes comparable gender systems as part of the training in the 1930s to 1950s at residential schools for Native Americans in North America. As part of the curriculum, girls were sent to work during summers as domestic workers, which was considered ideal training for their future lives as housewives, while boys apprenticed in trades that were meant to provide future income.

29. It is striking that the Evenk first names most often encountered in the Evenk District are Russian in origin. In contrast, Evenk surnames are distinctively Evenk in origin. Typical Evenk surnames in the region are Khutokogir, Chapogir, and Udygir; historically these were names for clans. David Anderson (2000:44) writes in regard to Khantaika surnames that missionaries in that region (to the north of the Evenk District), probably began the practice of using clan names as surnames for specific people. The relatively low percentage of Russian Orthodox conversions among Evenki in this region historically is reflected in their retention of Evenk surnames; by comparison, those identifying as Sakha in the Evenk District often have Russian surnames like Popov.

30. Okruzhnoi muzei EAO, Tura, kollektsiia Suslova, photograph 51, "Seriia fotosnimkov Filippa Iakovlevicha Babkina v bytnost' ego zaveduiushchim Kazymskoi kul'tbazoi (iz kollektsii I.M. Suslova), 1925."

31. As Grant notes in regard to the Nivkhi, a group concentrated on Sakhalin Island in the Russian Far East, the Soviet government viewed work with indigenous Siberians as a means for measuring the success of the new Soviet cultural project (Grant 1995a: 89).

32. In 1994 more than 840 people of the 25,000 population in the Evenk District were infected with tuberculosis (Statistika 1993). Those Evenki who worked in the now defunct government cooperatives (*sovkhozy*) were especially prone to tuberculosis because new "farming cooperatives" or private enterprises were not required to provide sick leave for their employees to receive treatment. Also, the former monthly government medical visits to villages and reindeer brigades were curtailed severely by the mid-1990s and were reduced to a single yearly screening for tuberculosis.

33. The pension was hardly enough for the elderly to finance basics, and they relied on generating extra income through sewing, borrowing from relatives, and receiving emergency monies from the town social service agency providing for pensioners and invalids. In December of 1993, a locally subsidized loaf of dark bread cost 300 rubles (about 25 cents, at the then exchange rate of 1,000 rubles to $1 U.S.). In 1995 it cost 1,200 rubles (about 25 cents, at the exchange rate of 4,500 rubles to $1 U.S.).

34. For a discussion of the dynamics of trade and the various routes traversed by different families in the broader region, see D. Anderson (2000: 136–39).

35. In her work based on extensive interviews with aboriginal Australians, Thies notes similar methods of avoidance of state schooling (1987: 24).

36. The term *stakhanovets*, or stakhanovite, was created in the intense Soviet industrialization period of the 1920s to indicate that a person was a diligent worker. It takes its name from one particularly accomplished worker. In the post-World War II period, the term "stakhanovite" took on some negative connotations among the urban intelligentsia in the Soviet Union; it came to be used to refer to a person who sped up work and forced coworkers to accomplish tasks faster than they preferred.

37. See Cruikshank (1997) for a discussion of the ways in which audiences factor into the practice of oral tradition.

38. Nikul'shin describes his perspective on social stratification in the early 1930s; he calculates that in 1931-32, 8.3 percent of the Evenk *kulaki* owned 73.5 percent of all reindeer in the Evenk District (1939: 15). Tugolukov (1971: 204) clarifies this analysis by emphasizing that this concentration of resources was limited to domesticated reindeer; there was no real difference between households in the number of boats, guns or other tools in their possession. See Grant (1995a: 68–89) for a discussion of early Soviet administrative structures such as native councils that were established in the North in the 1920s.

39. Right up to 1991 when the Komsomol was disbanded, many youngsters prized membership in the Young Pioneers in St. Petersburg; Markowitz notes that some of the students she interviewed about becoming Young Pioneers spoke of the pride they had felt upon being inducted in the mid-1980s (2000: 51–54).

40. "Red ties" apparently have some more contemporary resonances for this community as well. One story goes that in the 1980s residential school students would loiter around the airport building hoping for a ride home. The students from one of the villages located closest to Tura could be spotted easily because they were the only ones wearing the red handkerchiefs around their necks. The storyteller sardonically noted that when these students gave up waiting for a plane, at least in winter they could walk the twenty-five kilometers home along the frozen river. They supposedly continued to wear the red ties so they could ward off any wolves they might meet on the way (personal communication with Joachim Habeck, 1998).

Chapter 4. Young Women Between the Market and the Collective

1. With the economic hardship of the 1990s, pig farming became a popular small business enterprise in Russia. It is particularly popular in harsh climatic regions, where poor land and extremely short growing seasons make intensive agriculture and cattle farming impossible. Since the early 1990s, the growing reliance on homesteading, including raising pigs, chickens, cows, and goats, crosscuts social strata in Russia. One author writes of the importance of pigs for teachers, one of whom told him: "'See that pig? That will be a video player. That's my savings'" (Meshcheriakov 1996: 167).

2. Tsianina Lomawaima also suggests we should be cognizant of how memory, and therefore perspectives of an age cohort, shift with time (personal communication, 1996).

Chapter 5. Inside the Residential School: Cultural Revitalization and the Leninist Program

1. *Subbotniki*, or days for "voluntary" labor, date from 1918 in other parts of the Soviet Union and remained a common feature of Soviet life until the late 1980s. In Tura these were still being carried out in the residential school until late 1993. After a hiatus of nearly five years, some Tura organizations were reintroducing this practice of *subbotniki* in 1998.

2. The Russian word *vospitatel'*, caregiver (plural *vospitateli*), comes from the word *vospityvat'*, to raise or to bring up. The word *vospitatel'* has a formal ring to it. In the Evenk District the word was most often used to refer to the official work of looking after children in a day care or residential school setting.

3. This director was never prosecuted, and soon after her departure from the school she opened two commercial kiosks selling imported sausage, children's books, clothing, liquor, and other luxury goods.

4. In my interview with her (fieldnotes, April 22, 1994) the director of the residential school's division for special education estimated that the majority of the children under her supervision were there because of fetal alcohol syndrome. In 1993 there were 55 children enrolled in the division from throughout the Evenk District, but this number had dropped from 120 students in the 1970s, when it first began operating. The director explained that mentally challenged children were often kept home in the villages after 1993 when it was no longer required for them to attend school.

5. Not only was the language program curtailed significantly in 1998, but the Institute for Teacher Development was closed in 1999. The research conducted there was deemed "unnecessary" by the Evenk Department of Education (personal communication with Diana Andreevna Shchapeva, Tura, April 1999).

Chapter 6. Taiga Kids, Incubator Kids, and Intellectuals

1. In 1994 about one-tenth of the Evenk population in Tura belonged to the Association of Peoples of the North.

2. The clash over land use in Siberia has also been documented in film; for instance, see Soosaar's *Father, Son, and Holy Torum* (1989) examining intergenerational Ob-Ugrian attitudes toward widespread oil exploration on traditional lands in western Siberia.

3. In a converse manner, Stambach has written that schooling in rural Tanzania is more about perpetuating structural differences of unequal power relations and economic inequalities, and less about mastering practical skills (1996: 1). In central Siberia Evenki are recognizing the power of schooling to challenge structural inequalities and destabilize hegemonic power relations.

4. In 1989 9 percent of the Evenk population belonged to the Communist Party (Miller 1994: 335), while among the Khanty in western Siberia, for instance, Balzer notes that no more than 2 percent of the population belonged to the Party at any given time (1999: 263).

5. In a related way, Giddens writes that "social supervision" is one of the institutional dimensions of modern societies (1990: 58).

6. The households herding reindeer, hunting, or fishing as a sole means of subsistence were listed by the Evenk District Department of Statistics as belonging

to "nomadic" (*kochevye*) households. In 1992, for instance, 88 people, including 32women, were listed as belonging to "nomadic" households (Okruzhnoi otdel statistiki EAO 1992). Gurvich and Sokolova observe, however, that many households were not counted as herding reindeer if the households also maintained a residence in a village (1991: 213, cited in Anderson 2000). The number of domesticated reindeer in this area decreased from 64,000 in 1965 to 31,000 in 1989 and to only 8,700 by January 1996 (personal communication with Joachim Habeck, 1998). The number of households herding reindeer in the Evenk District had officially dwindled to about thirty in 1996 (Okruzhnoi otdel statistiki EAO 1996).

7. Here my definition of "intellectuals" is parallel to Drobizheva's use of the term "elite" (1996: 3). She defines the elite as those segments of society that affect the functioning of society through their strategic decision making in an official capacity or through their unofficial stature in society.

8. The *ispolkom* is the executive committee of a soviet (be it a city, region, district, republic, or all-union). It is not a Party organization but a state (that is, Soviet) body. Communist Party members dominated it, however, and enacted Communist Party policy (GA KK, f. 1845, o. 1, d. 239, l. 91. Krasnoiarsk komitet sodeistviia malym narodnostiam Severnykh okrain pri okrispolkome, "O rezul'tatakh kamandirovki v Tazovskii tuzemnyi raion—prezidiumu Turukhanskogo raiispolkoma," 1932).

9. The Institute for Teacher Development published more than twenty of these teaching aids with titles such as "Lessons in Evenk Decorative Arts for the Eleventh Grade" (Saf'iannikova 1994), "Evenk Games" (Udygir 1995), "Reindeer Sleds" (Amel'kin 1995), "Evenkiia—My Reindeer Region: Materials for Preschool Education" (Dmitrieva 1997), and "In the World of Northern Myths" (Osogostok 1995). All these materials are written in Russian and have some Evenk words interspersed. The Institute also published, however, a Russian-Evenk phrasebook, a Russian-Evenk children's dictionary, a Russian-Evenk teaching aid, and a Sakha-Russian thematic phrasebook. The publications, and the institute as a whole, were financed by the Evenk District Department of Education until it curtailed the funding in 1999.

10. In 1993 four levels of distinct administration relating to the Evenk District existed, with representatives elected to office at each level. First, three regional councils operated (one each in Tura, Vanavara, and Baikit), each of which met every few months to discuss such local issues as contracts for supplying aviation services to remote areas and development of public space like an open air market in Tura. Second, there was a district council that met sporadically in regard to regional issues of land use and negotiating contracts with investors such as multinational oil interests. The third layer of administration was at the level of the Territory Parliament; by the mid-1990s the Evenk Autonomous District elected a representative to this body. The fourth, and most distant layer of representation, was still at the level of the Russian Parliament in Moscow. Between 1993 and 2002 the Evenk District held three elections for two representatives to the Parliament of the Russian Federation, a representative to the Krasnoiarsk Territory parliament, and representatives to the district and local councils.

11. It was not rare for the CIA to be invoked in public gatherings in Russia in the 1990s. One Western reporter commenting on the 1996 presidential campaign trail describes a gathering in a vocational school in the Ural mountains in which candidate Gennady Ziuganov asserted that the CIA was taking over Russian television (Bivens 2000: 90). Given the energetic applause, the crowd gathered appeared to support his critical view of the state of Russian media. In

contrast, in the Evenk District campaign events held in the residential school in 1993, the teachers displayed little enthusiasm for the speaker's perspectives.

12. Zinaida Nikolaevna Pikunova, a vocal Evenk educator who gained extensive experience organizing as a Komsomol member, was instrumental in the establishment of the local Arun in 1990. Along with her late husband, who was the managing editor of the Evenk District newspaper *Sovietskaia Evenkiia*, the Evenk educator sought to establish an organization that would champion the rights of local native peoples (Evenki, Sakha, and Kety) living in the Evenk District. In 1993–94 the organization received most of its funding directly from Moscow, either through budget allocations lobbied by representatives or through the Department of the North.

13. The game warden had lived in Tura for nearly twenty years, and she could have avoided the designation of "newcomer" and come to be considered local, or *mestnaia/mestnyi*. It was not her profession that branded her as a newcomer; some of the Russians working as assistants to the game warden were not viewed as newcomers. Instead, the game warden was identified as a newcomer because of her disregard for local systems of knowledge regarding the spirit and animal worlds respected by other locals. In one case during a fishing trip, the game warden ordered one of her assistants to kill a young bear that was not bothering anyone. Those taking part in the fishing trip were appalled and considered this very bad luck; they refused to make use of any of the bear meat or bear's body parts such as bladder, skin, and fat that the warden offered to them. As noted in Chapter 1, bears are particularly respected among the Evenki and other indigenous Siberians. See Rethmann (2001: 49–53) for a similar discussion of the place of bears in Koryak views of the animal, human, and spirit worlds.

14. Okruzhnoi muzei EAO, Tura, kollektsiia Suslova.

Chapter 7. Representing Culture: Museums, Material Culture, and Doing the Lambada

1. Murashko (1996) and Schindler (1997) discuss how indigenous Siberians continue to seek control over traditional land and resources. Beginning in the early 1990s the Russian government continually granted private oil, gas, and timber interests access to lands traditionally used by indigenous peoples, while refusing to safeguard indigenous peoples' rights to land and renewable resources. In April, 1999, however, the Russian Parliament passed legislation regarding a range of rights for indigenous peoples, including those related to land use. It remains to be seen how this legislation will be enforced in various regions of Russia.

2. Personal communication with Anatol Donkan and Mareile Onodera (the organizers of the Amur Ethnic Art Museum in Vladivostok), April 15, 1998.

3. Personal communication with Andrei Khalkachan, August 2, 1999, about an "apartment museum" located in Gizhiga, the Russian Far East.

4. In the late 1990s, Evenk District store owners had not sponsored museum projects yet, but they occasionally provided refreshments for exhibit openings and graduation ceremonies held at the local School for the Arts and at the House of Culture.

5. According to recent Russian Federation legislation, rehabilitated persons and their direct family members were to receive a symbolic monetary compensation. Evenk District legislation also deemed such persons eligible for free housing in Krasnoiarsk.

6. The Popular Memory Group (1982: 205–10) provides an especially lucid

discussion of the "social production of memory," how it operates as histories are documented or passed on orally, and how various institutions, including museums, participate in this process.

7. In promoting cultural revitalization, Evenk intellectuals are not unlike other indigenous elite in other parts of the world. For instance, Kay Warren (1991: 100) describes how "culturalists" are "reviving the heroic imagery of Maya warriors in an attempt to deal with the passivity they see as one of the scars of Latino racism and its language of inferiority for indigenous populations." Maya identity politics, like Evenk identity politics, is using seemingly familiar units of identity to define nationhood. As Warren writes, "Continuity in descent, culture, and language is being constructed as a challenge to histories of conquest and assimilation" (1991: 100).

8. Panarin (1997) notes a similar generational disjuncture as being a problem for the consolidation of village stability in Buriatiia.

9. In 1993 the Evenk District newspaper changed its name from *Sovetskaia Evenkiia* (Soviet Evenkiia) to *Evenkiiskaia zhizn'* (Evenk Life). The original name, *Evenkiiskaia novaia zhizn'*" (Evenk New Life), dated from the newspaper's founding in 1933; the name was changed to *Sovetskaia Evenkiia* in the mid-1940s.

10. Alexandra Kudria, a woman of Evenk heritage and a specialist on Evenk language at the Institute of National Schools in Moscow, explains that native language programs were reintroduced in the North in the 1970s after a hiatus of nearly fifteen years (see Bartels and Bartels 1995: 61). See also Pikunova (1998) for an overview of the initiation of these language revitalization programs in the 1970s.

11. Personal communication with Khristina Ivanovna Chardu, former director of the Evenk District Regional History Museum, June 1998.

Bibliography

Aaltonen, Jouko, and Heimo Lappalainen. 1993. *Taiga Nomads.* Coproducers: Finnish Broadcasting Company (YLE); Swedish Television (SVT); Institute of Ethnology and Anthropology, RAN; AVEK The Nordic Film and TV-Fund; Nordic Anthropological Film Association. Production: ILLUME Ltd.

Abelmann, Nancy. 1997. Narrating Selfhood and Personality in South Korea: Women and Social Mobility. *American Ethnologist* 24 (4): 786–812.

Abriutina, Larisa. 1997. Narody Severa: Problemy, analiz prichin i perspektivy ikh preodoleniia. (The Peoples of the North and Their Problems: An Analysis of Causes and Perspectives for Overcoming the Problems.) *Zhivaia Arktika* 2–4 (6–8): 16–23.

Abu-Lughod, Lila. 1998. Introduction. In *Remaking Women: Feminism and Modernity in the Middle East,* ed. Lila Abu-Lughod. 3–31. Princeton, N.J.: Princeton University Press.

———. 1993. Introduction. In *Writing Women's Worlds: Bedouin Stories.* 1–42. Berkeley: University of California Press.

———. 1990. The Romance of Resistance: Tracing Transformations of Power Through Bedouin Women. *American Ethnologist* 17 (1): 41–55.

———. 1986. *Veiled Sentiments: Honor and Poetry in a Bedouin Society.* Berkeley: University of California Press.

Ackelsberg, Martha. 1992. Mujeres Libres: The Preservation of Memory Under the Politics of Repression in Spain. In *International Yearbook of Oral History and Life Stories,* vol. 1, *Memory and Totalitarianism,* ed. Luisa Passerini. 125–43. Oxford: Oxford University Press.

Aipin, Yu. 1989. Not by Oil Alone. *Moscow News* 2.

Alekseenko, E. A. 1988. Kety. In *Narody mira: istoriko-etnograficheskii spravochnik* (An Ethno-Historical Handbook to Peoples of the World), ed. Iu. V. Bromlei. 211–12. Moscow: Sovetskaia Entsiklopediia.

———. 1967. *Kety: istorichesko-etnograficheskie ocherki* (Kety: Historico-Ethnographic Traits). Leningrad: Nauka.

Alonso, Ana Maria. 1988. The Effects of Truth: Re-presentations of the Past and the Imaging of Community. *Journal of Historical Sociology* 1 (1): 33–57.

Amel'kin, A. G. 1996. *Kratkii slovar' po toponimike Evenkii* (*Short Dictionary of Evenk Toponymics*). Tura: Evenkiiskii okruzhnoi institut usovershenstvovaniia uchitelei.

———. 1995. *Narty* (Reindeer Sleds). Tura: Evenkiiskii okruzhnoi institut usovershenstvovaniia uchitelei.

Amosov, Anatolii. 1998. *Evenki: ocherk o gosudarstvennom regulirovanii zaniatosti malochislennykh narodov Severa v Evenkiiskom avtonomnom okruge.* (*Evenki: An Overview of the Government Regulation of Employment Among the Numerically Small Peoples of the North Residing in the Evenk Autonomous District*). Krasnoiarsk: Bukva.

Anderson, Benedict. 1983. *Imagined Communities: Reflections on the Origin and Spread of Nationalism.* London: Verso.

Anderson, David G. 2000. *Identity and Ecology in Arctic Siberia: The Number One Reindeer Brigade.* New York: Oxford University Press.

———. 1998. Surrogate Currencies and the Wild Market in Central Siberia. Presented at the Conference on Barter in Post-Socialist Societies held at the Møller Centre, Churchill College, Cambridge, December 13–14.

———. 1991. Turning Hunters into Herders: A Critical Examination of Soviet Development Policy Among the Evenki of Southeastern Siberia. *Arctic* 44 (1): 12–22.

Anderson, David G., and Nataliia A. Orekhova. 2002. The Suslov Legacy: the Story of One Family's Struggle with Shamanism. *Sibirica* 2 (1): 88–112.

Anisimov, A. F. 1950. Kul't medvedia u evenkov i problema evoliutsii totemisticheskikh verovanii (The Bear Cult Among the Evenki and the Problem of the Evolution of Totemic Beliefs). *Voprosy istorii religii i ateizma.* Moscow: Sbornik.

Appadurai, Arjun. 1996. *Modernity at Large: Cultural Dimensions of Globalization.* Minneapolis: University of Minnesota Press.

———. 1991. Global Ethnoscapes: Notes and Queries for a Transnational Anthropology. In *Recapturing Anthropology: Working in the Present,* ed. Richard G. Fox. 191–210. Santa Fe, N.M.: School of American Research Press.

Appadurai, Arjun, and Carol A. Breckenridge. 1992. Museums Are Good to Think: Heritage on View in India. In *Museums and Communities: The Politics of Public Culture,* ed. Ivan Karp, Christine Mullen Kreamer, and Steven D. Lavine. 34–55. Washington, D.C.: Smithsonian Institution Press.

Arendt, Hannah. 1966. *Totalitarianism.* Part 3, *The Origins of Totalitarianism.* New York: Harcourt, Brace.

Armitage, Andrew. 1995. *Comparing the Policy of Aboriginal Assimilation: Australia, Canada, and New Zealand.* Vancouver: University of British Columbia Press.

Asad, Talal, ed. 1973. *Anthropology and the Colonial Encounter.* Chicago: University of Chicago Press.

Attwood, Lynne. 1996. Young People, Sex, and Sexual Identity. In *Gender, Generation, and Identity in Contemporary Russia,* ed. Hilary Pilkington. 95–120. London: Routledge.

———. 1990. *The New Soviet Man and Woman: Sex Role Socialization in the USSR.* Bloomington: Indiana University Press.

Back, Les. 1993. Gendered Participation: Masculinity and Fieldwork in a South London Adolescent Community. In *Gendered Fields: Women, Men and Ethnography,* ed. Diane Bell, Pat Caplan, and Wazir Jahan Karim. 215–33. London: Routledge.

Bakhtin, Mikhail M. 1981. *The Dialogic Imagination.* Austin: University of Texas Press.

Balzer, Marjorie Mandelstam. 1999. *The Tenacity of Ethnicity: A Siberian Saga in Global Perspective.* Princeton, N.J.: Princeton University Press.

———. 1996. Flights of the Sacred: Symbolism and Theory in Siberian Shamanism. *American Anthropologist* 98 (2): 305–18.

———. 1993. Two Urban Shamans: Unmasking Leadership in Fin-de-Soviet Siberia. In *Perilous States: Conversations on Culture, Politics, and Nation,* ed. George E. Marcus. 131–64. Chicago: University of Chicago Press.

Bartels, Dennis A., and Alice L. Bartels. 1995. *When the North Was Red: Aboriginal Education in Soviet Siberia.* Montreal: McGill-Queen's University Press.

Barth, Fredrik. 1969. *Ethnic Groups and Boundaries: The Social Organization of Culture Difference.* London: Allen and Unwin.

Basso, Keith H. 1996. *Wisdom Sits in Places: Landscape and Language Among the Western Apache.* Albuquerque: University of New Mexico Press.

———. 1979. *Portraits of the "Whiteman": Linguistic Play and Cultural Symbols Among the Western Apache.* Cambridge: Cambridge University Press.

Battiste, Marie. 1999. Introduction. In *First Nations Education in Canada: The Circle Unfolds,* ed. Marie Battiste and Jean Barrman. vii–xx. Vancouver: University of British Columbia Press.

Bazanov, M. 1936. *Ocherki po istorii missionerskikh shkol na krainem Severe* (*An Outline of the History of Missionary Schools in the Far North*). Leningrad: Zvezda.

Behar, Ruth. 1993. *Translated Woman: Crossing the Border with Esperanza's Story.* Boston: Beacon Press.

Belianin, Nikolai N. 1990. Moi otets—olenevod. Text by Prokopia Iavtysaia, music by N. Belianin. In *Pesni nad Tunguskoi: Sbornik pesen iz repertuara detskogo fol'klornogo ansamblia Osikta* (*Songs over the Tunguska: Collection of Songs from the Repertoire of the Osikta Folk Ensemble*), ed. Nikolai Belianin. 12–14. Krasnoiarsk: Krasnoiarskoe knizhnoe izdatel'stvo.

Bell, Genevieve. 1995. Telling Stories Out of School: Rethinking the Documentary Record of the Carlisle Indian School. Presented at the 94th Annual Meeting of the American Anthropological Association, November 19, 1995, Washington, D.C.

Bentley, G. Carter. 1981. Migration, Ethnic Identity, and State Building in the Philippines: The Sulu Case. In *Ethnic Change,* ed. Charles F. Keyes. 117–53. Seattle: University of Washington Press.

Berdahl, Daphne. 1999. *Where the World Ended: Re-unification and Identity in the German Borderland.* Berkeley: University of California Press.

Béteille, André. 1998. The Idea of Indigenous People. *Current Anthropology* 39 (2): 187–91.

Bhabha, Homi. 1994. Between Identities, interview with Paul Thompson. In *International Yearbook of Oral History and Life Stories,* vol.3, *Migration and Identity,* ed. Rina Benmayor and Andor Skotnes. 183–200. New York: Oxford University Press.

Biolsi, Thomas, and Larry J. Zimmerman. 1997. Introduction: What's Changed, What Hasn't. In *Indians and Anthropologists: Vine Deloria, Jr., and the Critique of Anthropology,* ed. Thomas Biolsi and Larry J. Zimmerman. 3–24. Tucson: University of Arizona Press.

Bivens, Matt. 2000. Back to the USSR.: Special Report, Russia and the Media. *Brill's Content* 3 (6): 86–90.

Bledsoe, Caroline. 1992. Cultural Transformation of Western Education in Sierra Leone. *Africa* 62 (2): 182–202.

Bloch, Alexia. 2001. Cruise Ships and Prison Camps: Reflections from the Russian Far East on Museums and the Crafting of History. *Pacific Science* 55(4): 377–87.

Bloch, Alexia, and Laurel Kendall. 2004. *Museum at the End of the World: Travels and Conversations in the Post-Soviet Russian Far East.* Philadelphia: University of Pennsylvania Press.

Bloul, Rachel A. D. 1994. Veiled Objects of (Post)-Colonial Desire: Forbidden Women Disrupt the Republic Fraternal Space. *Australian Journal of Anthropology* 5 (1–2): 113–23.

Bogoslovskaia, Liudmilla. 1993. List of the Villages of the Chukotka Peninsula (2000 B.P. to present). *Beringian Notes* 2, 2. December 7. National Park Service.
Boitsova, A. F. 1971. Shkola narodov krainego Severa (School for the Peoples of the Far North). In *Osushchestvlenie Leninskoi natsional'noi politiki u narodov krainego Severa* (The Establishment of Leninist Nationality Policy Among the Peoples of the Far North), ed. I. S. Gurvich. 141–58. Moscow: Nauka.
Boldyrev, B. V. 1994. *Russko-evenkiiskii slovar'.* Novosibirsk: Nauka.
Bourdieu, Pierre. 1996. *Acts of Resistance Against the Tyranny of the Market.* New York: New Press.
———. 1984. *Distinction: A Social Critique of the Judgment of Taste.* Cambridge, Mass.: Harvard University Press.
———. 1977. *Outline of a Theory of Practice.* Cambridge: Cambridge University Press.
Bourdieu, Pierre, Luc Boltanski, and Monique de Saint-Martin. 1973. Les stratégies de reconversion: les classes socials et le système d'enseignement. *Information sur les Sciences Sociales* 12 (5): 61–113.
Breckenridge, Carol A. 1989. The Aesthetics and Politics of Colonial Collecting: India at World Fairs. *Journal of Society and History* 31 (2): 195–216.
Bridger, Sue. 2000. Rural Women in Russia: What Does Private Farming Mean? In *Making the Transition Work for Women in Europe and Central Asia,* ed. Marnia Lazreg. 42–49. Washington, D.C.: World Bank.
Briggs, Jean. 1970. *Never in Anger: Portrait of an Eskimo Family.* Cambridge, Mass.: Harvard University Press.
Bronfenbrenner, Urie. 1970. *Two Worlds of Childhood: U.S. and U.S.S.R.* New York: Russell Sage Foundation.
Brysk, Alison. 1996. Turning Weakness into Strength: The Internationalization of Indian Rights. *Latin American Perspectives* 23 (2) (89): 38–57.
Chatterjee, Partha. 1993. *The Nation and Its Fragments: Colonial and Post-Colonial Histories.* Princeton, N.J.: Princeton University Press.
———. 1989. Colonialism, Nationalism, and Colonized Women: The Contest in India. *American Ethnologist* 16 (4): 622–633.
Chatty, Dawn. 1996. *Mobile Pastoralists: Development Planning and Social Change in Oman.* New York: Columbia University Press.
Chaussonnet, Valerie. 1988. Needles and Animals: Women's Magic. In *Crossroads of Continents: Cultures of Siberia and Alaska,* ed. William W. Fitzhugh and Aron Crowell. 209–27. Washington, D.C.: Smithsonian Institution Press.
Chhachhi, Amrita. 1998. Who Is Responsible for Maternity Benefit: State, Capital, or Husband? *Economic and Political Weekly* 33 (22): 21–29.
Child, Brenda. 1998. *Boarding School Seasons: American Indian Families, 1900–1940.* Lincoln: University of Nebraska Press.
China Nationality Photography and Art Press. 1989. *Chinese Nationalities.* Beijing: China Nationality Photography Art Press.
Clifford, J. 1990. Four Northwest Coast Museums. In *Exhibiting Cultures: The Poetics and Politics of Museum Display,* ed. Ivan Karp and S. D. Lavine. 112–254. Washington, D.C.: Smithsonian Institution Press.
CNN. 1997. From Marxism 101 to Capitalism 101. June 26. www.cnn.com/WORLD/9707/26/russia.university
Cohen, Abner. 1974. Introduction: The Lesson of Ethnicity. In *Urban Ethnicity,* ed. Abner Cohen. ix–xxii. London: Tavistock.
Cohen, Ronald. 1978. Ethnicity: Problem and Focus in Anthropology. *Annual Review of Anthropology* 7: 379–403.

Cojtí Cuxil, Demetrio. 1996. The Politics of Maya Revindication. In *Maya Cultural Activism in Guatemala,* ed. Edward F. Fischer and R. McKenna Brown. 19–50. Austin: University of Texas Press.

Comaroff, John, and Jean Comaroff. 1992. *Ethnography and the Historical Imagination.* Boulder, Colo.: Westview Press.

Conklin, Beth A. 1997. Body Paint, Feathers, VCRs: Aesthetics and Authenticity in Amazonian Activism. *American Ethnologist* 24 (4): 711–37.

Conquest, Robert. 1990. *The Great Terror: A Reassessment.* London: Hutchinson.

Constable, Nicole. 1997. *Maid to Order in Hong Kong: Stories of Filipina Workers.* Ithaca, N.Y.: Cornell University Press.

Creuziger, Clementine G. K. 1997. Russia's Unwanted Children: A Cultural Anthropological Study of Marginalized Children in Moscow and St. Petersburg. *Childhood* 9 (3): 343–57.

Cruikshank, Julie. 1997. Negotiating with Narrative: Establishing Cultural Identity at the Yukon International Storytelling Festival. *American Anthropologist* 99: 56–69.

Cruikshank, Julie, and Tatiana Argounova. 2000. Reinscribing Meaning: Memory and Indigenous Identity in Sakha Republic (Yakutiia). *Arctic Anthropology* 37 (1): 96–119.

Cushman, Thomas. 1995. *Notes from Underground: Rock Music Counterculture in Russia.* Albany: State University of New York Press.

Czaplicka, M. A. 1926. Siberia, Sibiriaks, Siberians. In *Encyclopedia of Religion and Ethics,* ed. James Hastings. 488–96. Edinburgh: T. & T. Clark.

Dash, P. L. 1998. Education in Post-Soviet Russia: No More an Obligation of the State. *Economic and Political Weekly* 33 (21): 1232–34.

Davis, Catherine. 1997. *A Place in the Sun? Women Writers in Twentieth Century Cuba.* London: Zed Books.

Deloria, Philip. 1998. *Playing Indian.* New Haven, Conn.: Yale University Press.

Dewey, John. 1900. *School and Society.* Chicago: University of Chicago Press.

di Leonardo, Micaela. 1993. What a Difference Political Economy Makes: Feminist Anthropology in the Postmodern Era. *Anthropology Quarterly* 66 (2): 76–80.

———. 1991. Introduction: Gender, Culture, and Political Economy. In *Gender at the Crossroads of Knowledge: Feminist Anthropology in the Post-Modern Era,* ed. Micaela di Leonardo. 1–48. Berkeley: University of California Press.

Dmitrieva, O. V. 1997. *Evenkiia—krai moi olennyi: Materialy v pomoshch' vospitateliu DOU i nachal'nykh shkol* (*Evenkiia—My Reindeer Region: Materials for Preschool Education*). Tura: Evenkiiskii okruzhnoi institut usovershenstvovaniia uchitelei.

Dobrova-Iadrintseva, L. 1928. Tuzemnye shkoly-internaty Sibirskogo kraia (Native Residential Schools in the Siberian Region). *Prosveshchenie Sibiri* 11: 80–86.

Doi, Mary Masayo. 2001. *Gesture, Gender, Nation: Dance and Social Change in Uzbekistan.* Westport, Conn: Bergin and Garvey.

Dolgikh, B. O. 1960. *Rodovoi i plemennoi sostav narodov Sibiri v XVII v* (*The Composition of Clans and Tribes of the Peoples of Siberia in the Seventeenth Century*). Moscow: Institut etnografii i antropologii.

Dominguez, Virginia R. 1986. The Marketing of Heritage. *American Ethnologist* 13 (3): 546–55.

Donkan Anatol, and Mareile Onodera. 1998. Art Museum for the Indigenous Peoples of the Far East. Promotional brochure. Vladivostok.

Drobizheva, Leokadiia. 1996. *Govorit elita respublik Rossiiskoi Federatsii: 110 interv'iu*

(*Elites Speak: 110 Interviews with Elite in Republics of the Russian Federation*). Moscow: Rossiiskaia Akademiia Nauk, Institut etnologii i antropologii.

Dunn, Elizabeth. 1990. Slick Salesmen and Simple People: Negotiated Capitalism in a Privatized Polish Firm. In *Uncertain Transition: Ethnographies of Change in the Post-Socialist World*, ed. Michael Burawoy and Katherine Verdery. 125–50. New York: Rowman and Littlefield.

Dunn, Ethel. 1968. Educating the Small Peoples of the Soviet North: The Limits of Culture Change. *Arctic Anthropology* 5 (1): 1–31.

Duong, Thu Huong. 1995. *Novel Without a Name*. Trans. Phan Huy Duong and Nina McPherson. New York: W. Morrow.

———. 1993. *Paradise of the Blind*. Trans. Phan Huy Duong and Nina McPherson. New York: Penguin.

EastWest Institute. 1999. *Russian Regional Investor* 1, no. 45. December 2.

Ehrenreich, Barbara, and John Ehrenreich. 1978. Medicine and Social Control. In *The Cultural Crisis of Modern Medicine*, ed. John Ehrenreich. 39–79. New York: Monthly Review Press.

Einhorn, Barbara. 1993. *Cinderella Goes to Market: Citizenship, Gender and Women's Movements in East Central Europe*. London: Verso.

Eklof, Ben. 1990. *Russian Peasant Schools: Officialdom, Village Culture, and Popular Pedagogy, 1861–1914*. Berkeley: University of California Press.

Engels, Friedrich. 1972. *The Origin of the Family, Private Property, and the State*. New York: Pathfinder Press.

Eriksen, Thomas Hylland. 1993. *Ethnicity and Nationalism: Anthropological Perspectives*. London: Pluto Press.

Essig, Laurie. 1999. *Queer in Russia: A Story of Sex, Self and the Other*. Durham, N.C.: Duke University Press.

Fabian, Johannes. 1983. *Time and the Other: How Anthropology Makes Its Object*. New York: Columbia University Press.

Fischer, Edward F., and R. McKenna Brown. 1996. Introduction: Maya Cultural Activism in Guatemala. In *Maya Cultural Activism in Guatemala*, ed. Edward F. Fischer and R. McKenna Brown. 1–18. Austin: University of Texas Press.

Fleras, Augie, and Jean Leonard Elliott. 1992. *The "Nations Within": Aboriginal-State Relations in Canada, the United States, and New Zealand*. Toronto: Oxford University Press.

Fondahl, Gail A. 1998. *Gaining Ground? Evenkis, Land, and Reform in Southeastern Siberia*. Boston: Allyn and Bacon.

———. 1993. Siberia: Native Peoples and Newcomers in Collision. In *Nations and Politics in the Soviet Successor States*, ed. Ian Bremmer and Ray Taras. 477–510. Cambridge: Cambridge University Press.

Forsyth, James. 1992. *A History of the Peoples of Siberia: Russia's North Asian Colony, 1581–1990*. Cambridge: Cambridge University Press.

Foucault, Michel. 1990/1978. *The History of Sexuality*. Vol. 1, *An Introduction*. First American Edition. Trans. Robert Hurley. New York: Vintage.

———. 1980. Afterword. In *Power/Knowledge: Selected Interviews and Other Writings*, ed. Colin Gordon. 78–133. New York: Pantheon Books.

Gal, Susan. 1995. Language and the "Arts of Resistance," *Cultural Anthropology* 10 (3): 407–24.

Gal, Susan, and Gail Kligman. 2000. *The Politics of Gender After Socialism*. Princeton, N.J.: Princeton University Press.

Gamburd, Michele Ruth. 2000. *The Kitchen Spoon's Handle: Transnationalism and Sri Lanka's Migrant Housemaids*. Ithaca, N.Y.: Cornell University Press.

Geertz, Clifford. 1973. *The Interpretation of Cultures*. New York: Basic Books.

Gibson, Margaret A. 1988. *Accommodation Without Assimilation: Sikh Immigrants in an American High School.* Ithaca, N.Y.: Cornell University Press.
Giddens, Anthony. 1990. *The Consequences of Modernity.* Stanford: Stanford University Press.
Gilroy, Paul. 1987. "There Ain't No Black in the Union Jack": The Cultural Politics of Race and Nation. London: Hutchinson.
Giroux, Henry A. 1981. *Ideology, Culture, and the Process of Schooling.* Philadelphia: Temple University Press.
Goldman, Wendy Z. 1993. *Women, the State, and Revolution: Soviet Family Policy and Social Life, 1917–1936.* Cambridge: Cambridge University Press.
Golovnev, Andrei V., and Gail Osherenko. 1999. *Siberian Survival: The Nenets and Their Story.* Ithaca, N.Y.: Cornell University Press.
Gorbey, Ken. 1992. The Challenge of Creating a Bicultural Museum. *Museum Anthropology* 15 (4): 7–8.
Gosudarstvennyi Arkhiv Rossiikoi Federatsii (TsGA RF) (1925). f. 3977, o. 1, d. 1, l. 1.
Gramsci, Antonio. 1988. Observations on the School: In Search of the Educational Principle. In *An Antonio Gramsci Reader, Selected Writings: 1916–1935*, ed. David Forgacs. 311–22. New York: Schocken Books.
———. 1971. *Selections from the Prison Notebooks.* New York: International.
Grant, Bruce. 1995a. *In the Soviet House of Culture: A Century of Perestroikas.* Princeton, N.J.: Princeton University Press.
———. 1995b. Nivkhi, Russians, and Others: The Politics of Indigenism on Sakhalin Island. In *Rediscovering Russia in Asia, Siberia, and the Russian Far East*, ed. Stephen Kotkin and David Wolff. 160–71. New York: M. E. Sharpe.
Gray, Patty. "Pursuing a Native Movement in a Russian Space: The Predicament of Indigenous Peoples in Post-Soviet Chukotka." Ph.D. dissertation, University of Wisconsin, 1998.
Guha, Ranajit. 1983. *Elementary Aspects of Peasant Insurgency in Colonial India.* Delhi: Oxford University Press.
Gumilev, L. N. 1990. *Etnogenez i biosfera zemli* (*Ethnogenesis and the Earth's Biosphere*). Leningrad: Geodrometeoizdat.
Gurvich, Il'ia Samoilovich. 1980. *Etnogenez narodov Severa* (*The Ethnogenesis of the Peoples of the North*). Moscow: Nauka.
Guthrie, Sharon R., and Shirley Castelnuovo. 1992. Elite Women Bodybuilders: Models of Resistance or Compliance? *Play and Culture* 5 (4): 401–8.
Habeck, Joachim Otto. 1997. Sedentarization of Nomads in the Evenki Autonomous District (Siberia). Presented at the 35th International Congress of Asian and North African Studies, Budapest, Hungary, July 7–12.
Haig-Brown, Celia. 1991. *Resistance and Renewal: Surviving the Indian Residential School.* Vancouver, B.C.: Tillacum Library.
Handler, Richard. 1993. An Anthropological Definition of the Museum and Its Purpose. *Museum Anthropology* 17 (1): 33–36.
———. 1988. *Nationalism and the Politics of Culture in Quebec.* Madison: University of Wisconsin Press.
Haney, Lynne. 1999. "But We Are Still Mothers": Gender, the State, and the Construction of Need in Postsocialist Hungary. In *Uncertain Transition: Ethnographies of Change in the Postsocialist World*, ed. Michael Burawoy and Katherine Verdery. 151–89. New York: Rowman and Littlefield.
Hann, Chris. 1996. Land Tenure and Citizenship in Tazlar. In *After Socialism: Land Reform and Social Change in Eastern Europe*, ed. Ray Abrahams. 23–50. Oxford: Berghahn Books.

Harrison, Faye V. 1991. Anthropology as an Agent of Transformation: Introductory Comments and Queries. Moving Further Toward an Anthropology of Liberation: An Agenda from the Periphery Behind the Veil. In *Decolonizing Anthropology: Moving Further Toward an Anthropology of Liberation*, ed. Faye V. Harrison. 1–14. Washington, D.C.: American Anthropological Association.

Hendrickson, Carol. 1995. *Weaving Identities: Construction of Dress and Self in a Highland Guatemala Town.* Austin: University of Texas Press.

Hinsley, Curtis M. 1992. Collecting Cultures and Cultures of Collecting: The Lure of the American Southwest, 1880–1915. *Museum Anthropology* 16 (1): 12–20.

Hivon, Miriam. 1995. Local Resistance to Privatization in Rural Russia. *Cambridge Anthropology* 18 (2): 13–22.

Hobsbawm, Eric, and Terence Ranger. 1990. *Nations and Nationalism Since 1780.* Cambridge: Cambridge University Press.

Hosking, Geoffrey. 1987. Memory in a Totalitarian Society: The Case of the Soviet Union. In *Memory: History, Culture, and the Mind*, ed. Thomas Butler. 115–30. Oxford: Basil Blackwell.

Human Rights Watch. 1998. *Abandoned to the State: Cruelty and Neglect in Russian Orphanages.* New York: Human Rights Watch.

Humphrey, Caroline. 1999a. *Marx Went Away But Karl Stayed Behind* (updated edition of *Karl Marx Collective: Economy, Society and Religion in a Siberian Collective Farm*). Ann Arbor: University of Michigan Press.

———. 1999b. Traders, "Disorder," and Citizenship Regimes in Provincial Russia. In *Uncertain Transition: Ethnographies of Change in the Postsocialist World*, ed. Michael Burawoy and Katherine Verdery. 19–52. New York: Rowman and Littlefield.

———. 1995. Creating a Culture of Disillusionment: Consumption in Moscow, a Chronicle of a Changing Time. In *Worlds Apart: Modernity Through the Prisim of the Local*, ed. D. Miller. 43–68. London: Routledge.

———. 1994a. Remembering the "Enemy": The Bogd Khaan in Twentieth Century Mongolia. In *Memory, History, and Opposition Under State Socialism*, ed. Rubie Watson. 21–45. Santa Fe, N.M.: School of American Research.

———. 1994b. Casual Chat and Ethnic Identity: Women's Second-Language Use Among Buryats in the USSR. In *Bilingual Women: Anthropological Approaches to Second-language Use*, ed. Pauline Burton, Ketaki Kushari Dyson, and Shirley Ardener. 65–79. Oxford: Berg.

———. 1994c. Shamanic Practices and the State in Northern Asia: Views From the Center and Periphery. In *Shamanism, History, and the State*, ed. Nicholas Thomas and Caroline Humphrey. 191–228. Ann Arbor: University of Michigan Press.

———. 1983. *Karl Marx Collective: Economy, Society, and Religion in a Siberian Collective Farm.* Cambridge: Cambridge University Press.

Husby-Darvas, Eva V. 2001. Hungarian Village Women in the Marketplace During the Late Socialist Period. In *Women Traders in Cross-Cultural Perspective: Mediating Identities, Marketing Wares*, ed. Linda J. Seligmann. 185–207. Stanford, Calif.: Stanford University Press.

Im, Den Gioun. 1998. "*En Route to Sakhalin.*" B.A. honors thesis, Adelphi University (manuscript in author's possession).

Ing, Rosalyn N. 1991. The Effects of Residential Schools on Native Child-Rearing Practices. *Canadian Journal of Native Education* 18: 65–118.

Itygin, Egor. 1927a. Vserossiiskoe soveshchanie po vseobshchemu obucheniiu natsmen (The All-Russia Meeting on the General Education of National Minorities). *Prosveshchenie Sibiri* 8: 84–87.

———. 1927b. Prosveshchenie natsional'nykh men'shinstv Sibirskogo kraia nakanune 10oi godovshchiny oktiabria (Enlightenment of National Minorities of the Siberian Region on the Eve of the 10th Anniversary of the October Revolution). *Prosveshchenie Sibiri* 10: 124–28.

Ivanova-Unarova, Zinaida. 1998. Sibirskaia kollektsiia v Amerikanskom muzee estestvennoi istorii (The Siberian Collection in the American Museum of Natural History). *Iskusstvo*. 38–43.

Jin, Ha. 1999. *Waiting*. New York: Pantheon.

———. 1997. *Under the Red Flag: Short Stories*. Athens: University of Georgia Press.

Kan, Sergei. 1989. Cohorts, Generations, and Their Culture: The Tlingit Potlatch in the 1980s. *Anthropos* 84: 405–22.

Kaneff, Deema. 1996. Responses to "Democratic" Land Reforms in a Bulgarian Village. In *After Socialism: Land Reform and Social Change in Eastern Europe*, ed. Ray Abrahams. 85–114. Oxford: Berghahn Books.

Kaplan, Flora E. S. 1994. Introduction. In *Museums and the Making of "Ourselves": The Role of Objects in National Identity*, ed. Flora E. S. Kaplan. 1–15. London: Leicester University Press.

Karlov, V. V. 1982. *Evenki v XVIII–nachale XX v (khoziaistvo i sotsial'naia struktura) (Evenki from the Eighteenth to the Beginning of the Twentieth Century—Household and Social Structure)*. Moscow: Izdatel'stvo moskovskogo universiteta.

Kelm, Mary-Ellen. 1996. "A Scandalous Procession": Residential Schooling and the Re/formation of Aboriginal Bodies, 1900/1950. *Native Studies Review* 11 (2): 51–88.

Kendall, Laurel. 1996. Korean Shamans and the Spirits of Capitalism. *American Anthropologist* 98(3): 512–27.

Kerttula, Anna M. 2000. *Antler on the Sea: The Yup'ik and Chukchi of the Russian Far East*. Ithaca, N.Y.: Cornell University Press.

Keyes, Charles F. 1981. The Dialectics of Ethnic Change. In *Ethnic Change*, ed. Charles F. Keyes. 4–30. Seattle: University of Washington Press.

Khelol, N. K. 1997. Semeinyi muzei Khelol (The Khelol Family Museum). *Aborigen Kamchatki* (14) (March 24): 1.

Khronika smutnogo vremeni (den' pervyi) (Chronicle of a Dark Time—Day One). 1993. *Moscow News*, Saturday, October 2.

Khubova, Daria, Andrei Ivankiev, and Tonia Sharova. 1992. After Glasnost: Oral History in the Soviet Union. In *International Yearbook of Oral History and Life Stories*, vol.1, *Memory and Totalitarianism*, ed. Luisa Passerini. 89–101. Oxford: Oxford University Press.

Kideckel, David. 1993. *The Solitude of Collectivism: Romanian Villagers to the Revolution and Beyond*. Ithaca, N.Y.: Cornell University Press.

King, Alexander. 1998. Soul Suckers: Shamanic Vampires in Northern Kamchatka, Russia. Presented at the American Anthropological Association Annual Meeting, Philadelphia, December.

Kligman, Gail. 1998. *The Politics of Duplicity: Controlling Reproduction in Ceausescu's Romania*. Berkeley: University of California Press.

———. 1988. *The Wedding of the Dead: Ritual, Poetics, and Popular Culture in Transylvania*. Berkeley: University of California Press.

Krupnik and Vakhtin. 1997. Indigenous Knowledge in Modern Culture: Siberian Yupik Ecological Legacy in Transition. *Arctic Anthropology* 34 (1): 235–52.

Kumar, Nita. 1992. *Friends, Brothers, and Informants: Fieldwork Memoirs of Banaras*. Berkeley: University of California Press.

Kwon, Heonik. 1993. "Maps and Actions: Nomadic and Sedentary Space in a Siberian Reindeer Farm," Ph.D. dissertation, University of Cambridge.

Kytmanov, D. 1927. Tuzemtsy Turukhanskogo kraia. *Sovetskaia Aziia* 2: 37–51.

Lamphere, Louise. 1987. *From Working Daughters to Working Mothers: Immigrant Women in a New England Industrial Community*. Ithaca, N.Y.: Cornell University Press.

Lampland, Martha. 1995. *The Object of Labour: Commodification in Socialist Hungary*. Chicago: University of Chicago Press.

Lancaster, Roger. 1988. *Thanks to God and the Revolution: Popular Religion and Class Consciousness in the New Nicaragua*. New York: Columbia University Press.

Lapidus, Gail Warshofsky. 1993. Gender and Restructuring: The Impact of *Perestroika* and Its Aftermath on Soviet Women. In *Democratic Reform and the Position of Women in Transitional Economies*, ed. Valentine M. Moghadam. 137–61. Oxford: Clarendon Press.

———. 1978. *Women in Soviet Society: Equality, Development, and Social Change*. Berkeley: University of California Press.

Lemon, Alaina. 1995. "What Are They Writing About Us Blacks?": Roma and "Race" in Russia. *Anthropology of East Europe Review* 33 (2): 34–40.

Lempert, David H. 1996. *Daily Life in a Crumbling Empire: The Absorption of Russia into the World Economy*. Vols. 1–2. Boulder, Colo.: East European Monographs.

Leonov, M. 1928. Prosveshchenie malykh narodnostei Severa (The Enlightenment of the Small Peoples of the North). *Prosveshchenie Sibiri* 5: 111–22.

Le Roy Ladurie, Emmanuel. 1978. *Montaillou: Cathars and Catholics in a French Village, 1294–1324*. London: Scholars Press.

Levin, Ted. 1996. *The Hundred Thousand Fools of God: Musical Travels in Central Asia (and Queens, New York)*. Bloomington: Indiana University Press.

Linnekin, Jocelyn. 1998. Family and Other Uncontrollables: Impression Management in Accompanied Fieldwork. In *Fieldwork and Families: Constructing New Models for Ethnographic Research*, ed. Juliana Flinn, Leslie Marshall and Jocelyn Armstrong. 71–83. Honolulu: University of Hawaií Press.

———. 1991. Cultural Invention and the Dilemma of Authenticity. *American Anthropologist* 93: 446–49.

Loader, Jayne. 1983. *The Atomic Café*. New York: Archive Films.

Lomawaima, K. Tsianina. 1994. *They Called It Prairie Light: The Story of Chilocco Indian School*. Lincoln: University of Nebraska Press.

———. 1993. Domesticity in the Federal Indian Schools: The Power of Authority over Mind and Body. *American Ethnologist* 20 (2): 227–40.

Lutz, Catherine, and Lila Abu-Lughod. 1990. Introduction: Emotion, Discourse, and the Politics of Everyday Life. In *Language and the Politics of Emotion*, ed. Catherine Lutz and Lila Abu-Lughod. 1–23. Cambridge: Cambridge University Press.

Mahuika, Apirana T. 1992. Maori Culture and the New Museum. *Museum Anthropology* 15 (4): 9–11.

Makarenko, Anton. 1973. *The Road to Life: An Epic in Education*. New York: Oriole Editions.

Mamdani, Mahmood. 1996. *Citizen and Subject: Contemporary Africa and the Legacy of Late Colonialism*. Princeton, N.J.: Princeton University Press.

Mani, Lata. 1987. Contentious Traditions: The Debate on Sati in Colonial India. *Cultural Critique* 7: 119–56.

Marcus, George. 1986. Contemporary Problems of Ethnography in the Modern World System. In *Writing Culture: The Poetics and Politics of Ethnography*, ed. James Clifford and George Marcus. 165–93. Berkeley: University of California Press.

Markowitz, Fran. 2000. *Coming of Age in Post-Soviet Russia.* Urbana: University of Illinois Press.

Maybury-Lewis, David. 1997. *Indigenous Peoples, Ethnic Groups, and the State.* Boston: Allyn and Bacon.

Meshcheryakov, Aleksandr. 1996. Kollektivnyi avtoportret sel'skogo uchitelia v otdel'no vziatoi postsovetskogo prostranstva selo Tory, Tunkinskii raion, Buriatiia, iul' 1995 goda (A Collective Self-portrait of a Rural Teacher in a Specific Post-Soviet Space in the Village of Tory, Tunkinsk Region, Buriatia, July 1995). *Acta Eurasica* 1 (2): 166–69.

Meyers, Fred. 1994. Culture-making: Performing Aboriginality at the Asia Society Gallery. *American Anthropologist* 21 (4): 679–99.

Mikheeva, N. V., N. I. Syrovatskii, N. I. Nikolaev, I. A. Neustroeva, and K. V. Novikov. 1993. *Rodovye, rodoplemennye, kochevye obshchiny (metodologicheskie rekomendatsii) (Clan, Clan-Tribal, and Nomadic Organizations—Methodological Recommendations).* Moscow: Tsentr nauchno-tekhnicheskoi informatsii, propogandy i reklamy.

Miller, John. 1994. The Peoples of the Soviet North: Recent Developments. In *The Rights of Subordinated Peoples,* ed. Oliver Mendelsohn and Upendra Baxi. 324–66. Delhi: Oxford University Press.

Mironov, N. D., and S. M. Shirokogoroff. 1924. Sramana-Shaman: Etymology of the Word "Shaman." *Journal of the North China Branch of the Royal Asiatic Society* 55: 105–30.

Moghadam, Valentine M. 1993. *Democratic Reform and the Position of Women in Transitional Economies,* ed. Valentine M. Moghadam. Oxford: Clarendon Press.

Mohanty, Chandra Talpade. 1991. Under Western Eyes: Feminist Scholarship and Colonial Discourses. In *Third World Women and the Politics of Feminism,* ed. Chandra Talpade Mohanty, Ann Russo, and Lourdes Torres. 51–80. Bloomington: University of Indiana Press.

Monakhova, Z. V. 1999. *Zhizn' stoibishcha (Life in a Reindeer Herding Camp).* Tura: Evenkiiskii okruzhnoi institut usovershenstvovaniia uchitelei.

Moore, Henrietta. 1988. *Feminism and Anthropology.* Minneapolis: University of Minnesota Press.

Mordvinov, A. 1860. Inorodtsy, obitaiushchie v Turukhanskom krae (Natives Living in the Turukhansk Krai). *Vesti.* Russkoe Geograficheskoe obshchestvo. 28.

Murashko, Olga A. 1996. Introduction. In *Anxious North: Indigenous Peoples in Soviet and Post-Soviet Russia,* ed. Alexander Pika, Jens Dahl, and Inge Larsen. 9–13. IWGIA Document 82. Copenhagen: IWGIA.

Nagengast, Carole. 1993. *Reluctant Socialists, Rural Entrepreneurs: Class, Culture, and the Polish State.* Boulder, Colo: Westview Press.

Nandy, Ashis. 1983. *The Intimate Enemy: Loss and Recovery of Self Under Colonialism.* Bombay: Oxford University Press.

National Public Radio. 1999. Jehovah's Witnesses in Russia. *Weekend Edition,* February 14.

Nedjalkov, Igor. 1997. *Evenki.* New York: Routledge.

Nelson, Cynthia, and Shahnaz Rouse. 2000. Gendering Globalization: Alternative Languages of Modernity. In *Situating Globalization: Views from Egypt,* ed. Cynthia Nelson and Shahnaz Rouse. 97–158. New Brunswick, N.J.: Transaction Publishers.

Nemtushkin, Alitet. 1998. *Samelkil: metki na olen'em ukhe (Samelkil: Markings on a Reindeer Ear).* Krasnoiarsk: Fond severnykh literatur, KheiGLeiN.

———. 1992. Prervannaia pesnia (Severed Song). In *Evenki basseina Eniseia,* ed. V. I. Boiko and V. G. Kostiuk. 3–16. Novosibirsk: Nauka.

Nikul'shin, N.P. 1939. *Pervobytnye proizvodstvennye ob'edineniia i sotsialisticheskoe stroitel'stvo u evenkov* (*Primitive Productive Units and Socialist Construction Among the Evenk*). Leningrad: Nauka.

Nove, Alec, ed. 1993. *The Stalin Phenomenon.* London: Macmillan.

Nuttall, Marc. 1992. *Arctic Homeland: Kinship, Community, and Development in Northwest Greenland.* Toronto: University of Toronto Press.

Ocherednaia zadacha (An Immediate Task). 1939. *Evenkiiskaia novaia zhizn',* February 22.

Oegir, Nikolai. 1989. *Tropa k rodniku: stikhi* (*Paths to the Spring: Poems*). Trans. (from Evenk) Aida Fedorova. Krasnoiarsk: Krasnoiarskoe knizhnoe izdatel'stvo.

Ogbu, John. 1991. *Minority Status and Schooling: A Comparative Study of Immigrant and Involuntary Migrants.* New York: Garland.

Okamura, Jonathan. 1981. Situational Ethnicity. *Ethnic and Racial Studies* 4: 452–63.

Okruzhnoi arkhiv Evenkiiskogo avtonomnogo okruga (GA EAO). 1932. Materialy tverdo zadontsov po kulatskim khoziaistvom po Evenkiiskomu natsional'nomu okrugu. Tura. f.2, o.1, l. 68.

———. 1913. Esseiskii sviatoi Vasil'evskoi tserkvi Turukhanskogo kraia, Illimpiiskii raion za 1913. f.29, o.1, d.3, l.8.

———. 1868. Perepiska Eniseiskogo dukhovnogo konsistorii c Turukhanskoi pokhodnoi tserkov'iu. f.29, o.1, d.11, l.83.

———. 1859. Vedomosti Turukhanskoi pokhodnoi tserkvi, 1754–1859. f.29, o.1, d.1, l.3.

Okruzhnoi muzei Evenkiiskogo avtonomnogo okruga (EAO). 1927. Seriia fotosnimkov Turinskoi kul'tbazy (iz kollektsii I. M. Suslova). Tura.

Okruzhnoi otdel statistiki Evenkiiskogo avtonomnogo okruga (EAO). 1996. Gosudarstvennaia statisticheskaia otchetnost'—chislennost' kochuiushchego naseleniia v raionakh prozhivaniia malochislennykh narodov Severa na 1 ianvaria 1995g/1996g. Tura.

———. 1994. *Godovoi otchet.* Tura.

———. 1993a. Karta ucheta migratsii naseleniia za 1990, 1991, 1992, 1993 g.g. Tura.

———. 1993b. Gosudarstvennaia statisticheskaia otchetnost'—chislennost' kochuiushchego naseleniia v raionakh prozhivaniia malochislennykh narodov Severa na 1 ianvaria 1992g/1993g. Tura.

———. 1993c. Spisok sel'skikh naselennykh punktov Evenkiiskogo avtonomnogo okruga po sostoianiiu na 1 ianvaria 1992g/1993g. Tura.

———. 1992. Spisok naselennykh punktov Evenkiiskogo avtonomnogo okruga po sostoianiiu na 1 ianvaria 1992. Tura.

———. 1985. Nalichie naseleniia v Evenkiiskom avtonomnom okruge (1981–1985). Tura.

——. 1965. Nalichie naseleniia v Evenkiiskom natsional'nom okruge (1959–1965g.g.). Tura.

Ong, Aiwa. 1999. *Flexible Citizenship: The Cultural Logics of Transnationality.* Durham, N.C.: Duke University Press.

———. 1990. State vs. Islam: Malay Families, Women's Bodies, and the Body Politic in Malaysia. *American Ethnologist* 17 (2): 258–76.

——. 1987. *Spirits of Resistance and Capitalist Discipline: Factory Women in Malaysia.* Albany: State University of New York Press.

Ortner, Sherry. 1995. Resistance and the Problem of Ethnographic Refusal. *Society for Comparative Studies in Society and History* 37 (1): 173–93.

Osherenko, Gail. 1995. Indigenous Political and Property Rights and Economic/ Environmental Reform in Northwest Siberia. *Post-Soviet Geography* 36 (4): 225–37.

Osogostok, O. I. 1995. *V mire severnykh mifov: Elementy severnoi mifologii, personazhi mifov* (In the World of Northern Myths: Elements of Northern Mythology, Personages in the Myths). Tura: Evenkiiskii okruzhnoi institut usovershenstvovaniia uchitelei.

Ozyegin, Gul. 2001. *Untidy Gender: Domestic Service in Turkey*. Philadelphia: Temple University Press.

Pallot, Judith. 1989. Rural Depopulation and the Restoration of the Bolshevik Village Under Gorbachev. *Soviet Studies* 42 (4): 655–74.

Panarin, Sergei. 1997. *Buriatskoe selo Tory v 90-e gody: sotsial'naia i kul'turnaia readaptatsiia maloi poselencheskoi obshchnosti* (A Buriat Village of Tory in the 1990s: Social and Cultural Readaptation of a Small Settlement). Papers of the IV International Scientific Conference "Rossiia i Vostok: problemy vzaimodeistviia." Omsk, Russia. 149–52.

Parker, Andrew, Mary Russo, Doris Sommer, and Patricia Yaeger. 1992. Introduction. In *Nationalisms and Sexualities*, ed. Andrew Parker, Mary Russo, Doris Sommer, and Patricia Yaeger. 1–18. New York: Routledge.

Pilkington, Hilary. 1996. "Youth Culture" in Contemporary Russia: Gender, Consumption, and Identity. In *Gender, Generation, and Identity in Contemporary Russia*, ed. Hilary Pilkington. 189–215. London: Routledge.

Pika, Aleksandr Ivanovich. 1997. *Neotraditionalism in the Russian North: Indigenous Peoples and the Legacy of Perestroika*. Trans. Bruce Grant. Circumpolar Research Series 6. Edmonton: Canadian Circumpolar Institute Press.

———. 1989. Malye narody Severa: iz pervobytnogo kommunizma v real'nyi sotsializm (Small Peoples of the North: From Primitive Communism to Real Socialism). In *Perestroika, Glasnost', Demokratiia, Sotsializm: v chelovecheskom izmerenii*. Moscow: Progress.

Pika, Aleksander, and Prokhorov, A. 1996. Neotraditionalism in the Russian North: To Enter the Future Without Forgetting the Past. In *Anxious North: Indigenous Peoples in Soviet and Post-Soviet Russia*, ed. Alexander Pika, Jens Dahl, and Inge Larsen. 263–69. IWGIA Document 82. Copenhagen: IWGIA.

Pikunova, Zinaida Nikolaevna. 1998. Ne narod—tebe, a ty narody (Not What Your People Can Do for You, But What You Can Do for Your People). *Evenkiiskaia zhizn'*, December 7–14 (45–46): 8–9.

———. 1998. Politics, Education, and Culture: A Case Study of the Preservation and Development of the Native Language of the Evenkis. In *Bicultural Education in the North: Ways of Preserving and Enhancing Indigenous Peoples' Languages and Traditional Knowledge*, ed. Erich Kasten. 123–37. Berlin: Waxman Münster.

Pine, Frances. 1996. Redefining Women's Work in Rural Poland. In *After Socialism: Land Reform and Social Change in Eastern Europe*, ed. Ray Abrahams. 133–55. Oxford: Berghahn Books.

Popov, V. N. 1993. *Kul'tura semeinogo vospitaniia narodov Severa: proshloe i nastoiashchee* (*The Culture of Family Upbringing Among Peoples of the North: Past and Present*). Iakutsk: Institut usovershenstvovaniia spetsialistov obrazovaniia.

Popular Memory Group. 1982. Popular Memory: Theory, Politics, Method. In *Making Histories: Studies in History Writing and Politics*, ed. Richard Johnson, Gregor Mclennan, Bill Schwartz, and David Sutton. 205–52. Minneapolis: University of Minnesota.

Posadskaia, Anastasia. 1993. Changes in Gender Discourses and Policies in the

Former Soviet Union. In *Democratic Reform and the Position of Women in Transitional Economies*, ed. Valentine M. Moghadam. 162–79. Oxford: Clarendon Press.

Raheja, Gloria Goodwin, and Ann Grodzins Gold. 1994. *Listen to the Heron's Words: Reimagining Gender and Kinship in North India.* Berkeley: University of California Press.

Reed-Danahay, Deborah. 1996. *Education and Identity in Rural France: The Politics of Schooling.* New York: Cambridge University Press.

Regnier, Robert. 1999. The Sacred Circle: An Aboriginal Approach to Healing Education at an Urban High School. In *First Nations Education in Canada: The Circle Unfolds*, ed. Marie Battiste and Jean Barrman. 311–29. Vancouver: University of British Columbia Press.

Reiter, Rayna R., ed. 1975. *Toward an Anthropology of Women.* New York: Monthly Review Press.

Rethmann, Petra. 2001. *Tundra Passages: Gender and History in the Russian Far East.* University Park: Pennsylvania State University Press.

———. 2000. Skins of Desire: Poetry and Identity in Koriak Women's Gift Exchange. *American Ethnologist* 27 (1): 52–71.

———. 1999. Deadly Dis-ease: Medical Knowledge and Healing in Northern Kamchatka, Russia. *Culture, Medicine, and Psychiatry* 23: 197–217.

Ries, Nancy. 1997. *Russian Talk: Culture and Conversation During Perestroika.* Ithaca, N.Y.: Cornell University Press.

Rofel, Lisa. 1999. *Other Modernities: Gendered Yearnings in China After Socialism.* Berkeley: University of California Press.

———. 1994. Liberation Nostalgia and a Yearning for Modernity. In *Engendering China: Women, Culture, and the State*, ed. Christina K. Gilmartin. 226–49. Cambridge: Mass. Harvard University Press.

———. 1992. Eating Out of One Big Pot: Silk Workers in Contemporary China. In *Workers' Expressions: Beyond Accommodation and Resistance*, ed. John Calagione, Doris Francis, and Daniel Nugent. 79–97. Albany: State University of New York Press.

Romero, Mary. 1992. *Maid in the U.S.A.* New York: Routledge.

Rosaldo, Renato. 1989. *Culture and Truth: The Remaking of Social Analysis.* New York: Beacon Press.

———. 1980. *Ilongot Headhunting, 1884–1974: A Study in Society and History.* Stanford, Calif.: Stanford University Press.

Rosenberger, Nancy. 1992. Status, Individuality, and Leisure: Messages of Western Styles in Japanese Home Magazines. In *Remade in Japan: Everyday Life and Consumer Desire in a Changing Society*, ed. Joseph J. Tobin. 106–25. New Haven, Conn.: Yale University Press.

Rothenberg, Celia. 1999. Who Are We for Them? On Doing Research in the Palestinian West Bank. In *Feminist Fields: Ethnographic Insights*, ed. Rae Bridgeman, Sally Cole, and Heather Howard-Bobiwash. 137–56. Peterborough: Broadview Press.

Ruofu, Du, and Vincent F. Yip. 1993. Ewenki. In *Ethnic Groups in China.* 33–37. New York: Science Press.

Rushdie, Salmon. 1987. *The Jaguar's Smile: A Nicaraguan Journey.* New York: Viking.

Rytkheu, Yu. 1988. Slogany i amulety (Slogans and Amulets). *Komsomolskaya Pravda.* May 19.

Saf'iannikova. 1994. *Uroki dekorativno-prikladnogo iskusstva evenkiiskogo naroda, 11 klass* (*Lessons in Evenk Decorative Art for the Eleventh Grade*). Tura: Evenkiiskii okruzhnoi institut usovershenstvovaniia uchitelei.

Sangi, V. 1988. Otchuzhdenie (Alienation). *Sovetskaia Rossiia*, November 11.

Savoskul, Sergei. 1971. Etnicheskiie izmeneniia v Evenkiiskom natsional'nom okruge (Changes in Ethnicity in the Evenk National District). In *Preobrazovaniia v khoziaistve i kul'ture i etnicheskie protsessy u narodov Severa*, ed. I. S.Gurvich and V. O. Dolgikh. 256–79. Moscow: Nauka.

S bol'noi golovy na zdorovuiu (From Headache to Health). 1996. *Evenkiiskaia zhizn'* (May 20): 5.

Schein, Louisa. 2000. *Minority Rules: The Miao and the Feminine in China's Cultural Politics*. Durham, N.C.: Duke University Press.

Scheper-Hughes, Nancy. 1979. *Saints, Scholars, and Schizophrenics: Mental Illness in Rural Ireland*. Berkeley: University of California Press.

Schildkrout, Enid. 1999. Royal Treasury, Historic House, or Just a Museum? Transforming Manhyia Palace, Ghana, into a Site of Cultural Tourism. *Museum Anthropology* 22 (3): 14–27.

Schindler, Debra L. 1997. Redefining Tradition and Renegotiating Ethnicity in Native Russia. *Arctic Anthropology* 34 (1): 194–211.

Scott, James C. 1989. Everyday Forms of Resistance. In *Everyday Forms of Resistance*, ed. Forrest D. Colburn. 3–33. Armonk, N.Y.: M.E. Sharpe.

———. 1985. *Weapons of the Weak: Everyday Forms of Peasant Resistance*. New Haven, Conn.: Yale University Press.

Serge, Victor. 1937. *Russia Twenty Years After*. New York: Pioneer.

Sharp, Lesley A. 1990. Possessed and Disposessed Youth: Spirit Possession of School Children in Northwest Madagascar. *Culture, Medicine, and Psychiatry* 14 (3): 339–64.

Shchapeva, D. A. 1994. *Programma spetskursa po etnografii evenkov dlia uchashchikhsia X–XI klassov obshcheobrazovatel'noi shkoly* (*Evenk Ethnography Program for Tenth and Eleventh Grade Students*). Tura: Institut usovershenstvovaniia uchitelei.

Shebalin, Yuri Aleksandrovich. 1990. *Evenkiiskie dalekie kostry* (*Distant Evenki Campfires*). Krasnoiarsk: Krasnoiarskoe knizhnoe izdatel'stvo.

Sherbakova, Irina. 1992. The Gulag in Memory. In *International Yearbook of Oral History and Life Stories*, vol. 1, *Memory and Totalitarianism*, ed. Luisa Passerini. 103–15. Oxford: Oxford University Press.

Shimkin, Dimitri. 1990. Siberian Ethnography: Historical Sketch and Evaluation. *Arctic Anthropology* 27 (1): 36–51.

Shirokogoroff, Sergei M. 1933. *Social Organization of the Northern Tungus*. Shanghai: Commercial Press.

———. 1919. *Opyt issledovaniia osnov shamanstva u tungusov. Uchenye zapiski* (*Research Findings on the Foundations of Tungus Shamanism: Scholarly Observations*). Vladivostok: Istoriko-filologicheskii fakultet.

Shishkov, Vladislav Ia. 1987 (1961). *Ugrium-reka* (*The Gloomy River*). Moscow: Khudozhestvennaia literatura.

Shlapentokh, Vladimir. 1989. *Public and Private Life of the Soviet People: Changing Values in Post-Stalinist Russia*. New York: Oxford University Press.

Simon, Judith A. 1990. "The Place of Schooling in Maori Pakeha Relations." Ph.D. dissertation, University of Auckland.

Sirina, Anna. 1995. *Katangskie evenki v XX v.: rasselenie, organizatsiia sredy, zhiznideiatel'nosti* (*Katanga Evenki in the Twentieth Century: Settlement, Social Organization, and Lifeways*). Moscow: IEA, RAN.

Slezkine, Yuri. 1994. *Arctic Mirrors: Russia and the Small Peoples of the North*. Ithaca, N.Y.: Cornell University Press.

Smith, Linda Tuhiwai. 1999. *Decolonizing Methodologies: Research and Indigenous Peoples*. London: Zed Books.

Soosaar, Mark, director. 1989. *Father, Son, and Holy Torum.* 90 min. 16mm film. Weiko Saawa Film, Estonia and TVE, London.

Ssorin-Chaikov, Nikolai. 1998. "Stateless Society, State Collectives, and the State of Nature in Sub-Arctic Siberia: Evenki Hunters and Herders in the Twentieth Century." Ph.D. dissertation, Stanford University.

Stacey, Judith. 1988. Can There Be a Feminist Ethnography? *Women's Studies International Forum* 11 (1): 21–27.

Stack, Carol. 1974. *All Our Kin: Strategies for Survival in a Black Community.* New York: Harper and Row.

Stambach, Amy. 1996. "Seeded" in the Market Economy: Schooling and Social Transformations on Mount Kilimanjaro. *Anthropology and Education Quarterly* 27 (4): 545–67.

Stanley, Alessandra. 1996. Russian Traders Go Abroad for Some Serious Shopping. *New York Times,* November 9, p.1, 6.

Starovoitova, Galina Vasil'evna. 1987. *Etnicheskaia gruppa v sovremennom sovetskom gorode: sotsiologicheskie* ocherki (*Ethnic Groups in a Contemporary Soviet city: Sociological Characteristics*). Leningrad: Nauka.

Statistika (Statistics). 1994. *Krasnoiarskii rabochii* 131 (July 12): 1.

Statistika (Statistics). 1993. *Evenkiiskaia zhizn'* 41 (4954) (October 24): 8.

Stocking, George W. 1985. Introduction. In *Objects and Others: Essays on Museums and Material Culture,* ed. George W. Stocking. 3–14. Madison: University of Wisconsin Press.

Strakach, Iu. B. 1966. *Narodnye traditsii i podgotovka sovremennykh promyslovo-sel'skokhoziaistvennykh kadrov: taezhnye i tundrovye raiony Sibiri* (*Folk Traditions and the Training of Contemporary Industrial-Agricultural Cadres: The Taiga and Tundra Regions of Siberia*). Novosibirsk: Nauka.

———. 1962. Traditsii trudovogo vospitaniia u narodov Taimyra v nashe vremia (Current Traditions of Labor Education Among the Peoples of the Taimyr). *Sovetskaia etnografiia* 3: 35–48.

Svensson, Frances. 1978. The Final Crisis of Tribalism: Comparative Ethnic Policy on the American and Russian Frontiers. *Ethnic and Racial Studies* 1 (1): 100–23.

Sviridova, Natal'ia. 1995. *Priglashaem na tuiun: iz evenkiiskoi natsional'noi kukhni* (*You Are Invited to a Feast: Evenk Traditional Cooking*). Krasnoiarsk: Fond servernykh literatur KheiGLeiN.

Tertz, Abram. 1960. *On Socialist Realism.* Trans. George Dennis, intro. Czeslaw Milosz. 129–219. New York: Vintage Books.

Thies, Kaye. 1987. *Aboriginal Viewpoints on Education: A Survey in the East Kimberley Region.* National Center for Research on Rural Education, Research Series 5. Nedlands: University of Western Australia.

Thompson, E. P. 1966. *The Making of the English Working Class.* New York: Vintage.

Toer, Pramoedya Ananta. 1996. *Child of All Nations.* Trans. Max Lane. New York: Penguin.

———. 1982. *This Earth of Mankind.* Trans. Max Lane. Ringwood, Australia: Penguin Books.

Tokarev, S. A. 1988. Iakuty. In *Narody mira: istoriko-etnograficheskii spravochnik* (*An Ethno-Historical Handbook to Peoples of the World*), ed. Iu. V. Bromlei. 536–37. Moscow: Sovetskaia entsiklopediia.

Tsentral'noe statisticheskoe upravlenie USSR. 1927. *Pokhoziaistvennaia perepis' pripoliarnogo Severa* (Household Census of the Arctic North). Moscow.

Tugolukov, Vladilen Aleksandrovich. 1988. Eveny. In *Narody mira: istoriko-etnograficheskii spravochnik* (*An Ethno-Historical Handbook to Peoples of the World*), ed. Iu. V. Bromlei. 525–26. Moscow: Sovetskaia entsiklopediia.

———. 1980. *Idushchie poperek khrebtov* (*Riding Along the Ridges*). Krasnoiarsk: Krasnoiarskoe knizhnoe izdatel'stvo.

———. 1971. Preodolenie starogo v bytu i soznanii evenkov (Overcoming Old Ways in the Daily Life and Consciousness of the Evenki). In *Osushchestvlenie Leninskoi natsional'noi politiki u narodov krainego* Severa (Implementing Leninist National Politics Among the Peoples of the Far North), ed. I. S. Gurvich. 200–212. Moscow: Nauka.

Turner, Edith. 1996. *The Hands Feel It: Healing and Spirit Presence Among a Northern Alaskan People.* DeKalb: Northern Illinois University Press.

Udygir, I. T. 1995. *Evenkiiskie podvizhnye igry* (*Active Evenk Games*). Tura: Evenkiiskii okruzhnoi institut usovershenstvovaniia uchitelei.

Vakhtin, Nikolai. 1994. Native Peoples of the Russian Far North. In *Polar Peoples: Self-Determination and Development*, ed. Minority Rights Group. 29–80. London: Minority Rights Publications.

Vasilevich, G. M. and A. V. Smoliak. 1964. The Evenks. In *The Peoples of Siberia*, ed. M. G. Levin and L. P. Potapov, trans. Scripta Technica. 620–54. Chicago: University of Chicago Press.

Verdery, Katherine. 1999. Fuzzy Property: Rights, Power, and Identity in Transylvania's Decollectivization. In *Uncertain Transition: Ethnographies of Change in the Post-socialist World*, ed. Michael Burawoy and Katherine Verdery. 53–82. New York: Rowman and Littlefield.

———. 1996. *What Was Socialism and What Comes Next?* Princeton, N.J.: Princeton University Press.

———. 1983. *Transylvanian Villagers: Three Centuries of Political, Economic, and Ethnic Change.* Berkeley: University of California Press.

Vitebsky, Piers. 1991. Landscape and Self-determination Among the Eveny: The Political Environment of Siberian Reindeer Herders Today. In *Bush Base: Forest Farm, Culture, Environment and Development*, ed. Elisabeth Croll and David Parkin. 223–46. New York: Routledge.

V zerkale statistiki (In the Statistics Mirror). 1999. *Evenkiiskaia zhizn'* 38 (October 13): 1.

Wanner, Catherine. 1998. *Burden of Dreams: History and Identity in Post-Soviet Ukraine.* University Park: Pennsylvania State University Press.

Warren, Kay B. 1998. *Indigenous Movements and Their Critics: Pan-Maya Activism in Guatemala.* Princeton, N.J.: Princeton University Press.

———. 1991. Reading History as Resistance: Maya Public Intellectuals in Guatemala. In *Maya Cultural Activism in Guatemala*, ed. Edward F. Fischer and R. McKenna Brown. 89–106. Austin: University of Texas Press.

Watson, Rubie S. 1995. Palaces, Museums, and Squares: Chinese National Spaces. *Museum Anthropology* 19 (2): 7–17.

———. 1994. Memory, History, and Opposition Under State Socialism. In *Memory, History, and Opposition Under State Socialism*, ed. Rubie S. Watson. 1–20. Santa Fe, N.M.: School of American Research Press.

Wax, Murray L., Rosalie H. Wax, and Robert V. Dumont, Jr. 1989. *Formal Education in an American Indian Community.* Prospect Heights, Ill.: Waveland Press.

Willis, Paul. 1981/1977. *Learning to Labour: How Working Class Kids Get Working Class Jobs.* New York: Columbia University Press.

Wilmer, Franke. 1993. *The Indigenous Voice in World Politics.* Newbury Park, Calif.: Sage.

Wolcott, Harry F. 1989. *A Kwakiutl Village and School.* Prospect Heights, Ill.: Waveland Press.

Wolf, Eric. 1982. *Europe and the People Without History.* Berkeley: University of California Press.

Wolf, Marjorie. 1992. *A Thrice Told Tale: Feminism, Postmodernism, and Ethnographic Responsibility.* Stanford, Calif.: Stanford University Press.

Worsley, Peter. 1984. *The Three Worlds: Culture and World Development.* London: Weidenfeld and Nicholson.

Yanagisako, Sylvia. 1979. Family and Household: The Analysis of Domestic Groups. *Annual Review of Anthropology* 8: 161–205.

Yuval-Davis, Nira, and Flora Anthias. 1989. *Woman-Nation-State.* London: Macmillan.

Zhukovskaia, Natalia. 1995. Religion and Ethnicity in Eastern Russia, Republic of Buryatia: a Panorama of the 1990s. *Central Asian Survey* 14 (1): 25–42.

Index